DATE DUE

DE 15 94			
NO 9 95			

DEMCO 38-296

APOCALYPTIC
OVERTURES

APOCALYPTIC OVERTURES

Sexual Politics and the Sense of an Ending

...

RICHARD DELLAMORA

RUTGERS UNIVERSITY PRESS
NEW BRUNSWICK, NEW JERSEY

Portions of Chapter 2 appeared in somewhat different form as "Critical Impression-ism as Anti-Phallogocentric Strategy," in *Pater in the 1990s*, ed. Laurel Brake and Ian Small (Greensboro, N.C.: ELT Press, 1991), pp. 127–142. Chapter 3 appeared in somewhat different form as "E. M. Forster at the End," in *Victorian Literature and Culture* 21 (1993). Chapter 6 appeared in somewhat different form as "Apocalyptic Utterance in Edmund White's 'An Oracle,'" in *Writing Aids: Gay Literature, Lan-guage, and Analysis*, ed. Timothy Murphy and Suzanne Poirier, pp. 98–116, copy-right © 1993 by Columbia University Press, New York. Reprinted by permission of the publisher.

Library of Congress Cataloging-in-Publication Data

Dellamora, Richard.
Apocalyptic overtures : sexual politics and the sense of an ending /
Richard Dellamora.
p.   cm.
Includes bibliographical references (p.).
ISBN 0-8135-2056-8 (cloth) — ISBN 0-8135-2057-6 (pbk.)
1. Gays' writings, English—History and criticism.   2. English literature—Men authors—History and criticism.   3. American literature—Men authors—History and criticism.   4. Gays' writings, American—History and criticism.   5. Apocalyptic literature—History and criticism.   6. Homosexuality and literature.   7. AIDS (Disease) in literature.   8. Sex role in literature.   9. Gay men in literature.   10. Closure (Rhetoric)   I. Title.
PR120.G39D45   1994
820.9′920664—dc20   93-27242
CIP

British Cataloging-in-Publication information available

Alma Mater

CONTENTS

ILLUSTRATIONS

ACKNOWLEDGMENTS

A book is the record of the places where and the people among whom it has been written. This book was shaped by three seminars that I participated in during the past several years. The first was with Nancy K. Miller at the School of Criticism and Theory at Dartmouth College in Hanover, N.H., in the summer of 1988. The second, on the politics of deconstruction, was directed by Deborah Esch at the Twelfth International Summer Institute for Semiotic and Structural Studies at the University of Toronto in 1990. The third, again at the School of Criticism and Theory, was on aesthetic fetishism in postmodern culture and was conducted by Wendy Steiner. I thank the leaders of these seminars and my fellow students for making intellectual exchange what it should be. Finally, I thank Dominick LaCapra, whose lectures at the School of Criticism and Theory shaped my own reflections about traumatic aspects of group history.

Late in 1988, shortly after the manuscript of my first book was accepted for publication, I moved from the village of Keene, Ontario, to a neighborhood in central Toronto. In the writing of this book I have drawn on the confidence and strength that comes from living among Toronto's large, resilient, and highly visible lesbian and gay communities. I am also grateful for the access that living in Toronto affords to a number of highly creative cultural practitioners: Linda Hutcheon, Barbara Godard, and Kathleen Martindale, among others.

The final version of the manuscript was produced during a visiting fellowship in the department of English at Princeton University during the academic year 1992–1993. I thank Elaine Showalter, chair of the department, her colleagues, and Dean Robert C. Gunning for having made it possible for me to share in Princeton's wealth of personal and material resources. Finally, I thank the Social Sciences and Humanities Research Council of Canada, which funded my year at Princeton, for having once again provided me with that scarcest and most valuable of scholarly commodities—time.

Leslie Mitchner at Rutgers University Press has large claim to be named the "onlie begetter" of this book. Her encouragement from the outset and her insistence that the book be as good as I can write it have helped make it what it is. For her energy, determination, and attention, I am grateful. I would also like to thank the two external readers for the Press, who were extremely helpful, as well as the copy editor, Andrew Lewis.

INTRODUCTION

A*pocalyptic Overtures* deals with male sexual dissidence in late-nineteenth- and in late-twentieth-century culture. I focus on the ends of these two centuries because of the crises that accompanied each. The chapters that follow, however, are not, strictly speaking, about either Oscar Wilde or the AIDS epidemic. Nor are they confined to the immediate ends of centuries. Rather, they deal with the problematics of narrativizing the history of sexual and emotional attachments between men. What emerges cannot account for the construction of male homosexuality as an identity in the 1890s or articulate the vicissitudes of gay identity from the late 1960s, through the devastations of AIDS, to the end of the century. Such a master narrative would exclude the most notable feature of the history of the formation of male sexual minorities, namely the repeated catastrophes that have conditioned their emergence and continued existence.

Each chapter focuses on a text or set of texts—literary, critical, theoretical, cinematic, or visual—in which a narrative of individual and/or group history is constituted. In each case, what becomes most important is an experience of blockage that renders the story, in Jacques Derrida's phrase, "a non-totalisable totality."[1] This resistance to narrative coherence impels an attempt to return through art to an earlier history, which, if recovered, promises to explain and thereby remedy the inadequacies of identity and consciousness in the present. Usually, such remedies are not forthcoming. But what can occur is a better understanding of the circumstances that make gaps, losses, and ruptures in individual and group histories inescapable.

One way to pursue this analysis is to study how male-male sexual difference is articulated in relation to that particular way of structuring time called apocalyptic. The word *apocalypse* refers to the final book of the New Testament, the Revelation or, in Roman Catholic usage, the Apocalypse of St. John the Apostle. The Apocalypse projected for early Christians a series of types and events up to and including the very end of time when, as the messenger assures John, "a new heaven and a new earth" will descend and the "New Jerusalem" will be established (Rev. 21.1, 2). Christians have long attempted to decode the prophecies of Apocalypse, but they have not confined their readings to sacred history. Rather, they have also configured Western secular history in apocalyptic terms. Others, especially Jewish groups, have done likewise. Since the Enlightenment, the pattern has been translated to secular contexts—as in Hegel's view of "a fixed progression of ages, leading to a kind of perfect state."[2] Hegel envisaged this process as one of peaceful evolution. Taking an opposed view, Marx and Engels in *The Communist Manifesto* argued that revolution would be necessary in order to transform civil society permanently.[3] In modern Western societies, apocalypse has been translated into a continual "mood of end-dominated crisis. . . . We . . . are left with [a sense of] eternal transition, perpetual crisis."[4] Early on Christians also translated apocalypse into the terms of the history of the individual Christian set out as a narrative that ended with death and judgment, Heaven or Hell. This pattern has come to pervade secular society; the self is regarded as continually in crisis. In this context, "no longer imminent, the End is immanent."[5]

Frank Kermode first introduced apocalyptic narrative structure as a significant topic within literary studies in *The Sense of an Ending: Studies in the Theory of Fiction* (1967). Despite my disagreements with Kermode,[6] the subtitle of *Apocalyptic Overtures* acknowledges his study as a point of departure (and, occasionally, of return) for the contemporary study of apocalypse. Kermode's book appeared at the very moment when the hegemony of historical and New Critical approaches to the study of literature in anglophone countries was challenged by the emergence of postmodern cultural practices and the introduction of poststructuralist theory from France. These shifts occurred simultaneously with invocations of apocalyptic hope and anxiety from the Left and the Right as liberal consensus in the United States broke under the stress of the Vietnam War, a disabling series of assassinations, and widespread civil disturbances. Led by the struggle of African Americans for civil rights, minority politics in those years acquired a new and continuing importance. At this time too, the Stonewall Riots of June 1969 launched the lesbian and gay liberation movement of the 1970s.

The years since 1968 have seen a remarkable efflorescence of apocalyptic theory, especially in the work of Jacques Derrida, which ranges from his proclamation of the end of "Western collocution"[7] in a lecture delivered in New York City in 1968, to the analysis of apocalyptic catastrophe in philosophic tradition in *The Post Card* (1980), to the influential essay "No Apocalypse, Not Now," to "Of an Apocalyptic Tone Recently Adopted in Philosophy," a meditation on apocalyptic utterance in St. John. He addresses apocalyptic aspects of AIDS in his recently translated "The Rhetoric of Drugs." Derrida exploits new possibilities by considering apocalypse as a form of narrative, but I believe his exploration of apocalyptic tone to be even more significant because it provides a way to imagine alterity within conventional linguistic structures.

Finally, apocalyptic pattern and tone often exist in relation to sublime affect, the characteristic aesthetic mode within postmodernist practice and—in the argument of theorists like Jean-François Lyotard—a condition of the very possibility of democratic heterogeneity in contemporary society.

Among dominant groups apocalyptic narratives have often been invoked in order to validate violence done to others. Among subordinate groups apocalyptic thinking is frequently an effect of the pressure of persecution. Apocalyptic narratives have been mobilized to justify the imprisonment, torture, and execution of the subjects of male-male desire. Lee Edelman, for example, points out that in an English tract of 1692, "Jenny Cromwell's Complaint Against Sodomy," "sodomy is construed as exemplifying a logic of reversal with widespread and uncontrollable implications—implications that reenact a 'sodomitical' disturbance of temporal (and therefore narrative) positionality that threatens to reduce the play of history to the finality of an endgame."[8] The threat that sodomy was traditionally taken to pose to both the secular and the religious orders suggests that the association of sex between men with end times is embedded in the political unconscious of Christian societies. Accordingly, when persecution of such subjects increases at moments, such as the ends of centuries, when cultural anxieties about time become intensified, such responses are due not only to immediate but also to atavistic factors. Subjects of same-sex desire, however, invoke the Greco-Roman past as a period in which sexual and emotional ties between men flourished. This idealization has been closely associated with ideas of social and cultural renewal in "renaissances," whether that of fifteenth-century Florence, the High Renaissance in Rome, eighteenth-century neoclassicism, or the Victorian renaissance, whose advent Walter Pater and Oscar Wilde celebrated. In the work of the turn-of-the-century homosexual apologist Edward Carpenter, the emergence of male homosexuals or "Uranians" portends the perfection of the human species. Carpenter's vision, however, which is conditioned by the development of medical and juridical discourses of male homosexuality, is compensatory to a fault. He validates male homosexuality at the price of enlisting homosexual subjects within a sacrificial order whose telos is the greater good of humanity.

These examples do not determine that apocalyptic thinking is necessarily "good" or "bad." But they do recommend caution. The pervasive tendency to structure individual and group experience in apocalyptic terms can be easily abused. For this reason, Derrida insists that apocalyptic appeals must be subjected to continual critical analysis. Furthermore, his reflections on "the tone of the other" can play an important role in developing apocalyptic modes of utterance that resist the tendency to slip into binary oppositions between Self and Other. In the following chapters I do not offer a synthetic view of apocalypse in relation to the group history of sexual minorities. Rather, in each I adopt a double temporal focus in working through a particular problematic in apocalyptic thinking. I do so in the hope that this book will foster cultural analyses and practices that configure history in ways useful not only to those engaged in the study of sexualities but also to others with an interest in the cultural construction of minority experience.

Apocalyptic Overtures is in two parts. Between 1885, when passage of the Labouchère amendment criminalized "gross indecency" between men, and 1895, when Oscar Wilde was prosecuted and found guilty under its terms, male homosexuality was defined in medical and juridical discourses in England. Because of the coincidence of the end of the century with these moments, Part One is titled *Fin de siècle*. For my purposes, the Wilde trials provide something like an empty center around which a number of personalities, events, and texts can be configured. This void has an uncanny correlative in what Ed Cohen refers to as the "overwhelming absence" of transcripts and other trial records.[9] This fact suggests in turn a characteristic aspect of the history of the formation of sexual and other minorities: namely, that such histories, where they can be reconstructed at all, have to be shaped in relation to interruptions and suppressions in personal and institutional memories. These erasures provide one kind of testimony to the violence that has been visited on minority subjects.

In the opening chapter I focus on a paradigmatic instance of the preoccupation that gay writers have recently shown in re-presenting the present by reimagining it in relation to the past. Neil Bartlett's *Who Was That Man? A Present for Mr Oscar Wilde* (1988) responds to the apocalyptic end of 1970s gay culture by returning to seek Oscar Wilde in the nocturnal maze of London streets. Bartlett attempts to chart a narrative of desire that can evade apocalyptic closure while avoiding the sorts of exclusions on which the gay narratives of the 1970s were predicated.

In Chapter 2 I deal with texts by Pater, Wilde, Carpenter, and John Gray but take a lead from Bartlett in moving back even earlier than the 1890s to the apocalyptic climate with which the nineteenth century opened. I focus on the *other* tradition in Greek male-male sexuality, the one associated not with Socrates, Plato, and the Athenian Academy but with the sexual and emotional ties between men at Sparta. This tradition is represented in Jacques Louis David's sublime image of *Leonidas at Thermopylae*. The painting casts its protagonists in an apocalyptic narrative in which the nation faces dramatically contrasting possibilities of salvation or total defeat. Such a presentation demands total sacrifice by its citizens—particularly its young men eligible for military service. In

Spartan tradition, however, sublime sacrifice is supplemented with military pederasty, which enlists devotion between a younger and an older warrior in the service of the common safety. Although views about the sexual implications of love between Spartan soldiers varied, philological discussions of Spartan-model pederasty provided a rare opportunity for nineteenth-century writers to discuss male-male relations outside conventional moral and religious contexts. In this way, the science of philology became an important site for imagining the possibility of sexual and emotional ties between men.

Translated into English and put to use in the public schools and at Cambridge and Oxford, German studies of Greek philology and history were used to shape an expanding cadre of military officers and civil servants in England and its colonies overseas. Writers like John Ruskin and Matthew Arnold sought in the Spartan model of state organization clues to how political democracy could be reconciled with national solidarity. This development sets the context for the discussion of how in the early 1890s writers like Pater and Wilde mobilized a homosexual reverse discourse that challenged the exploitation of desire between men for military purposes.

I invoke deconstruction in this book as a site of apocalyptic theory. Theory, however, is not a metadiscourse somehow protected from gender effects. Deconstruction is implicated in the work of gender, by which, in this case, I mean the construction and contestation of masculinity.[10] In Chapter 3 I begin an analysis of this work in the context of the American appropriation of French deconstruction. The chapter contains two arguments. In the first I focus on the revival of interest in Pater in the United States during the 1970s and analyze the appropriation of the critic as a patron saint of deconstruction *avant la lettre* in the work of J. Hillis Miller. In the second I trace the development of homosexual polemic in Pater's aesthetic criticism and fiction—a development that Miller ignores. In particular I focus on *Marius the Epicurean*, a novel of ancient Rome that appeared in 1885, the same year in which increasing social purity agitation was pushing Parliament toward enacting legal reforms that expanded eventually to include the antihomosexual Labouchère amendment.[11] Like Carpenter, who in these years linked his attraction to other men to his commitment to socialist politics, Pater attempted to reimagine relations between men in a context of apocalyptic hope.[12] In his portrait of a Christian community at Rome during the reign of Marcus Aurelius, Pater translates the Johannine apocalypse into a model of social conciliation and renewal under an aegis that is at once partly Christian, partly homoerotic. Pater, who was a masterful analyst of the psychological and social mechanisms of homophobia, registers the fragmentary and interrupted character of projects like those of Marius and the Christians. The novel ends during an outbreak of plague that provokes renewed persecution. Swept accidentally into the net, Marius dies in captivity, claimed by the Christians, in ironic misrecognition, as a Christian martyr.

In the fourth and final chapter in Part One I turn to E. M. Forster's first published short story, "Albergo Empedocle" (1903). Reflecting the loss of philology as a site at which sexual and emotional ties between men could be imagined, Forster's story tells about a young man who has a vision of life as an ancient Greek—only to find that unless he relinquishes that vision he will not be permitted to live in contemporary England. This loss exists in relation to a number of other endings—of the century, of Victoria's reign, of the ability of hegemonic male discourse to contain a proliferation of minority discourses, of the relatively open possibilities for homosexual cultural production that Wilde had fostered with immense energy and intelligence.

As indicated by its title, *Fin de millennium*, Part Two looks toward the year 2000. The approaching millennium has raised gender anxieties even more than the decade of the 1890s did. In the United States, moreover, the fin de siècle began early, with the advent of AIDS, initially described as GRID (gay-related immunodeficiency), in 1981.[13] By 1990, an array of apocalyptic narratives had been inscribed in mystified, homophobic representations of AIDS in the mass media.[14] Part Two ends with two studies of AIDS-related fiction. Edmund White's short story, "An Oracle" (1986), registers the impact of AIDS among upper-middle-class white New Yorkers. I argue that White's use of oracular utterance in the story opens the narrative (and the social, economic, and national closures that it implies) to "the tone of the other." Given the rapidly increasing incidence of AIDS among members of other minority groups, the capacity of men in the gay "mainstream" to attend to new political and medical needs is of the utmost importance.

Alan Hollinghurst's *Swimming-Pool Library* (1988) is set in an even more rarified social milieu in London in the summer of 1983. In Hollinghurst's novel, the challenge that AIDS poses to narrativity is suggested not only by the absence of the word "AIDS" from the book but, more significant, by the significant absence from the narrative of the history of the politically motivated prosecutions of elite male queers in Great Britain during the early 1950s. This absence is symptomatic of the privileges on which the young aristocratic protagonist's sexual forays depend. But the missing historical referent also signals that the history of male-male sexualities in Britain has been constituted in relation to cultural constructions of ignorance that contribute to the continuing subordination of minorities. Even when the historical record is reconstituted, the process of recovery is incomplete, and the divisions among men who desire other men persist.

In Chapter 5 I focus on the displacement of gay contexts in David Cronenberg's 1992 film adaptation of William Burroughs's novel *Naked Lunch*. The appropriation of material within hegemonic culture remains a major factor in the obliteration of minority cultural practices even in work like Cronenberg's, which to a degree resists mass marketing and is inflected by *other* minority experience—in Cronenberg's case by his positioning as a Jewish intellectual and a filmmaker based in anglophone Canada. In the course of the chapter I double back to the apocalyptic narrative of the autobiographical novel *Queer*, which Burroughs wrote in the mid-1950s but did not publish until 1985. I consider how "Burroughs" was translated into a figure of apocalyptic disorder in a mid-1960s Battle of the Books, in which traditionalists like M. H. Abrams and liberals like Kermode countered the challenges to literary humanism that theorists like Paul de Man and J. Hillis Miller were beginning to pose as they shifted from existentialist and phenomenological positions to deconstruction. In this chapter I recover significant moments in the engendering of deconstruction in America, a process in which the antagonists of deconstruction have repeatedly associated it with queer perversity.

In Chapter 6 I continue this work by showing how one of the most influential critical/theoretical contributions to the description of contemporary postmodernism is inflected by an unacknowledged attraction-repulsion to homosexual sensation. Fredric Jameson's attack on Andy Warhol, the most significant postmodern artist, demonstrates how thoroughly sexualized is the deployment of sublime affects and apocalyptic narratives in postmodern theory. Nonetheless, Jameson acknowledges that the hegemonic structure of masculinity is a central factor in the loss of agency that he sees as characteristic of postmodernity. This concession does at least indicate the crucial role that the analysis of masculinities must play in addressing questions about agency in contemporary existence. Finally, I suggest how the critique of Jameson's presentation of postmodernity opens possibilities for envisaging a politics beyond the year 2000 in which individual and group agency will have an important place. This suggestion opens a prospect into the next century not of redemption or annihilation but of focused effort among a continually shifting array of actors.

Foucault *and* Derrida

Jacques Derrida is the foremost theorist of apocalypse in the late twentieth century. He has written about apocalypse as a narrative, as a tone, as a mode of discourse, as a metadiscourse, as one among a number of genres, and as a mode of individual or group history. I draw on this array to supplement the constructionist approach to the history of gender and sexuality that I took in *Masculine Desire*. To some readers, supplementing constructionism with deconstruction may seem contradictory; Michel Foucault, after all, repudiated deconstruction in 1972.[15] But readers of my earlier book will remember that Foucault himself had second thoughts about the single-minded vigor with which students of his work took up his description of the construction of "the homosexual" as a "species" in sexology of the fin de siècle.[16] In the introduction to *The Use of Pleasure*, the second volume of *The History of Sexuality*, he remarks that the term "sexuality did not appear until the beginning of the nineteenth century," a fact that, he says, "should be neither underestimated nor over-interpreted."[17]

In the same introduction, Foucault critiques the approach he took in volume 1, which he describes as "a history of the experience of sexuality, where experience is understood as the correlation between fields of knowledge, types of normativity, and forms of subjectivity in a particular culture." In preparing further volumes, Foucault encountered difficulties that prompted him to reformulate the inquiry. Central to the development of ideas of sexuality was the idea of the male-as-subject-of-desire, yet the notion served simply as an axiom, whereas "desire and the subject of desire were withdrawn from the historical field." For this reason, he felt a need to shift the focus of his attention: "In order to understand how the modern individual could experience himself as a subject of a 'sexuality,' it was essential first to determine how, for centuries, Western man had been brought to recognize himself as a subject of desire." This effort induced yet a third shift as Foucault found himself posing the questions, What is the subject? How does one become a subject? These questions led him in turn to fashion a hermeneutics of the self based on the connections between male-male sexual practices and the structure of personal relations and awareness in Classical Greece.[18]

The ethical emphasis of what eventually came to be volume 2 of *The History of Sexuality* has not endeared Foucault to social constructionists, since it acknowledges the problematic relationship between "fields of knowledge" and "forms of subjectivity" in his earlier formulation. In particular, Foucault had permitted himself no way to address questions about the agency of subjects in the field of discourses. Some readers also found disturbing Foucault's return, by way of philology, to a conception of "aesthetics" that had been held by elite male homosexuals of the late nineteenth century. The phrase, "aesthetics of existence," which he uses to describe male-male erotics in ancient Greece, echoes the use of the phrase by the homosexual polemicist John Addington Symonds. In "The Genius of Greek Art" in volume 2 of *Studies of the Greek Poets* (1875), Symonds recommends a return to an eroticized ideal of *aesthesis* as a guide to moral conduct. Symonds makes this proposal in defense of desire between men against Christian disapproval and against the belief, deeply embedded in Western culture, that sexual inversion implies gender inversion.[19] Although his text literally predates the definition of male homosexuality in late Victorian sexology, already in 1875 Symonds sought to frame alternatives to the strictures around "homosexuality" that were later to shape the subjectivities of men with sexual and emotional ties to other men. Regenia Gagnier criticizes Foucault's advocacy of an "aesthetic 'care of the self,'" which in her eyes betokens "mere nostalgia for an autonomous community of honorable men or the private luxury of an aesthete's regime of self-regulation in a finely 'disciplined' world."[20] Yet Foucault argues that a literal translation of Greek subjectivity into contemporary mores is neither possible nor desirable. And he explicitly dissociates his interest in the "care of the self" from Classical virility: "The Greek ethics of pleasure is linked to a virile society, to dissymmetry, exclusion of the other, an obsession with penetration, and a kind of threat of being dispossessed of your own energy, and so on. All that is quite disgusting."[21] What Foucault's "return" to Greek culture does betoken is his increasingly open engagement with gay culture, especially as a result of his trips to Toronto, to California, and to the East Coast in the late 1970s and early 1980s. This engagement reflected his growing interest in sexual practices as sites at which new modes of relationship can be constituted. The concern acquires added poignancy after Foucault developed AIDS in the early 1980s. As Ed Cohen has pointed out, within the high-culture context in which the name "Foucault" circulated, this association provoked embarrassment and disavowal.[22]

In *The Use of Pleasure*, Foucault implicitly addresses the dilemmas facing those who are liable to be termed homosexual. He does so within his larger view of what he refers to as "individualizing power," the power of the institutions of the modern state to define personal subjectivity.[23] The search for an alternative to this operation leads him into Greek tradition, in which he finds a technology of the self in relation to male-male sexual practices that is aesthetic rather than confessional in character. In this context, the term *aesthetic* refers to a specific set of practices, especially apt for gay men, that can be articulated in resistance to "individualizing power." Foucault conceives this resistance—in its use of bodily pleasures and in its use of *becoming-gay* to invent new modes of sociality—as creative: "I should like to say 'it is necessary to work increasingly at being gay', to place oneself in a dimension where the sexual choices that one makes . . . must be at the same time creators of ways of life. To be gay signifies that these choices diffuse themselves across the entire life; it is also a certain manner of refusing the modes of life offered; it is to make a sexual choice the impetus for a change of existence."[24] One project that this Foucauldian politics requires is a return to moments in the history of the formation of sexual subjectivities in the late nineteenth century. Although this return is necessary to gay self-reflection, its relevance is by no means limited to subjects of sexual minorities. Rather, recent work within the spectrum of gay studies provides, in Foucault's words, "a historic opportunity to open up potential relationships and emotions, not so much by means of specific qualities which gay people possess, but for the reason that their position 'off center', in a certain way, together with the diagonal lines they can draw through social structures allows people to see these possibilities."[25]

Because of the controversy that attended Derrida's critical review of *Madness and Civilization*, Foucauldian analysis and Derridean deconstruction have usually been regarded as incompatible.[26] In responding to Derrida, Foucault accuses him of "the reduction of discursive practices to textual traces; the elision of the events produced therein and the retention only of marks for a reading; the invention of voices behind texts to avoid having to analyse the modes of implication of the subject in discourses; the assigning of the originary as said and unsaid in the text to avoid replacing [i. e., resituating] discursive practices in the field of transformations where they are carried out."[27] But Foucault's criticism is unwarranted.

In "The Ends of Man," for example, a lecture delivered in New York City in 1968, Derrida announces apocalypse as a major topic within his work. Contrary to Foucault's contention, Derrida foregrounds the discursive siting of the paper and the conference on philosophic anthropology of which it was a part. He points out the political implications of participating in an international colloquium of Western philosophers on this subject in a country that at the time was involved in a major land war in Southeast Asia. Derrida makes explicit both his refusal to support the U.S. war effort in Vietnam and his implication within that effort as a result of accepting an offer to speak at an academic conference held in the United States. He sites his text as a declaration from within a philosophic tradition that should not ignore its "evil complicities" in warfare and in civil and racial strife. Nor does the narrow diversity of views tolerated in American civil society represent or respond to the challenge posed by the emergence of new agencies on the world stage. Derrida characterizes these forces as a "difference which . . . bears down, with a mute, growing and menacing pressure on the enclosure of Western collocution."[28] If this statement sounds apocalyptic, it is, exemplifying one of Derrida's principal points, namely, that philosophic reflection in the West always occurs within an apocalyptic metadiscourse. Thought about *the ends of man* carried on within the confines of philosophic anthropology is always enclosed within Western assumptions that are erroneously construed as universal.

This error motivates Derrida's relentless critique of apocalyptic pattern, but the inescapability of apocalypse also compels him to theorize it in ways that acknowledge and enable agency exerted from outside the "enclosure." Hence the potential interest of Derridean apocalypse to subaltern subjects, to gay men, and to members of other minorities. Derrida argues that an apocalyptic tone can unfix the meaning of messages as well as the definition of their senders and receivers. He locates these processes in relation to discourses in which different and contradictory subject positions are and can be put in play. In other words, Derrida directs his presentation of apocalypse toward what Foucault refers to as "the modes of implication of the subject in discourses." Although it is true that Derrida has resisted equating subject positions with particular individual and collective identities, the deconstruction, both analytic and affirmative, that he practices offers a powerful supplement to Foucauldian discourse analysis. Moreover, his emphasis on the mutual implication of aesthetics and discourses of truth adds a new element to the theory of the production of discursive knowledge.

Derrida's interest in apocalypse has focused on the functions of apocalyptic tone within institutions. When he hypothesizes the existence of "*one* apocalyptic tone, a unity of the apocalyptic tone," he has in mind the unified tone sought by those who claim to have special access to the truth—whether they be politicians, preachers, philosophers, or experts in another discipline.[29] In response to continual attacks, Derrida has repeatedly emphasized the connection between institutions and the analysis of foundational discourses. In *Truth in Painting*, for example, he argues: "Deconstruction . . . attacks not only the internal edifice, both semantic and formal, of philosophemes, but also what one would be wrong to assign to the philosophic institution as its external housing, its extrinsic conditions of practice: the historical forms of its pedagogy, the social, economic or political structures of this pedagogical institution. It is because deconstruction interferes with solid structures, 'material' institutions, and not only with discourses or signifying representations, that it is always distinct from an analysis or a 'critique.'"[30] Derrida portrays "the unified tone" in philosophy as a mirage that can be sustained only by seduction or coercion. His analyses of the discursive disruptions of a unified tone provide examples of tactics that disempowered subjects and groups can use to subvert the claims to special knowledge that elite cadres use to justify their attempts to monopolize power.

Derrida's emphasis on how the apocalyptic tone can be used either to open or to close the possibilities of democratic exchange is congruent with the emphasis in Foucault's later writing on how the power effects of discourses can be redirected from marginal subject positions. Formulating the concept of reverse discourse, Foucault argues that "discourses . . . can . . . circulate without changing their form from one strategy to another, opposing strategy. We must not expect the discourses on sex to tell us . . . what ideology—dominant or dominated—they represent; rather we must question them on the two levels of their tactical productivity (what reciprocal effects of power and knowledge they ensure) and their strategical integration (what conjunction and what force relationship make their utilization necessary in a given episode of the various configurations that occur)."[31] In contending that a reverse discourse can be literally indistinguishable from the discourse that it reverses, Foucault suggests the effectiveness of aesthetic means within sexual politics.

Both writers have had a similar recourse to the late political writings of the philosopher Immanuel Kant. Foucault argues that Kant initiates both main lines of contemporary philosophic thought: the analysis of truth-claims in foundational discourses and the analysis of what Foucault refers to as "an ontology of the present, an ontology of ourselves."[32] He finds evidence of the second project in Kant's post-Revolutionary reflections. A proponent of republican self-government, Kant faced a dilemma when the Reign of Terror canceled the promises of the Constitution of 1791. He responded by urging that the ground for belief in the possibility of human progress is not whether or not the Revolution succeeds but in the "*sympathy*" with which the revolutionary situation was greeted.[33] In Foucault's words: "What is meaningful and what is to constitute the sign of progress is that, around the Revolution, there is, says Kant, 'a sympathy of aspiration bordering on enthusiasm.' What is important in the Revolution is not the Revolution itself, but what takes place in the heads of those who do not make it or, in any case, who are not its principal actors; it is the relationship that they themselves have with that Revolution of which they are not the active agents."[34] Derrida's project follows both lines of Kant's thought much as Foucault understands them. The analytic project of deconstruction carries forward Kant's foundational critique by applying it not only to Hegel and later philosophers but to the very points in Kant's own work where he suspends the analysis of basic postulates.[35] The affirmative project of deconstruction, like Kant's political essays, projects hope forward in the face of contemporary catastrophe. This moral tone—

in Kant, Derrida, and Foucault—has a special significance as the *fin de millennium* approaches, and for no group more so than for lesbians and gay men, whose experience of relative emancipation in the 1970s was followed by the onset of AIDS in the early 1980s. Since then, lesbians and gay men have continued to make gains; but they have also experienced strategic defeats and many losses.

Postmodernity, the Sublime, and the Spectacle of AIDS

In *Looking Back on the End of the World*, Dietmar Kamper and Christoph Wulf assert that the concept of the world produced by the social and historical sciences of the nineteenth century "has begun to crumble" late in the twentieth. Paradoxically, this collapse has been triggered by the contemporary "obsession with the last moment," a fantasy a number of whose many forms Kamper and Wulf outline. The obsolescence of the concept of one world can be interpreted both positively and negatively. Kamper and Wulf find grounds for hope in the need to move beyond "a retrospective view of the end of the world" to "new vistas."[36] Both their assertion of the end of the world and their call to imagine new vistas beyond that end are apocalyptic. Both also belong to narratives about the meaning of existence in time. As such, they have a place within an apocalyptic metanarrative, described by Dominick LaCapra among others, that locates a defining moment in the shift from religious to secular thinking in Western culture in the late eighteenth century.[37] LaCapra emphasizes the anxious sense of displacement that accompanies this shift. In the nineteenth century, writers in disciplines such as philosophy, philology, anthropology, and biology attempted to overcome the loss of a sense that time is providentially ordered by inventing new ways of ordering time that possess a universal human significance.[38]

Jean-François Lyotard has defined postmodernism in relation to a lapse of confidence in the grand narratives of Western thought constructed during the nineteenth century. He attempts to hasten this collapse by subverting "the discourse of the master, the magisterial discourse," a discourse that depends for its authority on its ability to determine "the conditions of truth" on the basis of which claims to knowledge and power are put forward. Lyotard refers to this "meta-discourse . . . within the magisterial discourse" as the discipline of philosophy.[39] The critique of foundational statements within philosophy permits the search "for new presentations, in order to impart a stronger sense of the unpresentable."[40] The political goal of this effort is, as he remarks, to develop "the strength of the weak." Through a variety of rhetorical means, the tactical use of silences and tonal inflections and the mobilization of reverse discourses, "the weak" can, in Lyotard's words, "play these rules—or rather the Rule of these rules against itself by including the so-called metastatements in its own utterances. . . . Our weakness (I don't really know who 'we' is), can tap the strength of power to neutralize it."[41] Although Lyotard may be uncertain about who can benefit from this play, his analysis suggests strategic possibilities for those who stage political interventions from minority subject positions.

In the somewhat different terms set forth in *The Postmodern Condition*, Lyotard declares his goal to be to "activate the differences" implicit in that which is "unpresentable" within the dominant ideology.[42] Reference to the "unpresentable" frames Lyotard's distinction between modernist and postmodernist culture in terms of the sublime, since Kant defines the sublime in terms of the limits of representation. Lyotard adapts Kant's general definition of the sublime as *"that, the mere capacity of thinking which evidences a faculty of mind transcending every standard of sense."*[43]

In experiential terms, the sublime is "a pleasure which surges up only indirectly, i.e., in such a way that it is produced by the feeling of an instantaneous inhibition of the vital forces, followed at once by an outpouring of these same forces, an outpouring that is all the stronger for the inhibition."[44] This description refers to the sort of aesthetic experience an observer might have while gazing at the pyramids of El Gizeh or an Alpine gorge or at a landscape painting by Caspar David Friedrich. But this particular kind of aesthetic experience contains a narrative structure with three distinct moments: the initial viewing; a spontaneous experience of check, blockage, or "inhibition of the vital forces"; and a final release. This threefold structure makes it possible to translate sublime affect from its immediate context in aesthetics to a number of other contexts,[45] and no one has exploited this possibility more aggressively than has Lyotard. In discussing the political field that has opened in the late twentieth century as a result of the failure of the grand narratives, for example, Lyotard describes democratic heterogeneity as a mode of the sublime: "It is not only the Idea of a *single* purpose which would be pointed to in our feeling, but already the Idea that this purpose consists in the formation and free exploration of Ideas *in the plural*, the Idea that this end is the beginning of the *infinity of heterogeneous finalities*."[46] As Thomas Yingling has argued in defending the interventions of ACT UP (AIDS Coalition to Unleash Power), the ground rules under which supposedly heterogeneous agencies function often exclude PLWAs (persons living with AIDS) from the game.[47] Nonetheless, Lyotard's description of the field of contemporary cultural politics is extremely useful in strategic terms.

Kant describes two modes of the sublime. The first mode takes the form of what I term the infinite sublime, that is, the feeling produced by imagining a "numerical series progressing *ad infinitum*." The second mode, the dynamic sublime, is the feeling of awe, terror, and pleasure that the subject perceives in witnessing a natural phenomenon, such as a volcanic eruption, from a position of safety.[48] These modes of the sublime are subject to very different interpretations depending on how one understands the term *transcending* in the general definition. In the sense of overcoming, surpassing, and excelling, the word suggests the triumph of the human capacity of reason over the limits of sensation even in face of a representation that literally exceeds the limits of human comprehension. In the psychoanalytic terms in which much contemporary discussion of the sublime has been couched, this ability reinforces the identification of the ego with the superego. Quoting Thomas Weiskel, Neil Hertz writes: "The Kantian sublime, in both its manifestations, becomes 'the very moment in which the mind turns within and performs its identification with reason. The sublime recapitulates and thereby reestablishes the oedipus complex,' with Kant's reason taking the role of the superego, that agency generated by an act of sublimation, 'an identification with the father taken as model.'"[49] The sublime need not, however, be represented exclusively in this way. It is possible, rather, to focus on the moment of "inhibition"— that is, the moment when the subject is bewildered by perceiving items in an endless series or by seeing something that evokes awe. In this context, the sublime can be understood as expressing a differential relation between "spectacle" and cognitive capacity. This sort of relational understanding resists the identification of the subject with either "reason" or "the father." In this light, "transcending every standard of sense" can refer to a differential relation within the experience of the sublime that corroborates the character of the sublime as a mode of resistance to confidence about the adequacy of rational comprehension. The succeeding "outpouring" of "vital forces," then, is not final; the experience of the sublime can always revert to the moment of resistance that Hertz refers to as "blockage."[50]

Paradoxically, the sublime is a mode of representation that adduces something that lies outside the limits of representation. Lyotard argues that in twentieth-century culture, the sublime thus conceived operates in two contrasting ways. The modernist sublime emphasizes "the powerlessness of the faculty of presentation, . . . the nostalgia for presence felt by the human subject." This nostalgia has regressive implications since it prompts desire for a politics that will enable the subject to identify with a power in such a way as to overcome the resistance inherent to the experience of the sublime. In contrast, the postmodern sublime emphasizes "the power of the faculty to conceive" that which it cannot present.[51] What is "unpresentable" within artistic or political discourse can nonetheless become "conceivable," and what is conceivable can become part of a political agenda.

In the final years of the twentieth century, the special circumstances attending the AIDS epidemic have tended to prompt responses in both modes of the sublime. By early 1992, 133,000 persons had died of AIDS in the United States alone.[52] Although persons of all sorts are included in this number, to date, most of the deceased are gay or bisexual men. In Canada, this group accounts for 83 percent of all reported cases.[53] The incidence of AIDS, moreover, is localized in certain cities, regions, and fields of work. For those most immediately affected, AIDS can prompt a sense of the infinite sublime. The number of those affected seems to extend without limit. Since the epidemic has yet to reach its maximum, the sense that a limitless number of persons is affected will be exacerbated in the next few years. Those most exposed to risk of infection can also experience the epidemic in terms of the dynamic sublime, only with this difference, that the security from direct personal threat that Kant includes in his initial definition of this mode is absent. Among gay men, this effect is intensified by the long period that may occur between initial infection with HIV and the onset of AIDS. At different times and over extended periods, gay men can be HIV-positive, HIV-negative, or PLWAs. The dynamic sublime, whose subject/object can actually be exposed to threat of destruction, is uncannily apt in relation to a range of extraordinary emotional effects produced by the representation of AIDS in the media and in private experience. In both ways, then, in the sense that those affected are a number without limit and in the sense that one is already or may soon be drawn into that number, AIDS fascinates and fills with dread.

In this situation, the self-resisting character of the sublime can have significant moral and political effects. The discrepancy between representation (or spectacle) and the effort to comprehend phenomena that exceed comprehension can prompt subjects to interrogate the spectacle and the connection between it and a number of different politics. Subjects of the sublime need not be transfixed in states of fear, terror, or wonder. The sublime can motivate continuing efforts to understand the conditions that produce it. But if the sensations roused by the spectacle of the wasted bodies of PLWAs are relieved by appeals to specious "answers" posed by authoritative voices, the sublime can be a powerful means for enforcing the identification of subjects with constituted authorities. This possibility makes yet yet more urgent the cognitive interrogation of the experience of the sublime.

Engendering Philosophy

During the 1970s, Derrida's evocations of the affirmative project of deconstruction often turned on the figure of woman. This is particularly true of *Spurs*, which he first presented as a lecture at a colloquium on Nietzsche in 1972.[54] In the published version, Derrida celebrates woman "as an affirmative power, a dissimulatress, an artist, a dionysiac" (97). This affirmation becomes possible as a result of a concurrent critique of sexual difference, meaning the binary opposition of male and female: "There is no truth in itself of the sexual difference in itself, of either man or woman in itself. All of ontology, nonetheless, with its inspection, appropriation, identification and verification of identity, has resulted in concealing, even as it presupposes it, this undecidability" (103). Derrida contends that, like other binaries, sexual difference is grounded not in nature but in culture. Accordingly, in *Spurs* there is no simple relation between woman as sign and woman, women, femininity, or feminism as referents. Indeed, at the outset, Derrida expresses uncertainty whether his subject is "woman" or "style" (37, 35). In *Spurs*, woman usually refers to the wide range of genres and styles that Nietzsche employs. Derrida considers them as examples of the rhetorical figures that veil the truth that is the usual object of the "philosopher-knight" (53).

The primary intertexts of *Spurs* are to be found in Plato, Nietzsche, Freud, and Heidegger. This location within male tradition plus Derrida's emphasis on "Nietzsche's indictment of feminism" (103) makes *Spurs* an unsuitable text on the basis of which to affirm sexual dissidence. Any attempt to do so needs to situate the text within ongoing debates about philosophy, deconstruction, and feminism in France in the early 1970s. Derrida signals the existence of these contexts without, for the most part, naming them.[55] As a result, the text conserves the male philosophic monopoly that he elsewhere satirizes.

Contexts are even more complex for "Choreographies" (1982), the first of several interviews given by Derrida to North American feminists. It ends with one of the best known passages in his writing, the oracular expression of Derrida's "dream" of "a sexuality without number."[56] Nonetheless, apocalyptic narrative in the text functions in an exclusionary way that permits Derrida to "dance" with heterosexual feminists while exiling lesbian feminists, as though they were perverse Ariadnes, to a dim outer world in which their difference makes no difference. In Derrida's words, "homosexuality and heterosexuality . . . come to the same thing."[57] Apocalypse operates in the interview for the most part in a singular tone, a mode that Derrida usually subjects to caustic irony.[58]

Philosophic tradition is framed within binary oppositions of male and

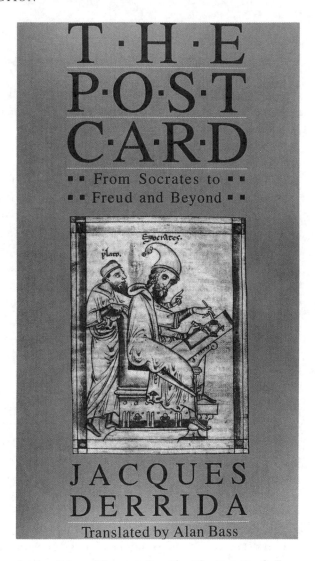

1. The cover to the paperback edition of Jacques Derrida, *The Post Card: From Socrates to Freud and Beyond* (Chicago: University of Chicago Press, 1987).

female, heterosexual and homosexual, which lend it the authority of the compulsory heterosexuality that it also enforces. In *The Post Card*, Derrida uses a number of apocalyptic fictions to address how truth is produced and transmitted in this tradition. In "Envois," the opening section of the book, Derrida defines "apocalypse" as the process of inversion whereby, since the time of Plato, writers have declared the priority of their

2. And what are these male homosocials up to? Jacques Derrida has some ideas. Matthew Paris of St. Albans (d. 1259), *Plato and Socrates*. Frontispiece to *The Prognostics of Socrates the King* (MS Ashm. 304, fol. 31v [detail]). Courtesy Bodleian Library, University of Oxford.

predecessors, then attributed to those predecessors concepts of their own in place of those which were supposedly prior. Derrida finds a further inversion signaled in the frontispiece by Matthew Paris to a medieval fortune-telling book. A reproduction of this image appears on the cover of the paperbound edition of *The Post Card*. In Paris's illumination, "plato" stands behind "Socrates," who writes at a lectern. Plato's gesturing hands appear to indicate that he is dictating material to his predecessor! Derrida uses this second inversion to invert and thereby demystify the first. Speaking as "Derrida," the autobiographical protagonist of "Envois," he exclaims: "An apocalyptic revelation: Socrates writing, writing in front of Plato." Continuing, "Derrida" writes: "What a couple. *Socrates* turns his *back* to plato, who has made him write whatever he wanted while pretending to receive it from him."[59] Again a little later, "Derrida" writes: "I see *Plato* getting an erection in *Socrates'* back and see the insane hubris of his prick, an interminable, disproportionate erection traversing Paris's head like a single idea and then the copyist's chair, before slowly sliding, still warm, under *Socrates'* right leg, in harmony or symphony with the movements of this phallus sheaf, the points, plumes, pens, fingers, nails and *grattoirs*, the very pencil boxes which address themselves in the same direction."[60] Plato's dictation to Socrates produces a "catastrophe" that conserves tradition's authority while usurping it. In this inversion, the moment of origin disappears in a fictional regress since foundational writing is the product of the founder's disciple or "son."[61] Taking this scene of writing as paradigmatic within philosophy, Derrida uses the image on the post card to shift attention from moments when original, fundamental postulates are written to those later moments when those fundamental postulates are *re*written. This Derridean inversion critiques the prior inversion, which has enabled successive philosophers from Plato to Nietzsche to Heidegger and Freud to attach their own doctrinal formulations to the signatures of earlier philosophers.

Apocalyptic "inversion" as it usually occurs within philosophy is an aspect of logocentrism. Although it has referents both in love-hate between male rivals and in the erotic scenes of instruction in which philosophy originates and in which it continues to be instilled, this particular kind of inversion exists within the terms of hegemonic sexuality.[62] As such, it is by no means the same inversion as that which is subjected to scrutiny by late nineteenth-century sexologists. Rather, the "truths" that this inversion establishes are opposed to what sexologists refer to as "sexual inversion," which they define as the negation of the normal rules of sex and gender.[63]

The apocalyptic fictions that I have just traced are only two of the apocalyptic narratives that Derrida deploys in "Envois." There are others. In the biblical genre of apocalypse, a scribe writes down eschatological revelations that are communicated to him by one or more mediators, called angels. As with philosophic truths, these revelations are reversible; that is, the scribe authorizes his text by claiming that he simply records what someone higher on the ontological ladder has told him. When Derrida discusses the Apocalypse of St. John as an example of the genre, he emphasizes this structure: "John is the one who already receives mail [*courrier*] through the further intermediary of a bearer who is an angel, a pure messenger. And John transmits a message already transmitted, testifies to a testimony that will again be that of another testimony, that of Jesus; so many sendings, *envois*, so many voices, and this puts many people on the line."[64] But what happens when the angel, far from being "a pure messenger," is an object of desire? What happens when the inverted pederasty of philosophic tradition affects the message that it is supposed to transmit without alteration? This question, which has been a perennial source of defensiveness within the institution of philosophy, is foregrounded in *The Post Card*.

"Envois," the long opening section, which Derrida calls "a kind of false preface," is an epistolary novel, in which the letter-writer, "Derrida," carries on a love affair with an(other) whose gender, given the rules of French grammar, can shift in mid-sentence.[65] The "direction" of this affair is given by the double inversion described above.

> The di-rection, the dierection of this couple, these old nuts, these rascals on horseback, this is us, in any event, *a priori* (they arrive on us) we are lying on our backs in the belly of the mare as if in an enormous library, and it gallops; it gallops, from time to time I turn to your side, I lie on you and guessing, reconstituting it by all kinds of chance calculations and conjectures, I set up [*dresse*] within you the *carte* of their displacements, the ones they will have induced with the slightest movement of the pen, barely pulling on the reins. Then, without disengaging myself I resettle [*redresse*] myself again.[66]

This "dierection" exists both within compulsory heterosexuality and in opposition to it. At times, a male lover, "mon doux amour," appears to be in question: "I owe it to you to have discovered homosexuality, and ours is indestructible," writes "Derrida."[67] More often, the lover is described in female pronouns: "Elle me touche, elle me prend dans sa voix, en m'accusant elle me berce encore, elle me nage, elle m'envague, tu m'ennuages comme un poisson, je me laisse aimer dans l'eau."[68] In either case, gender appears to be an effect of signifying practices rather than of bodily difference. Derrida makes this point even in his choice of the genre of the epistolary novel, which is usually associated with a feminine narrator. He invokes this convention early in "Envois" when he parodies the opening lines of the *Letters of a Portuguese Nun*. In choosing to write "à la Portugaise," that is, in the style of an impassioned woman, he likewise parodies the conventional male ventriloquism of the genre and thereby renders vulnerable the autobiographical persona through which he writes.

This effect is intensified by the frequent use of middle voice in "Derrida's" address.[69] "Derrida's" rhetorical becoming-woman finds a further context in the practice of gay writers to write camp fiction about protagonists who are nuns and of gay performance artists to masquerade as nuns. One of these writers, Ronald Firbank, wrote his novels on post cards just as "Derrida" purports to write "Envois."[70] Whether referred to as male or female, the lover(s) remain veiled, as does "Derrida" with his equivocally discovered homosexuality.

The uncertainties are significant, especially in relation to philosophic tradition, in which the body as an object of desire has been a continual object of scandal.[71] They are also pertinent to theoretical discussions that occur in subsequent portions of *The Post Card*. In the long section on Freud's *Beyond the Pleasure Principle*, Derrida argues that "all the interweavings of fort-da . . . can only be called oedipal if one names it, by synecdoche, by means of only one of its effects"; the child's game of throwing and retrieving the spool (fort-da) is oedipal by virtue of "a reductive, regulative fiction."[72] The representation of the narrator of "Envois" and his addressee(s) testifies to erotic divagations not compassable within the oedipal triangle.[73] Derrida/"Derrida" is a failed Oedipus, who cannot get the lines of desire straight. I am, he says, "a lame inheritor. . . . I fall all the time." Later, he becomes literally lame when apparently he suffers a broken ankle.[74]

Derrida/"Derrida" behaves improperly within both philosophic and sexual discourses. The relationship in "Envois" between the two "monstrous angels" who are sender and receiver produces a secondary apocalypse that generates considerable static in the transmission of truth.[75] Derrida implies that the acknowledgment of a desire between men that falls outside the kind of inversion sanctioned within philosophy challenges the very meaning of "authority," "discipline," and "truth." These terms depend on the production of oedipal masculinity and vice-versa. But "Derrida"'s private life contradicts this sexual economy. Although married, he is romantically involved—with his readers, with one or more women, and, possibly, with a man or men too. As a delirious lover who finds both men and women attractive, he calls into question the high ethical tone of philosophy. As the latest overturner within philosophic tradition, he acts as other sons have before him. But in pointing out the ruse whereby these men "bugger" their fathers, he puts in question the propriety of their claim to be true heirs. As for himself, he declines to claim that he simply restates what Heidegger or Freud or Lacan have already said. Instead, at a moment rife with gender irony, he lets a *female* antagonist make that claim about *his* work.[76]

These ambiguities permit Derrida to indulge himself in the myth drawn from *Phaedrus* that love between men can be "salvific," to use the word favored by the contemporary gay critic Claude Summers.[77] But Derrida also questions, through parody, to whether sexual and emotional ties between men can lead to philosophic knowledge. Both sorts of claims, those within philosophy and those within homosexual polemic, are queried. The telephone calls, letters, and post cards that shuttle between "Derrida" and his lover(s) emphasize not only detours of desire but also how operations of desire contribute to knowledge-formation while simultaneously producing interference effects in its transmission. In contrast, philosophic tradition needs to repress awareness of the desire that motivates it in order to accomplish the transfer of pederastic desire into knowledge-production and a philosophic rivalry as intense as it is disavowed.

Derridean Apocalypse

Published in France in 1980, "Envois" may be read as responding to Luce Irigaray's critique of "hom(m)o-sexualité" in philosophic tradition. Irigaray exclaims: "What mockery of generation, parody of copulation and genealogy, drawing its *strength* from the same model, from the model of the same: the [masculine] subject."[78] Derrida agrees but makes conscious use of what Irigaray describes as unwitting parody. He subverts tradition from inside. Like Roland Barthes's *Lover's Discourse* (1977), "Envois" is an experiment in critical theory rendered through the medium of desire in language. And just as Barthes's book has helped shape subsequent gay fictions such as Robert Glück's *Jack the Modernist*, Derrida's book, translated into English in 1987, is likely to have a similar effect. Yet, during the 1980s, the conditions of amorous discourse were irrevocably altered. As Glück states in a note on the reverse of the title page: the novel "is set in 1981. Before the onset of the AIDS epidemic, I would have gone (did go) to the baths and liberally exchange bodily fluids; now I don't."

When, at the end of the decade, Derrida turns to AIDS, he does so in emphatically apocalyptic terms. In an interview, "The Rhetoric of Drugs," he describes the advent of AIDS as "one of the major events facing humanity, one of the most revealing and, what amounts to the same thing, one of the most 'apocalyptic' in its most essential and 'interior' history— that is, AIDS." AIDS has given a new sense to the meaning of the word *trauma*: "Even should humanity some day come to control the [HIV] virus (it will take at least a generation), still, even in the most unconscious symbolic zones, the traumatism has irreversibly affected the experience of desire and what we coolly call intersubjectivity, the rapport to the alter ego, etc." In view of the disruption of concepts of the subject and inter-subjectivity, Derrida predicts that "reactions are largely unforeseeable and entirely capable of bringing forth the worst political violence."[79]

Emphasizing trauma as they do, Derrida's comments suggest the need for additional analysis of the blockage experienced by subjects in face of AIDS. In psychoanalysis, trauma is a condition in which the analysand has suppressed the memory of a devastating past experience. This suppression has a positive function insofar as it permits individual and collective subjects, through analysis, to reclaim material so disturbing that it otherwise would remain permanently inaccessible. History recovered in this way, however, is necessarily constituted on the basis of loss, since it is a defining characteristic of trauma that a crucial portion of memory continues to escape consciousness. "Trauma evokes the difficult truth of a history that is constituted by the very incomprehensibility of its occurrence."[80] Derrida contends that, as a result of AIDS, loss inhabits not only individual and group history but the very "experience of desire." In this sense, the subject of male-male desire will, "in the future," not ever be the same as he and other subjects were in the past. Moreover, as Derrida argues, the experience of desire has also been transformed for other subjects of desire.

In addition to suggesting how basic philosophic concepts have been affected as a result of AIDS, deconstruction provides ways of analyzing apocalyptic rhetoric in AIDS discourses, whether these originate in the mass media or in gay polemic.[81] In addition, some theorists argue that Derridean deconstruction is a mode of theory especially hospitable to gay textuality.[82] In "What Will Have Been Said about AIDS," Alexander García-Düttmann draws an analogy between the impertinence of the practice that in the 1970s was called "tricking" and the impertinence of deconstructive thought, which "must always think that which cannot be reduced to itself. If it must always think that which exceeds it and if it is only on this condition that we think at all, then there is no thought that would not be excessive and would not prove to be essentially impertinent."[83] But "tricking," which today borders upon anachronism, is only one gay practice among many. Moreover, García-Düttmann refrains from explicitly linking Derrida's name to the association of deconstruction with sexual perversity. Instead, he links "impertinence" to Barthes, who in the preface to Renaud Camus's *Tricks*, remarks: "What society will not tolerate is that I should be . . . nothing, or to be more exact, that the something that I am should be openly expressed as provisional, revocable, insignificant, inessential, in a word: impertinent."[84]

The question of alterity arises in connection with "Of an Apocalyptic Tone Recently Adopted in Philosophy," an essay in which Derrida focuses on both the last book of the New Testament and a lampoon in which Kant derides the "apocalyptic tone" that religious enthusiasts adopted in late eighteenth-century Germany. In this essay, Derrida's own tone is less confident and audacious, more urgent and qualified than in "Envois." He adduces a wide range of meanings for *apocalypse*: the term can refer to eschatology, prediction, prophecy, vision, contemplation, gaze, inspiration, mystical illumination, catastrophe, the unveiling of "secrets," such as those of the male or female genitalia, and so on. Despite this range of possibilities, Derrida emphasizes that in early Christianity the term *apocalypse* mostly referred to the imminent unveiling of the truth. Its negative meanings of onrushing judgment and destruction came to the fore later.[85]

Derrida once again stresses two opposing meanings of apocalypse. Like Kant, he argues that apocalyptic claims depend on appeals to intuitive knowledge at the expense of rational analysis. These appeals are always made in the interest of the mystagogues who utter them: "What effect do these noble, gentile [*gentils*] prophets or eloquent visionaries want to produce? In view to what immediate or adjourned [i. e., deferred] benefit? What do they do, what do we do in saying this? To seduce or subjugate whom, intimidate or make whom come?"[86] These questions direct attention to the institutional and other political contexts in which apocalyptic anxieties are provoked. In face of claims to truth and power based on these grounds, Derrida concurs with Kant in affirming apocalypse in another sense of the word: "We cannot and we must not—this is a law and a destiny—forgo the *Aufklärung*, in other words, what imposes itself as the enigmatic desire for vigilance, for the lucid vigil [*veille*], for elucidation, for critique and truth, but for a truth that at the same time keeps within itself some apocalyptic desire, this time as desire for clarity and revelation, to demystify, or if you prefer, to deconstruct the apocalyptic discourse itself and with it everything that speculates on vision, the imminence of the end, theophany, parousia, the last judgment." This "vigilance" resists the pleasure of being seduced. Deconstruction declines to accept the "delirium" of oracular utterance, which Derrida describes as "a leap from concepts to the unthinkable or the irrepresentable, an obscure anticipation of the mysterious secret come from the beyond. This leap toward the imminence of a vision without concept, this impatience turned toward the most crypted secret sets free a poetico-metaphorical overabundance."[87]

Yet if Derrida resists oracular utterance in this sublime mode, he endorses oracular meaning in another sense. Once oracular utterance is recognized to be a linguistic fiction, it can be used to derail claims that apocalyptic tone should be understood in one way and one way only. In this sense, oracle affects the meaning not only of messages but also of their senders and receivers. "Let us imagine," says Derrida,

> that there is *one* apocalyptic tone, a unity of the apocalyptic tone, and that *the* apocalyptic tone is not the effect of a generalised derailment, of a *Verstimmung* multiplying the voices and making the tones shift [*sauter*], opening each word to the haunting memory [*hantise*] of the other in an unmasterable polytonality, with grafts, intrusions, interferences [*parasitages*]. Generalised *Verstimmung* is the possibility for the other tone, or the tone of another, to come at no matter what moment to interrupt a familiar music. (Just as I suppose this is readily produced in analysis, but also elsewhere, when suddenly a tone come from one knows not where cuts short, if that can be said, the tone that tranquilly seemed to determine (*bestimmen*) the voice and thus insure the unity of destination, the self-identity of some addressee [*destinataire*] or sender [*destinateur*]. Henceforth *Verstimmung*, if that is what we call the derailment, the sudden change [*saute*] of tone as one would say *la saute d'humeur*, the sudden change of mood, it is the disorder or the delirium of destination (*Bestimmung*), but also the possibility of all emission or utterance.)[88]

I cite these difficult passages at length because they are central in describing the two major phases of Derridean deconstruction: the analytic and the affirmative.[89] Both have important roles to play in relation to apocalypse. The first is necessary in order to resist the manipulative use of apocalyptic discourse. The second is necessary in order to mobilize the discourse on behalf of subordinated individuals and groups. Oracular utterance needs to retain "enough apocalyptic desire" to motivate both the pursuit of social renovation and the continuing critique of "the apocalyptic discourse itself."

As in *The Post Card*, Derrida recognizes that philosophical polemic is a gendered discourse that likewise produces gender effects. He notices that Kant characterizes his antagonists as a secretive coterie of effeminate/emasculate aristocrats. This group expresses its claim to privileged access to the truth by means of a metaphor: they alone know "the secret" behind "the veil of Isis." Kant mocks their assertion of manliness: he accuses them "of behaving like 'musclemen (*Kraftmännern*)'" who . . . claim they have caught this goddess by the end of her robe and thus have made themselves her masters and lords." Borrowing from his antagonists the use of sexualized language and apocalyptic tone, Kant contends that their position represents "the death of philosophy," a process that he also describes as an unmanning. Derrida says that Kant accuses his antagonists "of castrating the *logos* and of defalcating off its phallus."[90] Tracking gender through Kant's text, Derrida shows that hegemonic masculinity inhabits philosophical discourse. Kant's remedy for castration is the removal from philosophy of metaphorical language or the "veiled Isis." Yet his critique of the mystagogues exemplifies the impossibility of achieving this goal, not only because language itself is a series of figures that veil truth but also because the play of veiling and unveiling underwrites the masculine investment in truth and vice-versa. In other words, philosophy depends on a gendered discourse in which "woman" (Isis) is the object of (male) knowledge. In addition, philosophical argument both produces and is structured by a secondary binary difference between men who know and emasculates who seduce. In this dyad, the male/female opposition is converted into a psychological structure of "masculinity" and "femininity" in individual males. Furthermore, the pair is transformed into a relational structure of masculinity in which "more" manly men dominate those who are deemed "less" manly and, somehow, "feminine." This division is homologous with relational definitions of masculinity that are important in antihomosexual polemic of the late nineteenth century. In England in the 1890s, Tory politicians and radical journalists inveighed against a clique of effete men of privilege who debauched the virtuous sons of the working class.[91] In sexology, the structure is validated within "third-sex theory," which claims that homosexuals are persons who possess female souls within male bodies.[92]

In succeeding years, Derrida has continued to use apocalyptic terms to express a range of tonalities of gender and sexuality.[93] He has also turned his attention to other apocalyptic sites: to the threat of atomic warfare during the nuclear scare of the first Reagan administration and to reflections on the Holocaust.[94] Recently, Derridean apocalypse has been most prominent in relation to what Christopher Norris terms the nuclear sublime. In the United States, "nuclear criticism" is a form of literary criticism that focuses on the changes in awareness that have accompanied the possibility of universal nuclear destruction. Nuclear criticism in this mode is sometimes depoliticized as a mode of ethical reflection cut off from questions of social policy.[95] In addition, in American deconstruction, Derrida's arguments about the rhetoric of nuclear deterrence are sometimes used to deny any reality other than textual to the ongoing debates.[96] Both tendencies abuse his intervention. Derrida calls into question the authority to determine social policy that specialists claim on the basis of nuclear expertise. He argues that these claims must be subjected to the most rigorous possible rhetorical analysis. Since the expertise needed to do so exists within the humanities, policymakers have a responsibility to involve students of the humanities in the debate over nuclear strategy.[97]

But Derrida has other things to say which are pertinent to the situation in which gay men have found themselves now for over a decade. Derrida's nuclear commentary is framed within the biblical genre of apocalypse. Like the angel of the Apocalypse, he carries messages about ultimate ending. His warnings come in the form of "missives" that draw attention to the unsuspected fictions that comprise the logic of nuclear deterrence. And he warns that nuclear war would "irreversibly destroy the entire archive and all symbolic capacity, would destroy the 'movement of survival,' what I call 'survivance,' at the very heart of life."[98]

AIDS has not destroyed the memory of gay existence, but it has made such destruction imaginable. Under the circumstances, gay writers have been pressed into service as angels of the millennium. Bearing messages to gays and to others, they remind us that an archive does exist and that it is our responsibility to carry its words. In gay writing, the trope of nuclear disaster has been used, in displaced fashion, to signify unspecified anxieties about continued individual and group existence in face of AIDS. This is the case with Glück's novel, which he wrote in the mid-1980s, after the onset of AIDS, but whose events are set before the definition of GRID in 1981. Given the chronology, "AIDS" is literally unsayable for the characters and the fictionalized, autobiographical narrator. But that narrator does express nuclear anxieties, widespread at the time, that carry subliminal messages about AIDS:

> Believing in a future would mean so much to Jack and me in our love-making . . . , you have no idea. At worst it would make Jack's reserve easier to bear, not to mention the melting ice-cap, the ruined ozone layer, nuclear proliferation, the polluted oceans and the corresponding rallies and marches. First we stopped having grandparents and extended families so each life came to equal its biological span. It's really the end of religion and I'm less disturbed by the implication than by all the mess to clean up. Now the race numbers its own days so again we are thrown back on ourselves: Dread Prospect.[99]

Glück as narrator is thrown back on the prospect of annihilation: his, the couple's, and ours. The "we" whom the passage addresses can be the narrator or everyone. It is also the more limited group of those who value love between men and who need each other to (re)construct the knowledge of an existence with a "future."

ONE

... # FIN DE SIÈCLE

(*Overleaf*) 3. Stephen Andrews, *A Change of Heart,* 1990. Photo by Isaac Applebaum. Courtesy Garnet Press Gallery, Toronto.

1

· · ·

LOOKING BACK
TOWARD THE FUTURE:
NEIL BARTLETT'S GIFT
FOR OSCAR WILDE

To speak of historicizing the future is to speak of apocalypse. Upper-case Apocalypse prophesies the imminence of Christ in His Second Coming. More generally, apocalypse refers to the four last things: death and judgment, Heaven or Hell. Translated into practices such as nuclear criticism, the four elements become a variable typology. In his book *In a Dark Time: The Apocalyptic Temper in the American Novel of the Nuclear Age*, Joseph Dewey distinguishes between "the cataclysmic imagination, the millennialist spirit, and the apocalyptic temper." In his schema, the first term emphasizes the horrors that accompany the end; the second projects the advent of a paradisal future; the third refers to a contemplative response that provides grounds for "hope" by plotting "an order as wide as the cosmos itself, an order that points humanity toward nothing less than the finale of its history."[1] When used to structure a particular series of events, typologies like Dewey's produce errors, in part because they carry residues of significance from religious or other contexts such as national history, in part because existence does not usually comply with a human desire for neat formulations. These efforts are at odds with basic elements of the genre, such as oracular utterance, which are designedly equivocal. And a single apocalyptic narrative may implicate all three of Dewey's phases simultaneously. These ambiguities are central to ethico-political aspects of apocalypse, which require a response that often resembles the religious experience of conversion. Without such changes in subjects, the social engagements toward which apocalyptic appeals are directed cannot be achieved.

Male homosexual history in England in the 1890s and gay history in the United States after Stonewall can both be articulated within a three-part model like Dewey's. The Wilde trials of the 1890s brought to an abrupt, catastrophic close an unprecedented efflorescence of middle-class male homosexual culture in England. The advent of AIDS occurred at the end of a decade of dramatic gay subcultural development. The evident contrast between these crises and the aspirations, efforts, and accomplishments of the immediately preceding years makes it inevitable that both periods will be cast within apocalyptic narratives of Before and After. In this typology, both the early 1890s and the 1970s are represented in millennialist terms. The periods after the trials and after the onset of AIDS are both seen as cataclysms.

The Wilde trials can be compared with the onset of AIDS in another way: both phenomena were used by hegemonic institutions to define the meaning of homosexual identity while negating the capacity of subjects of male-male desire to represent themselves. This public response has intensified the negative effects of AIDS for gay men, who have been faced not only with the danger of being erased by disease but who have also been denied agency by politicians, the media, and others who are all too ready to *represent* gay men and the members of other so-called risk groups.[2] Since what Wayne Koestenbaum refers to as the carceral sense of homosexual identity dates from the time of the trials, the intensified scapegoating of gay men that has occurred within the past decade gives the events of the 1890s new pertinence. Koestenbaum comments: "Post-Wilde gay readers discover they are gay as if it were a fact already there, when it is precisely their mourning of Wilde, their acknowledgment of a likeness, that guides them toward that identity."[3]

For most of the twentieth century, literary critics seemed to be capable of little more than translating Wilde's writings, especially *The Picture of Dorian Gray*, into cautionary moral tales. Yet within the past decade, a number of powerful new readings of Wilde's texts have emerged, all of which are sited in the context of late nineteenth-century male homosexual culture.[4] Faced with the disruptions posed by AIDS and the evident analogies between the 1890s and the present, gay writers seeking to imagine a future with and *after* AIDS have turned to the past. Among these efforts, Neil Bartlett's *Who Was That Man? A Present for Mr Oscar Wilde* (1988) is paradigmatic.

Bartlett casts recent gay history in London in terms of an apocalyptic narrative of Paradise Found and Lost. But just as in Derrida's comment or Glück's novel of San Francisco in the early 1980s, Bartlett follows the line of desire back to an earlier millennium and fall. He attaches his text's desire to the elusive figure of Oscar Wilde, whom he cruises. With its attractions, detours, and deferrals, however, the text that cruises evades typologies and returns to a present whose future remains to be determined. Bartlett addresses the book to Wilde but also includes autobiographical material and improvises a number of ways of constructing time in response to transformations in the existence of men with sexual and emotional ties to other men. Resisting the tendency to impose apocalyptic closure on the extraordinary development of gay culture since Stonewall, Bartlett produces an ending that refuses to conclude or sum up.

The defining recent moment of *Who Was That Man?* is an interruption that occurred in what had, by the late 1970s, become a complacent millennialist account of recent gay history. Bartlett portrays the decade as one in which young gay men could come to London and find abundant access to sexual partners. "And now," writes Bartlett, "this sexual ease, the one thing that we have in common, has been taken from us. The arrival of a fatal, sexually transmissible disease, the perfect image to revive the most ancient and popular hostilities against us and within us, is rearranging the practical details of our lives, the imagery of our lives, our self-perceptions." Writing from a moment after this break in gay sociality, Bartlett does not reject the self-representation of 1970s gay culture as Paradise Now even though subsequent knowledge necessarily ironizes that presentation. Rather, he acknowledges this story to be his story. "Sex," he writes, "has been our Paradise."[5] This story is also the narrative of what the struggle for gay liberation had achieved by the end of the decade. "We thought, for a moment, that we had finally arrived. The white, affluent, urban, male, butch, American style of the late seventies was, both as fiction and as reality, the real thing, the goal of all our struggles. (Not for nothing was our biggest discotheque opened under the name of *Heaven*.)"

Since Bartlett arrived in London more or less simultaneously with AIDS, the gay paradise that he evokes was receding even as he mastered its rituals. "The first British case of the rare cancer Kaposi's sarcoma . . . was reported in the [British medical journal, the *Lancet*]," in December 1981.[6] Bartlett acquired a gay lifestyle at the very moment when the multiple vulnerabilities of that style were about to be revealed. Writing with this double awareness, Bartlett is also aware that the earlier narrative could be installed as *the* gay lifestyle only at the price of certain exclusions. "It was a style that explicitly proposed a single culture. It offered to embrace everybody, to erase all differences in a generous, homogeneous, successful style. Commercially promoted on a mass scale, it seemed to absorb all the other, older styles. It arrived from elsewhere, fully developed and packaged, complete with a distinctive physique, costume, music and sexual code of practice" (220–221). Without denying the importance of the emergence of visible gay culture, the passage provides the elements of an ironic analysis of a commodified version of gay millenarianism. Bartlett poses a problematic switch between the rhetoric and politics of gay liberation ("all our struggles") and the *return* of this message as a commodity, "the real thing." Exactly who the return sender is is not clear—as presumably it was unclear to the men who enjoyed the benefits of the urban ghetto without inquiring about its (re)sources. Nor are the effects of this culture stated, though some are implicit in what "the package" excludes: what is *not* white, affluent, metropolitan, butch or "American." It is as much in response to these exclusions as to subsequent calamity that Bartlett sets in motion the search for Wilde and a London past shut outside the gate of "Heaven."

Bartlett could represent Paradise Lost as a portrait from Hell. In the passage in which he refers to "the arrival of a fatal, sexually transmissible disease," he begins to unfold new stories or, rather, new repetitions of old stories. Homosexuals carry plague; homosexuals are exemplary sufferers.[7] Bartlett knows that "sexual ease" is not the only thing that "we" have in common; "we" also have in common the experience of homophobia. But he defines his narrative neither in terms of oppression nor in terms of the paradise that he remembers. Faced with the failure of one apocalyptic narrative, Bartlett avoids converting it into another. Instead, he resorts to cruising as a motive that can organize a text that is at once both pre- and postmillenarian. This motive does not relinquish apocalyptic desire, since to cruise is to seek a momentary site of bliss that will redeem cruising as mere repetition. But cruising also functions as an archaeological search for the historical traces of subjects of male-male desire in London. Bartlett pieces together the codes that such subjects have devised in order to identify themselves to each other in a world in which officially they have no place.

This process dislocates the gay man who is the phantasmic object of Bartlett's cruising. The gay subject/object Bartlett searches for eludes him—not just in the person of Wilde but in the persons of many men: gays, homosexuals, queers, queens. Some of these men conform to stereotypes. Ernest Boulton and Frederick William Parke, for instance, were arrested in 1871 after entering in cross dress the retiring room for women in the Strand Theatre. Men like Boulton and Park continue to be subject to the play of visibility and invisibility projected by the dominant culture. At their trial, however, the play worked to their benefit since they were found not guilty of criminal charges on the grounds that they so flaunted their effeminacy that it could not possibly signify prurient and unspeakable acts.

Bartlett returns to the 1890s by way of a serial, open-ended narrative motivated by desire between men. He cruises Oscar Wilde, the subject/object of his study: "What if I rounded the corner of Villiers Street at midnight, and suddenly found myself walking by gaslight, and the man looking over his shoulder at me as he passed had the same moustache, but different clothes, the well-cut black and white evening dress of the summer of 1891—would we recognize each other? Would I smile at him too, knowing that we were going to the same place, looking for the same thing? Would our eyes meet? What would we talk about?" (xx–xxi). To answer these questions, Bartlett has to imagine the objects of Wilde's desire: the young men who received money in return for testifying against him; Robert Ross, his lover before and after the trials; and, of course, Bosie. As Bartlett researches the book, he finds that "it seemed a mistake to focus my attention on a single subject":

> Why is it that whenever the famous are exposed or eulogized, when their pictures appear in the paper alongside a scandal or reappraisal of an illustrious career, I always want to turn away, to go back to the parts of the city we've forgotten, to get lost in the strange streets? I'd rather talk about some ordinary queen I know, I'd rather relate the story of some man I've met, describe the face of some dancer or beauty. A book which gives a picture of that part of my history which is called "Oscar Wilde" would have to include all these stories and others besides. (30)

The line of desire quickly divides, requiring that Wilde's objects of desire become subjects of their own stories.

This process of ramification reverses the process that consolidated a gay "we" within the highly commodified "style" of the 1970s. It also poses an impossible task, since the track of desire pursued in this way can only end in a labyrinthine "city we've forgotten," in "strange streets" to get lost in. History and identity-formation will be replaced by tracing and losing track of individual lines. Hence, the *fin* of history, at least of gay history. In this sense, Bartlett, impelled by the onset of AIDS, enters the terrain of "post-gay" history, where globalizing narratives of gay liberation, whether in radical or commodified forms, are no longer credible. But there is a tension between this tendency toward negation and Bartlett's counterinsistence on inscribing the subject as "we." Who is this "we" that moves so easily between the urban gay lifestyle of the 1970s, with its evident exclusions, and the "post-AIDS," decentered collective subject that finds its way through a maze? The politics of the new situation incite Bartlett to cruise. In this way he hopes to begin to be able to describe the "we." Demarcations between writer, listener, reader, and object of study overlap. Bartlett's subject is also the "I" that writing produces and the addressee in middle voice to whom that writing is directed. The text produces the subjects of a gay textuality that include "I," "you," "Wilde," "some ordinary queen I know," and all those others.

The "I" who addresses this reader is a latter-day Lucien de Rubempré, the good-looking, ingenuous young man who came to the capital to make his fortune.[8] He also presents himself as the subject of a popular genre of gay pulp fiction in the 1970s: the coming-out story. Born in 1958, he arrives in London in 1981. His story is that of the young man from a small town who is drawn to the big city by sex and glamor. London is identified with "the other," with the man who has already successfully made the transition from outsider to insider in gay urban existence. This other is a latter-day Oscar Wilde, the phantasmic object of Bartlett's desire. His own particular story arrives at a conventional happy ending. He becomes familiar and comfortable with the pubs, clubs, restaurants, and other cruising grounds of gay London. He finds a lover. Success. Finale. Lights out.

Bartlett poses the reader whom he also cruises as the subject/object of a similar narrative. Cruising results in successful socialization as a gay man. Bliss is a way station en route. Entering the precincts of paradise, he says: "If we are ever going to get there, then surely it will be at half past one on a Sunday morning. When the music bites, when everyone you look at is so handsome, as the temperature rises, you can feel yourself sweat for joy. In the middle of town, in the middle of the night, the walls of Jericho are about to fall. Surely here, and now, the rules no longer apply. We are about to escape. The world is about to change" (215). The apocalyptic inflection of this passage, however, interferes with the message. Within the terms of the biblical analogy, gay men should be "the children of Israel" about to take Jericho and enter the Promised Land as the angel has foretold (Josh. 6.1, 5.14). But Bartlett appears to have more sympathy with the Canaanites within the city, whose walls for the moment protect them from slaughter by the elect. The identification of a gay reader oscillates between the two parties.

Invoking biblical types does not stabilize group identity or chart its future. The "we," the "walls" of the Philistine city, the "world" that "is about to change" refer to a destiny larger, more dangerous, and more obscure than that of gay acculturation. Once this possibility becomes audible, "Bartlett" can no longer assume that he and other gay men are "looking for the same thing." He becomes aware of the need to undertake a genealogy of sexual difference: "We abolish time and distance, difference, in exclaiming, *Oh! He's just like us.* We refuse the task (and pleasure) of identifying where he is like us, where he differs. We admire his face, but we don't want to talk to him in case he has the wrong accent. We wouldn't follow him along the street in case this familiar geography were to shift under our feet" (217). How does one cruise once desire becomes variable? In the description of dancing "at half past one," narrative begins to become its own imaginary double, since read in the shadow of AIDS, the apocalyptic projection of fantasies of collective "escape" is all too ironic. Yes, "the world is about to change," but not as "I"/"you" intend(ed) or suppose(d).

The task of genealogy determines the generic structure of the book. Without a model of lineal descent or collective election, representation of individual and group history is necessarily composite. *Who Was That Man?* includes straightforward narrative history, fragments of confession, diary excerpts, pieces of literary criticism, and entries from a commonplace book. Important connections are made *across* genres so that, for instance, it is by means of an exegesis of Wilde's "Portrait of Mr W. H." (1889) that Bartlett theorizes (by showing that Wilde theorizes) the importance of stereotypical images of desire in producing desire between men. These connections between texts and across genres are crucial because they testify to what Bartlett refers to as the textual character of homosexual and gay desire. Equally important, they indicate the fugitive and incomplete character of that desire. Accordingly, while the rhetorical gambit of *Who Was That Man?* to tell yet again the story of the young man from the provinces, presupposes the familiarity of the story to be told, gay lives remain persistently outside the satisfactory closure of conventional life stories. At the end of *Who Was That Man?* Bartlett turns his attention away from "I," "you," and "Wilde" and focuses instead on seven different accounts of history, some of them single-line citations from Wilde (for example, "The only real people are the people who never existed" [236]). In this way, Bartlett shifts from presenting identity as consciousness to presenting it as a textual event. Recourse to citation indicates the inadequacy of the voice of the "I" to articulate relations of desire between men within history. Because the citations from Wilde yield no single narrative, the reader needs to supplement Bartlett (and Wilde's) intentionality with his (or her) own. The shift to textuality functions as an address, provoking the reader to a response whose content is not already prescribed in Bartlett's text. Thus addressed, the reader is no longer solely the object of Bartlett's cruising.

"The only real people are the people who never existed." The sort of response that *could* be made to this is a line spoken by a character in Virginia Woolf's *Between the Acts* (1941), a fiction both feminist and apocalyptic which disrupts the narrative of compulsory heterosexuality. One of the protagonists is a married woman who is held immobile by the play of "love and hate" in her marriage. At the end of the book, she complains: "Surely it was time someone invented a new plot, or that the author came out from the bushes."[9] Isa ("Is a . . ."/, "I sa[y]," "Isaiah," the prophetic type of one who comes after and who saves mankind by taking its sufferings upon him/herself) is one of those characters that "never existed." The narrative into which she has been impelled as wife and mother is not "real." It does not address needs and desires that remain outside verisimilitude because verisimilar existence is, for her, existence within *someone else's* story. Isa's name suggests a different, apocalyptic trajectory that is especially haunting in a novel written early in World War II. In this second narrative, her exemplary sufferings, like those of the Jewish prophet, are the type of yet other sufferings that could redeem the time in which she is caught. This other narrative remains an elusive possibility.

Bartlett focuses on gay identity as a double representation that is thoroughly prescribed but that also resists prescription. The moral of his text is the conviction that the denial of either set of operations is delusive. The final words of Bartlett's text refer to Dorian Gray's attempt to destroy the portrait that by disclosing a man's desire for him, had first prompted Dorian to recognize himself as a subject of desire: "*The Picture of Dorian Gray* ends when Dorian, on the last page of his story, picks up a knife and slashes to ribbons the image which has haunted his life" (237). In the fantastic conclusion to Wilde's novel, Dorian's attempt to destroy the image has the opposite effect of restoring it to its original beauty. It is Dorian himself, not his image, that is caught within the terms of Wilde's tendentious moral parable. Moral causes have inescapable effects. What triumphs intact is the power of representation in the figure of the unmarred portrait.

Bartlett argues that the coming-out story was the dominant representation of gay identity during the 1970s. A remarkably efficient genre, identity, politics, community, and desire coalesce in it. Bartlett describes the narrative in three forms: as an autobiographical narrative whose basic structure is already familiar ("We knew it all along" [23]); as the story of emergence of a collective gay identity after Stonewall; and as the writing of gay history and identity by deciphering the life of some great figure of the past, say Tchaikovsky. "Layers of clues, suggestions and distortion (letters, works of art, symptoms) are stripped away until we arrive at the truth" (24). This truth is exemplary: Tchaikovsky becomes the figure of prophecy. He is revealed to be the suffering servant, the surplus value from whose victimization is the emergence of gay identity.

When Bartlett scrutinizes Wilde, he finds something else. An Isaiah-figure, yes, but that's it, a *figure*. Until the moment of the trials Wilde defined himself in oppositional terms as a satirist within the upper classes. The success of his comedies in the theater depended on inverting the customary values of the privileged world that he and his dramatis personae inhabited. Wilde was ejected from that world by being forced to coincide with the representation of himself as homosexual. As Ed Cohen argues, this effect was produced in the course of the three trials, at the end of the first of which the *Daily Telegraph* states: "As for any further influence which Wilde can exercise upon social, literary, or artistic matters, and the contempt and disgust felt for such a character being fully met by the hideous downfall of the man and of his theories, we may dismiss the prisoner without further remark."[10] That is, the trial and its coverage in the press "revealed" the "truth" that Wilde was a pathological, criminal "type."[11] After that, the only mode of writing left to him was that of confession under the eyes of his warders. Hence his final work, *De Profundis*, addressed to his former lover, Alfred Douglas.

Wilde did not go easily. It took three trials and the active participation of the Solicitor-General finally to convict him.[12] Once released from prison, he refused to represent the "truth" that had been produced with so much effort and expense by his superiors. Deprived of an oppositional role in British society, he departed for the Continent under the assumed name of Sebastian Melmoth. The name suggests Wilde's revisionary representation of the identity impressed upon him. Saint Sebastian is a Christian martyr who is usually portrayed as a handsome young male nude shot with arrows. This name connotes both Wilde as martyr to British justice and the interdicted object of his desire. Melmoth is the name of the Byronic hero of a Gothic novel "by Charles Maturin, our hero's maternal great-uncle." The character is "a hideous, heartless man, condemned to wander the earth, homeless for eternity, in penance for some . . . unnamed, unnameable crime." Bartlett comments: "The choice of names indicates the bitterness and the care with which the new personality was to be forged. What had in fact been imposed (exile, loss of family, being a criminal) was made to appear chosen, a chosen role" (165). Bartlett registers this assumption of a new identity under the term "camp": "The characteristic name for the heroic life of things or people which have no right to exist was invented, along with so many other features of our lives, during the life and times of Mr Oscar Wilde. It is a word that we still use. We still consider inventing a new life to be an ordinary, even inevitable activity. If you can't be authentic (and you can't), if this doesn't feel like real life (and it doesn't), then you can be *camp*" (167). Bartlett reminds his reader that camping is a response to the exclusionary effects of hegemonic culture. Men like Wilde reject a compelled, negative authenticity by forging fictitious identities for themselves from the second-hand trappings and the hand-me-down costumes and decor of camp.

The reminder that hegemonic culture denies authenticity to homosexuals and that they have been compelled to devise an identity out of inauthentic materials puts readers on guard against the formula of the coming-out narrative, which attempts to stabilize gay selves, community, and politics by asserting the authenticity of gay identity. This project must always be qualified by the fact that the "truth" about gay men has been produced elsewhere and as such is always negative. Denying this fact means denying the ways in which gay men have repeatedly been identified as "Canaanites." Gay existence is always at least potentially hazardous. Reclaiming or fashioning an identity does not sequester it from the political effects of others. Recalling the intensified legal prosecutions of the early 1950s, one man writes: "The temperature of the time was quite unpleasant. We thought we were all going to be arrested and there was going to be a big swoop. The newspapers were full of it. I got so frightened I burnt all my love letters."[13] Faced with the threat of destruction, the camp persona writes his or her life as *somebody else's*. Bartlett asks readers to see their existence as in opposition to the naturalizing structures that Wilde resisted and in collaboration with many homosexuals and gay men who have resisted by camping. Camp is not just a current mode. Rather, it is a work of *bricolage* shared across time and across class and other differences and motivated by opposition to those who criminalize and pathologize the pleasures of same-sex desire.

Although commercial gay culture today is on the rebound from the devastating effects of AIDS, it can never again be the place of arrival that it was, for some, for a moment, during the 1970s. Henceforth, gay culture will always exist at a number of different sites, including, as even *The New York Times* has acknowledged, the expressly political.[14] If the style of the 1970s was "white, affluent, urban, male, butch, American," then it excluded or subordinated those who were, variously, people of color, ethnic, poor or just getting by, small town or rural, poorly educated, closeted, married or bisexual, effeminate or crossdressing or transsexual. One might also add to this number those who were either too young or too old. In short, the myth that those answering the description constituted gay sociality in the 1970s is just that—a myth. As such, it was continually challenged.[15] Nonetheless, this particular representation defined the terms in relation to which other views were put forward. The assertion of "queer" sexualities in the 1980s, for instance, was determined by their dis-identification from a homogeneous representation of the white, urban middle-class lifestyle along with the liberal variant of gay politics with which it is associated. The emergence in Britain during the 1980s of gay cultural producers such as Bartlett, Isaac Julien, and Sunil Gupta, among others, has made it possible to represent male sexualities in new ways despite the efforts of the Tory Government to impose a singular meaning on nonheterosexual relations.[16] Even in mass cultural vehicles, such as Neil Jordan's film *The Crying Game* (1992), one glimpses the possibility that the representation of marginalized sets of social relations can provide new contexts for sexual politics—though apparently the British public, which ignored the film on its initial release, is not eager to listen.

Bartlett's reader is left in a position like that in which Bartlett finds himself after he tries to share his discoveries with "another man, one of the older men whose story I'd missed—a middle-aged Irishman who lives alone in the block next to mine—and he got angry. He'd heard it all before. He stood up and looked out of the window, away from me, and said: *That's it; there's nothing new in it. You should watch those old queens sometimes, they had their own way of doing it, their own performance. A lot of those queens paved the way for you, that was my generation. You should watch us a bit, you boys, you young men, you might learn something"* (128–129). Bartlett comments: "I try to remember what he said when I'm copying out these stories. The fact that men like him are invisible, whether in the 1980s, the 1950s, or the 1870s is incredible. When I find traces of his life, and of other lives, I'm not sure how to react, whether to celebrate, or turn away and look out of the window like he did, angry, angry that all these stories have been forgotten" (129). Bartlett's encounter suggests what can happen when the object of study begins to talk back. Other gay men have their own versions of gay history. These accounts can include fixed characterizations ("old queens") and axiomatic narratives ("A lot of those queens paved the way for you"). The narrators are often of a different age and ethnicity from "you." And their experience of desire for other men may have left them alone and embittered—as Bartlett's interlocutor seems to be. Gay subjectivity is not only a site, it's a turf that has always been already visited and claimed. Men who think they've already "been there" are liable to be angered by new proclamations of what to them is old news or by efforts to destabilize familiar truths about what it means to be gay. Similarly, the new kid on the block is liable to resent someone else telling him what it means to be sexually different. An inquiry like Bartlett's is bound to provoke resentment and anger. Interestingly, both the older man and Bartlett have anger in common. But anger will not overcome their disarray. Looking out the window at a cityscape during a strained and interrupted exchange in which narratives to be told, heard, and reheard remain in suspension—this is the end to which Bartlett's search comes.

This kind of ending avoids closure. It is anti-apocalyptic, since narratives of social existence that end at some ultimate place can do so only by excluding other trajectories and endings. In *Who Was That Man?* Bartlett mingles apocalyptic with anti-apocalyptic modes of narration because the demand that gay existence yield truth has been a condition of the construction of gay identities. Moreover, the quest for a visionary locus has been a motivating desire within male-male sexual polemic. On neither ground can the existence of apocalyptic pattern in gay narrative be merely denied. Yet to acquiesce in either would be to produce a story that forecloses others, many of which have not yet been heard.

2

•••

DORIANISM

In this chapter I follow Neil Bartlett's example in looking back to the 1890s as a site at which key issues in relations between subjects of male-male desire become evident. As these subjects were increasingly specified as "homosexual," the old patterns that mobilized male-male libidinal energies in service of the nation-state or in the production of high culture came under severe pressure. I conclude this chapter with a discussion of works by male homosexuals in which are set in play reverse discourses that challenge the construction of desire in elite culture. Men like Pater, Wilde, and Carpenter were interested in drawing a distinction between emergent male homosexual culture and the male homosocial culture in which homosexual desire was regularly induced, then directed to hegemonic purposes. In order to be able to do so, such writers needed at some point to turn their attention to the critical analysis of the erotics of pedagogy in the public schools and at Oxford and Cambridge. Pater does so in one of his final works, "Emerald Uthwart" (1892). In this short fiction, he shows how two young Englishmen are drawn into love by the discipline of school life and the place in it of Greek studies. Subsequently, they place their devotion in service of Great Britain in the armed struggle against Napoleon, and both die. Similarly, in *The Picture of Dorian Gray* (1890), Wilde casts a skeptical eye on Basil Hallward's unsuccessful attempt to validate his attraction to a beautiful young aristocrat by placing it in the service of high art. In Wilde's novel too, both young men die.

The reverse discourses of Pater and Wilde pose a major question concerning sexual and emotional ties between men. If the traditional enlistment of these ties in cultural production of various sorts is to be challenged, what new rationales will be offered in its place? Or will writers, defending such ties on aesthetic grounds, argue that they are characterized—as Kant contends that art is characterized—by a *"finalité sans fin,"* a "finality without [moral, social, political or some other] end." [1] Late Victorian writers offer a variety of proposals. Pater, perhaps with Dorian and Basil in mind, deals with the question by arguing that desire between men needs to be translated from artistic commodification into existence, into the "real portrait of a real young" man. John Gray, a former friend and, probably, lover of Wilde, sees the idolization of young male beauty as leading inevitably first to sexual and gender inversion and then to death. Edward Carpenter attempts to validate homosexual desire by enlisting it in the service of the evolution of the race.

In order better to understand the argument in which these writers are involved, it is worthwhile to follow Bartlett's lead yet further in time to the very beginning of the century when apocalyptic anxieties and hopes were focused on the figure of Napoleon and his armies. In early nineteenth-century invocations of love between comrades-in-arms, three sorts of ends are invoked: the sacrifice of soldiers' lives, the moral purpose to which that sacrifice is devoted (that is, saving civilization from the enemy), and the catastrophic end that threatens if one's own party is defeated. The writers of the 1890s rejected this triple linkage of the ends of individual lives to the ethical and eschatological "ends" of humanity. During the Napoleonic period and afterward, sexual and emotional ties between men were mobilized in England, France, and Germany as a way to consolidate national brotherhood. Patriotic brothers were subject to a sacrificial logic in which their "collective casualties *within* war" validated the ideals—"freedom," "national sovereignty," and so on—in whose name the war was being fought.[2]

This set of factors was usually alluded to when what I call Dorianism was invoked in the nineteenth century. Dorianism refers to the institution of pederasty as it existed in the army of ancient Sparta. In Foucauldian terms, the idealization of love between soldiers might be described as yet another "technology of the self," "centering on the body as a machine: its disciplining, the optimization of its capabilities, the extortion of its forces, the parallel increase of its usefulness and its docility, its integration into systems of efficient and economic controls."[3] Between the defeat of Napoleon at Waterloo in 1815 and the early 1900s, writers in England frequently considered the subject of "Greek love," a phrase that David Halperin describes as a "coded phrase for the unmentionable term *paederasty*." In these discussions, pederasty, defined as "the sexual pursuit of adolescent males by adult males," usually means pederasty in the form of the educational, at times philosophic institution that existed at Athens.[4] This institution, whose meaning hinges on the induction of young male citizens into the privileges and responsibilities of adult citizenship through friendship with an older male, I refer to as Athenian-model pederasty. In ancient Greece, there was another form of pederasty, namely, the practice at Sparta of friendship and love between an adult male citizen/soldier and a younger one preparing to achieve the same status.[5] This relationship I refer to as Spartan-model pederasty.[6] Because nineteenth-century philologists associate it with the Dorian invaders of Lacedaemon, I refer to its invocation in painting and writing as *Dorianism*.

Framing their representations in terms of the social uses of desire between men, the apologists of Dorianism raised questions of continuing interest in relation to ethical aspects of desire between men. On the one hand, nineteenth-century approaches demonstrate how desire can be constructed in terms of nationalist and ethnic ambitions. These ends are served by invoking apocalyptic narratives and by other aesthetic means, especially the exploitation of sublime affects. On the other hand, the attempt by Pater and Wilde to sever emergent homosexuality from service to the state prompted urgent questions about how modes of sociality among homosexuals could be developed and sustained.

In the nineteenth century the willingness of some writers to validate sexual and emotional ties between men when these bonds were exercised in military action in effect effaces these relations. Desire between men is praiseworthy only when merged in nationalist fraternity or even, as in the painting of Jacques-Louis David, in a model of father-son relationship. When, as occurred later in the century, sexual ties between males began to become evident, they fell outside the normalizing representation of masculinity in nineteenth-century middle-class culture that links respectability with purity and virility. Under these circumstances, such ties were construed as signs of a criminal conspiracy against the state.[7]

Leonidas at Thermopylae

After one group of Dorian warriors gained ascendancy in ancient Lacedaemon, they found themselves surrounded by other Greeks. In order to guarantee the hegemony of this one group while suppressing conflict within it, the Spartan lawmaker Lycurgus followed the example of Crete by converting this group of Dorian fighting men into a permanent military corps.[8] He inscribed pederasty within the constitution as a prime means of socializing young men into this organization. This account of the origin of Spartan-model pederasty associates Dorianism with military expansion as well as with the dominance of one ethnic and class group over others within the boundaries of a particular state. The Lycurgan constitution was installed in the face of imminent internal collapse. Similarly Dorianism in the nineteenth century was usually invoked in the face of fears of catastrophic apocalypse. This atmosphere is readily reinforced by assumptions about cultural and social decadence, especially in the fin de siècle, and by invocations of a sacrificial logic that make a seductive appeal to subjects of male-male desire. Such men are subliminally offered an exchange: their lives for validation of their desires for other men.[9]

When the French state under Napoleon was extending its dominion across Europe, the French painter David glorified Dorianism. In the context of the German nationalism provoked by French expansionism, the philologist C. O. Müller did too. At Oxford, where Müller's *History and Antiquities of the Doric Race* became a standard undergraduate text, sages like Ruskin, Arnold, and Benjamin Jowett endorsed prescriptions drawn from the Spartan constitution as refracted through Plato in *The Republic*. These endorsements of the disciplinary organization of male sociality were underwritten by the general principle within late eighteenth-century humanism that the structure of individual psychology should mirror the structure of the state and vice-versa. As Paul de Man says of the end of Friedrich Schiller's *Letters on Aesthetic Education* (1795): "The 'state' that is here being advocated is not just a state of mind or of soul, but a principle of political value and authority that has its own claims on the shape and the limits of our freedom."[10] The metaphoric relationship between individual and corporate organization remained a potent one in nineteenth-century writing.

Apocalyptic narrative, decadence, ethnic prejudice, sacrificial logic, and the aesthetic ideology all figure in Immanuel Kant's representation of the sublime. In the immediate aftermath of the French Revolution, of which he was a partisan,[11] Kant includes in his analysis of the dynamic sublime the following paean to the military man:

> Even where civilization has reached a high pitch there remains this special reverence for the soldier; only that there is then further required of him that he should also exhibit all the virtues of peace—gentleness, sympathy and even becoming thought for his own person; and for the reason that in this we recognize that his mind is above the threats of danger. And so, comparing the statesman and the general, men may argue as they please as to the pre-eminent respect which is due either above the other; but the verdict of the aesthetic judgement is for the latter. War itself, provided it is conducted with order and a sacred respect for the rights of civilians, has something sublime about it, and gives nations that carry it on in such a manner a stamp of mind only the more sublime the more numerous the dangers to which they are exposed, and which they are able to meet with fortitude. On the other hand, a prolonged peace favours the predominance of a mere commercial spirit, and with it a debasing self-interest, cowardice, and effeminacy, and tends to degrade the character of the nation.[12]

An interesting shift occurs in the course of this passage from "the soldier" (*der Krieger*), who is liable to die, and "the general" (*der Feldherr*), who will most likely survive. The experience of the sublime varies with one's position within a hierarchy. Kant endorses "civilization" as superior to the "mere commercial spirit," a phrase that alludes to the petty bourgeoisie and to Jews.[13] To achieve something higher, in the name of the state, renders the immolation of individual soldiers sublime and saves "the character of the nation" [*die Denkungsart des Volks*] from contamination by "effeminacy."

David's painting *Leonidas at Thermopylae* provides a paradigmatic example of the aesthetic inscription of Spartan pederasty within the rhetoric of the nation-state in crisis. Referring to the sheer mass of nude male flesh in this unusually large painting, Robert Rosenblum terms the scene "the Davidian equivalent of a classical locker room," offering "the sexualized male counterpart" of contemporary academic paintings of nude females in Turkish baths.[14] In David's painting, however, the male nude is enlisted against a racial Other. At the right center of the painting, David emphasizes the institutional role of pederasty within Spartan life by portraying a fully mature soldier tenderly embracing a male ephebe garbed in sword, scabbard, and garland. The only nude figure whose genitals are not partly or altogether concealed from view is another ephebe, tying his sandal in the left foreground. The suffusion of a wide range of male relations with desire and love is signaled by the young men who dance together to the left and right while the thoroughly masculinized body of Leonidas at center is the object of an admiring look from another male in full prime.[15] In these representations, sexualized desire includes a wide range of relations of age and body type. According to Müller, in Crete and Sparta "the youth . . . wore the military dress which had been given him [by his φῐλήτωρ]; and fought in battle next his lover, inspired with double valour by the gods of war and love . . . ; and even in man's age he was distinguished by the first place and rank in the course, and certain insignia worn about the body."[16]

Although the Napoleonic Code of 1810 retained the decriminalization of sodomy included in the penal code of 1791, the evident homoeroticism of David's painting is not due to a relatively tolerant attitude toward sexual intimacy between men. Rather, the painting provides at once a demonstration and an analysis of the inscription of desire in the public order, in part through the dance, whose members are of one sex only, in part by the look of the soldier seated at right center. This look pertains to male homosocial culture, which by visual address fixes in place the idealized and idealizing figure of Leonidas, the king of Sparta killed by the Persians at Thermopylae in 480 B.C. If look and gesture inscribe male homosocial relations of power, the process of inscription is figured in literal fashion in the soldier at upper left who incises into the wall of the defile the epitaph: "Passerby, go tell Sparta that her children have died for her."[17] This use of prosopopeia is particularly chilling when written by and for men who are still alive. In the dance, indeed, men offer themselves to this process of memorialization. Equally chilling is the attempt to construct individual and collective memory before the fact. In

4. Jacques Louis David, *Leonidas at Thermopylae*, 1799–1803, 1813–1814. Louvre, Paris. Courtesy Giraudon/Art Resource, New York.

5. Man and young boy. David, *Leonidas at Thermopylae* (detail)

6. Leonidas and admirer. David, *Leonidas at Thermopylae* (detail)

the cultural modernity of Charles Baudelaire and Marcel Proust, memory is represented as the most individual aspect of consciousness. But already at the beginning of the century, David regarded memory as to be written in stone before the birth of future children. David's painting is organized in accord with this operation, not only by virtue of the impact of its overwhelming size but also by how the viewer's attention is focused on the central figure. In this way, the viewer is positioned within a male homosocial system. If there is any space of resistance to these processes, it occurs in the exploitation of an aspect of the work which belongs to all painting; namely, its poignant silence.[18] This limitation of the medium permits the viewer to enter into the mute world of those who will soon be dead and in this way remember aspects of existence that the memory excludes.

The inscription of male love within a statist project ennobles aesthetically and morally both male relations and the political aim. The implicit apocalyptic narrative of the painting, the setting at Thermopylae where this panoply of flesh is about to be sacrificed, endows devotion with the sublime value of dying for the sake of civilization itself. This raising of levels is signified in Leonidas's upward glance, which can be described as the sublimating operator of the painting, and by the open sky behind the defile as well as by "the fortified city" in the distance, "which is supposed to represent Athens."[19] The Doric temple facade behind the king, which was to be favored for the facades of nineteenth-century institutions such as universities, museums, and banks, serves a like function, as do the movements of the dancing warriors, whose arabesque stance, invented in 1790 by Pierre Gardel, choreographer and ballet master of the Paris Opéra, was used in huge, outdoor pantomimes celebrating the Revolution. The arabesque, with its connotations of both flight and elevation, signified purity and transcendence in fin de siècle French art and thought.[20]

Although David began working on this subject as early as 1799, by 1814, the year of its completion, when he showed the painting in his studio, the parallel between Leonidas and Napoleon, in exile at Elba, was evident, even to Napoleon when he visited David's studio during his brief return to Paris. During the earlier phase in which David had worked on the painting, he portrayed a number of the more lyrical figures: the ephebe tying his sandal and the young boy with the warrior. Only a decade later did David fix the position of Leonidas and his admirer and add the soldier with spear and helmet to the far left. In this shift in looks and body types, David registers the experience of ten more years of war. Vulnerability could be portrayed when one could still hope that young soldiers might return, alive and uninjured from battle. Later, the nude wears its musculature as though it were armor. This masculinizing of the body signifies casualties already incurred. Similarly, in inception, the painting included among its addressees David's son, who was instructed thereby in exemplary virtue. David returned to the subject shortly after his son, now grown to adulthood, was feared to have been lost in action at Leipzig.[21] The epitaph of the painting, then, is both prospective and retrospective: in 1800, David looks forward to victory, but by 1813 he was looking back on mass destruction and defeat.

Thinking Greek

German nationalism awoke in the resistance to French control of the German states in the opening years of the nineteenth century. Aryan "purity" was opposed to both English materialism and Jewish "effeminacy"—a construction that has survived well into this century.[22] After Waterloo, philologists like Friedrich Gottlieb Welcker and his successor at the university of Göttingen, Carl Ottfried Müller, invoked the Spartan model for their own ends. The idealization of Hellenic culture in the writings of Schiller and Johann Winckelmann had already guaranteed that it "would play a privileged role in the creation of German national identity and values."[23] For Welcker and Müller, there was the additional favorable association of the Dorians, northern invaders of the Peloponnesus, with Germany. Martin Bernal has argued that "the university of Göttingen, founded in 1734 by George II, Elector of Hanover and King of England, and forming a cultural bridge between Britain and Germany," was the prime source of the "Aryan Model" of Greek ethnic purity. Müller, who was "extreme in his Romanticism and ahead of his time in the intensity of his racialism and anti-Semitism," made use of modern source criticism in order to disavow North African and Semitic elements in Greek culture.[24] The attraction to Sparta was especially appropriate since "it was the Greeks themselves who first drew a sharp contrast between Asia and Europe, between 'Us' in the democratic West and the 'Barbarians' in the royal, imperial East." It was, as well, the Greek victories over the Persians between 490 and 479 B.C. that prompted Athenians to dreams of imperial grandeur that were soon to result in disaster.[25]

German responses to pederasty were both defensive and innovative. Welcker invoked the Greek poet Sappho as the model of a celibate *male* pederasty that provided one of "the foundations of Greek nationalism and the source of Greek artistic power."[26] In Welcker's desexualizing model, the attempt to achieve *Deutschheit* had homophobic, misogynistic, and erotophobic aspects.[27] Yet in his defense of *Männerliebe*, love of men, he extends his discussion to "the larger context of all homoerotic relations. Secondly, unlike many of his followers, Welcker refuses to deny completely the sensual content of 'love of men' by claiming that the phenomenon existed solely for pedagogical purposes." Müller seconded Welcker in "his history of the Dorians, in which he proposes this civilization as the model for the Greek genius and *pederastia* as the origin of that genius."[28] In this book, which in its English translation (1830, 1839) became a fixture of undergraduate education at Oxford, Müller expresses his intention to discuss pederasty "without examining it in a moral point of view, which does not fall within the scope of this work."[29] Müller considers pederasty without casting it in terms of a Christian antithesis between purity and "vice."[30] Instead he challenges his readers to discern the meaning of this institution within the terms of ancient Dorian existence or, in other words, to think Greek.[31] *Thinking Greek* in this sense becomes a permanent challenge (and problem) to latter-day Dorians. Although the tendency, as Müller himself in part exemplifies, is to relapse into a "Christian" view, through the remainder of the nineteenth century the problem of pederasty as Müller situates it remains central to Dorianism. The key questions are the ones that he implicitly poses: What is the Dorian understanding of pederasty? How do I as a modern man enter into that understanding? How does success in that effort change me and, potentially, my society? The questions have a utopian aspect, since implicit in the representations of Müller and others I consider is a metaphoric apprehension of the Dorian/modern analogy.

In *A Problem in Greek Ethics*, written for the most part in 1873 but published only posthumously in 1897 and then only until its publisher "was convicted on a charge of obscenity,"[32] Symonds associates pederasty with the Dorian invasions of the Peloponnesus: "To be loved was honourable, for it implied being worthy to be died for. To love was glorious, since it pledged the lover to self-sacrifice in case of need. In these conditions the paiderastic passion may have well combined manly virtue with carnal appetite, adding such romantic sentiment as some stern men reserve within their hearts for women. A motto might be chosen for a lover of this early Dorian type from the Aeolic poem ascribed to Theocritus: 'And made me tender from the iron man I used to be.'"[33] In Symonds's text, at least as later revised, Dorianism changes its character, since he speaks of utilizing "homosexual passions . . . for the benefit of society" with an eye not primarily to the needs of the nation but on behalf of himself and other homosexuals who sought to decriminalize sexual activities between men. Hence he addresses the text "to medical psychologists and jurists."[34] In contrast, Müller's discussion is compromised by the return of Christian moral conceptions. Still, Müller's final discussion does open a space for "this pure connexion": "In early times this proximity never would have been permitted, if any pollution had been apprehended from it."[35] *Thinking Greek* means apprehending this space, which exists between celibacy and *stuprum*, the Ciceronian term that Symonds translates with the word "outrage."[36]

Of course, for those less carefully decorous than Müller and Symonds, "pure connexion" could be basely parodied. The term "fellator," with which A. C. Swinburne peppers his correspondence, may be read as a transliteration of Müller's φιλήτωρ, the Cretan term for the male lover in pederasty.[37] Swinburne's point is not to specify which sexual practices were involved in Spartan-model pederasty. Rather, his abusive translation is designed to bring into view the general connection between intimate male bonding and sexual practices about which Müller is so discreet.

Müller's position, which Symonds draws on, is by no means the most daring one that exists in texts written in German. In *Mother Right* (1861), Johann Bachofen, a Swiss university professor and friend of Jakob Burckhardt and Friedrich Nietzsche, releases Sappho from the bonds of celibacy to which she had been relegated by Welcker and his successors. Declining to assess her "according to the ethical concepts of Christianity," Bachofen argues that "the love of women for their own sex was equivalent to the Orphic ἄρρενες ἔρωτες. Here again the sole purpose was to transcend the lower sensuality, to make physical beauty into a purified psychic beauty." Despite the sublimating rhetoric, purification in Bachofen's genuinely dialectical context means not celibacy but a fully embodied love in contrast to the "hetaerism" or profligacy that he associates with archaic or pre-Hellenic culture. Bachofen observes: "the madness of her heart . . . accomplished greater things than human reason." Sappho's eros, like Diotima's in the *Symposium*, is "not unitary and absolutely pure, but of twofold origin."[38] When Friedrich Engels drew on Bachofen's theory of mother right in his account of the genealogy of the family, he excluded this aspect of his thought. Instead, in an aside on Athenian pederasty, Engels condemns it as a corruption that issued from the reduced status of the wives of Athenian citizens: "This degradation of the women was avenged on the men and degraded them also till they fell into the abominable practice of sodomy."[39]

Discourse and Counterdiscourse at Oxford

In his introduction to *The Republic*, Benjamin Jowett writes: "The good man and the good citizen only coincide in the perfect State; and this perfection cannot be attained by legislation acting upon them from without, but, if at all, by education fashioning them from within."[40] The metaphoric relationship that Jowett draws between the structure of the state and the structure of the citizen is a commonplace of mid-Victorian social theory. John Ruskin makes use of it in *Unto This Last* (1860), as does Arnold in *Culture and Anarchy* (1869). All three writers draw on Plato's use of the metaphor in *The Republic*. Since Plato modeled his republic on Sparta, Victorian uses of the metaphor allude to Sparta. Given the importance that Plato and the Victorians both attach to "education," Dorianism, the special institution of Spartan pedagogy, is also implicated in these discussions. In "Emerald Uthwart," in which Pater analyzes the consciousness effects of Spartan-model pedagogy in nineteenth-century England, he comments at one point: "The social type [Plato] preferred, as we know, was conservative Sparta and its youth; whose unsparing discipline had doubtless something to do with the fact that it was the handsomest and best-formed in all Greece."[41] The surprising direction that this sentence takes from "discipline" to male beauty draws attention to the unspecified connections that exist between these two terms. Does "discipline" produce the "best-formed" body? Does a "handsome" face inspire disciplinary energy? The relations of cause and effect remain unspecified in Pater's deliberately vague phrasing.

Like the Plato of *The Republic*, Arnold in *Culture and Anarchy* appeals to a metaphoric relation between the structure of the subject and the structure of the state in order to provide a bulwark against the "anarchy" that he apprehends from the extension of the vote in 1867 to previously unenfranchised members of the middle, lower-middle, and working classes. Given the warring factions of Barbarians, Philistines, and Populace, as Arnold terms them, the extension of suffrage poses major challenges to civilization. These challenges can be met only by developing the idea of the State as subsuming and transcending particular persons and interests. "What if we tried to rise above the idea of class to the idea of the whole community, *the State*, and to find our centre of light and authority there? Every one of us has the idea of country, as a sentiment; hardly any one of us has the idea of *the State*, as a working power." In this context, individual culture is important primarily because the organization of the self provides an internal model of the discipline necessary to convert *the State* into "a working power." Whereas *Culture and Anarchy* does promise to enhance individual freedom, it proposes to achieve that end by turning the individual into a good citizen. Arnold proposes the State as the "organ of our collective best self, of our national right reason." Though this "reason" is to be formulated in cultural terms, persisting from Plato's adaptation of the Spartan model is the emphasis on "the power to respect, the power to obey."[42]

Arnold's reviews during the early 1870s of English translations of succeeding volumes of Ernst Curtius's *History of Greece* put national and imperial issues to the fore. Curtius was a proponent of Athenian democracy and a critic of Müller's claim of ethnic purity (and superiority) for the Dorians. In Arnold's reviews, democracy, which becomes synonymous with demagogy, accounts for the Sparta's ultimate triumph over Athens.[43] In his 1876 review of Curtius's fifth and final volume, Arnold asks "whether it is inevitable, then, that the faultier side of a national character should be always the one to prevail finally; and whether, therefore, since every national character has its faultier side, the greatness of no great nation can be permanent?" Faced with the prospect of decline, he concludes his review by urging his readers to "remain faithful to those moral ideas which, however they may be sometimes obscured or denied, are yet in the natural order of things the master-light for men of the Germanic race, for both Germans and Englishmen. And in our common, instinctive appreciation of those ideas lies the true, the indestructible ground of sympathy between Germany and England."[44] In the face of the rising tide of democracy, Arnold returns for comfort to the security of racial identity and recommends that England ally herself with the emergent Continental power of the 1870s.

Pater did not believe in such myths. In his account of ancient Sparta, he resists the validation of warfare that is fueled by the same beauty, love, and enthusiasm that it expends. In "Lacedaemon," published in the *Contemporary Review* in June 1892, he contrasts the operation of desire within Athenian- and Spartan-model pederasty by interpolating an interpretive figure, that of "some contemporary student of *The Republic*, a pupil, say! in the Athenian academy," who is "an admiring visitor" of Sparta and through whose eyes Lacedaemon is presented.[45] This figure opens the hermeneutic space known as "thinking Greek." In contrast are the "idle bystanders, . . . Platonic loungers after truth or what not," presumably practitioners or fantasists of what Cicero refers to as *stuprum*, whom the Spartans exclude from their gymnasia.[46] Pater insinuates his listeners into the subject-position of the young traveler, schooled in the institution of Athenian pederasty. But Pater also attempts to correct that position insofar as it participates in the regressive aspects of Dorianism. This correction is necessary historically since, as the Peloponnesian War devolved toward victory for Sparta, Athenians and in particular Plato in *The Republic*, had constructed Sparta as their imaginary (and superior) Other.[47] In Victorian terms, the correction is also necessary because, in the words of "Emerald Uthwart," "none" of the Greek models of pederasty "fits exactly."

"Emerald Uthwart" is a story of schoolboy friendship set at the time of Waterloo. In it, a pair of passionate but celibate friends embrace military service, are posted to the Continent, launch a raid of their own only to miss orders to advance, and are subsequently court-martialed. One is executed; the other dies shortly thereafter. Despite or perhaps in part by means of these individual apocalypses, Pater, in Lesley Higgins's term, *recodes* Plato's dialogue and makes it the eloquent expression of adolescent male romance.[48] For the protagonist and "James Stokes, the prefect, his immediate superior" (184), *thinking Greek* means attempting to find a model for their "antique friendship" in the Latin and Greek "books they read together." In the story, the Athenian model vies with the Spartan one. Though the latter appears to win out, Pater's point is that perfect translation from the Greek is not possible.

James and Emerald's friendship has strong overtones of Athenian-model pederasty. As the narrator remarks:

> In every generation of schoolboys there are a few who find out, almost for themselves, the beauty and power of good literature, even in the literature they must read perforce; and this, in turn, is but the handsel of a beauty and power still active in the actual world, should they have the good fortune, or rather, acquire the skill, to deal with it properly. It has something of the stir and unction—the intellectual awaking with a leap—of the coming of love. So it was with Uthwart about his seventeenth year. He felt it, felt the intellectual passion, like the pressure outward of wings within him—ἡ πτεροῦ δύναμις, says Plato, in the *Phaedrus*; but again, as some do with everyday love, withheld, restrained himself. (190)

At Emerald's school, the influence of texts like *Phaedrus* is overmastered by a "monastic" ("Hebraic" in Arnold's term) discipline that is repeatedly figured in the schoolboys' singing in choir. This singing, in turn, is both Christian and Greek, achieving the aesthetic effect of individual subordination within a larger unit that had earlier been produced in Lacedaemon. Athenian-model pederasty is subordinated to the Spartan model—so that, as the narrator observes—"It is of military glory that [the schoolboys] are really thinking" (185). Indeed, the relation between the two models, the potentialities of each, and the process whereby one is subordinated to the other are central concerns of Pater's study. The result is a portrait of the construction of male-male desire within English schooling that is framed in silent irony by the ongoing discussion within late Victorian sexology of homosexuality as a perversion. The categorization of attraction between men as *abnormal* gives Pater reason for setting the events of the story two generations earlier during the romantic period, when the intensification of sentiment between men was celebrated in aesthetic discourses in England and Germany.[49] Yet for a polemicist on behalf of sexual and emotional ties between men such as Pater, the same pressure impels a latter-day effort to frame new relations between masculine desire and cultural and social formations.

Attempting to think Greek, the narrator of "Emerald Uthwart" chooses two Greek words to indicate the powerful effects of the Spartan model. In contrast to the love between two young men that dawns over shared schoolbooks and which leads to self-reflection on Emerald's part, the narrator stresses that ἄσκησις, the beauty associated with "discipline," exerts its determining power over the young man *unconsciously*: "It would misrepresent Uthwart's wholly unconscious humility to say that he felt the beauty of the ἄσκησις (we need that Greek word) to which he not merely finds himself subject, but as under a fascination submissively yields himself, although another might have been aware of the charm of it, half ethic, half physical, as visibly effective in him" (182). "Another" here might be the narrator, who describes himself earlier as "the careful aesthetic observer" (177). Or it might be his friend James, whose wish to pursue a military career encourages Emerald's similar wish. Or it might be a schoolmaster who consciously manipulates the blend of physical and moral charm, perhaps the same schoolmaster who helps seal Emerald's fate by "frankly" recommending that he relinquish his dawning intellectual ambitions (190). Or it might be "others" whom Emerald meets during his brief stay at Oxford and who likewise "tell him, as if weighing him, his very self, against his merely scholastic capacity and effects, that he would 'do for the army'" (198).

During their first year at Oxford, the two young men take "advantage of a sudden outbreak of war to join the army at once" (195). Pater sets the period of their service in Europe immediately before Waterloo.[50] He does so in order to put in question the social utility of Spartan-model pederasty as well as the use of military service as a model of social organization generally in the opening chapter of Ruskin's *Unto This Last*. By setting the climax of the story in 1815, Pater concedes the maximum to his antagonists, since the final struggle against Napoleon can be construed as a supremely fitting moment of sacrifice. Yet even in this context he undercuts male sublimation. The narrator chooses a second Greek word to mark Uthwart's seemingly inevitable path, "a special word the Greeks had for the Fate which accompanied one who would come to a violent end. . . . Κήρ, the extraordinary Destiny, one's Doom, had a scent for distant blood-shedding; and, to be in at a sanguinary death, one of their number came forth to the very cradle, followed persistently all the way, over the waves, through powder and shot, through the rose-gardens;—where not? Looking back, one might trace the red footsteps all along, side by side" (185). Although the mythic presentation of this fate poses it as individual, it is socially constructed, incised in the ideal of male self-sacrifice. Given how Uthwart's pedigree combines Anglo-Saxon antiquity, Norman supersession, and Druid prehistory, the shadowed cradle may well be that of English manhood itself and specifically of the aristocratic caste to which Emerald belongs.[51]

The suggestion of class catastrophe signals Pater's view that neither the Athenian nor the Spartan model are serviceable in the contemporary world. Rather, men like Emerald and James require space in which to live their relationship in a way that alters their social surround instead of making them vulnerable to destructive manipulation at the behest of national interest. The love that Emerald finds in *Phaedrus* "is but the handsel of a beauty and power still active in the actual world." The key words are "active" and "actual": desire between men can work to help transform everyday life. This passage introduces a second apocalyptic possibility in sharp contrast to the individual fates pre-scribed in the main line of the narrative. The second possibility is of a power between men capable of transforming the conditions of social existence. By 1892, when the story was published, this utopian vision could be termed, properly speaking, homosexual. But to achieve the power and beauty suggested to the two students by *Phaedrus* requires an ethical knowledge and a shared experience that is not given but earned. In other words, unlike some other projections of utopian existence in homosexual polemic, Pater's comes back to ordinary contingencies. The transformation is to be not just dreamt but accomplished.

In a number of later writings modeled on the myth of Dionysus, Pater repeatedly invokes the return of the idealized young male body from the grave. But in "Emerald Uthwart" he grows impatient with mortality and insists instead on the "skill" needed to *think Greek*. The narrator contends that the return of the "'Golden-haired, scholar Apollo'" (191) is a delusion. One has to find something "better; . . . more like a real portrait of a real young Greek, like *Tryphon, Son of Eutychos*, for instance, (as friends remembered him with regret, as you may see him still on his tombstone in the British Museum) alive among the paler physical and intellectual lights of modern England" (191). In this passage, Pater denies the possibility of the perfect "Englishing" (196) of Greek. One is removed from the "real young Greek" by a series of figures: of a sculpture in relief, of an epitaph written by friends, and by the fact that England is not Greece, that in "modern England" the light is "paler."[52] He also concedes a necessary mourning within what he takes to be the sculptural figure of desire. Loss is inseparable from memory and from apocalyptic hope. Together with this multiple resistance to metaphoric identification occurs Pater's insistence that one can find something "better" than the sublime figure of Apollo. One can find something or, rather, someone who is "alive" today.

Shades of Gray

Given Pater's critique of Dorianism, what is one to make of the proximity of Dorian style to the style that a public schooler might aspire to, including even "that expressive brevity of utterance" associated with the stiff

7. *Tryphon, Son of Eutychos,* Roman funerary sculpture, A.D. 54–68 (in fifth century B.C. Greek style). Courtesy Trustees of the British Museum, London.

upper lip? And, in a section of "Lacedaemon" in which Pater repeatedly refers to public schools, what is one to make of his emphasis on "youthful friendship, 'passing even the love of woman,' which, by system, . . . elaborated into a kind of art, became an elementary part of education?"[53] Partial answers to these questions may be found in *The Picture of Dorian Gray*, the novel by Oscar Wilde whose parodic critique of Pater's aestheticism helped impel Pater to the analysis of pedagogic eros that he makes in his writing of the early 1890s.

In its earlier, magazine version, the novel combines a moral fable that is intimately associated with pederastic idealization and a discussion of the good life reminiscent of the Platonic dialogues most closely associated with the Athenian model. The first key moment in Wilde's version of Platonic conversation combines both Athenian and Dorian elements. The painter Basil Hallward declares at once his faith in cultural renaissance and the central place in it of his devotion to Dorian Gray.

> I sometimes think, Harry, that there are only two eras of any importance in the history of the world. The first is the appearance of a new medium for art, and the second is the appearance of a new personality for art also. What the invention of oil-painting was to the Venetians, the face of Antinoüs was to late Greek sculpture, and the face of Dorian Gray will some day be to me. . . . His personality has suggested to me an entirely new manner in art, an entirely new mode of style. I see things differently, I think of them differently. I can now re-create life in a way that was hidden from me before. . . . Unconsciously he defines for me the lines of a fresh school, a school that is to have in itself all the passion of the romantic spirit, all the perfection of the spirit that is Greek. The harmony of soul and body—how much that is! We in our madness have separated the two, and have invented a realism that is vulgar, an ideality that is void. Harry! Harry! if you only knew what Dorian Gray is to me![54]

Hallward's representation of Dorian recalls the homoerotic aesthetic culture of the essays on Leonardo and Winckelmann produced by Pater at Oxford in the 1860s. In these essays, desire works to desublimate what Hallward calls a false "ideality." Pater validates bodily existence, masturbation, and sexual and emotional ties between men both as valuable in themselves and as contributing to democratic change. In addition, in the years around 1867, Pater and other liberals hoped for legislative reform that would decriminalize sexual activities between men.[55] The loss of these hopes is a necessary precondition of the outcomes of pederasty in Wilde's novel. Following passage of the antihomosexual Labouchère amendment in 1885, Hallward's evocation is most remarkable for what is left unsaid: he dissociates masculine desire and the art it prompts from hope for social transformation.

Although the relation between culture and the state remains tacit, Basil reports that he has already painted Dorian in the guise of Antinoüs: "Crowned with heavy lotus-blossoms, he has sat on the prow of Adrian's barge, looking into the green, turbid Nile." Antinoüs was the beloved of the emperor Hadrian, who purportedly arranged the young man's death in the Nile before having him declared a god.[56] Represented in Hallward's portraiture as an object of the male homosocial gaze, Dorian's beauty connotes subjection, sacrifice, and idealization. These suggestions render Basil's cultural ideal ominous, a tone that echoes in Wilde's suggestion that Dorian sits for his portrait "with the air of a young Greek martyr" (185). A "martyr" of and to what?[57]

In Basil's statement, absence of confidence in the civic meaning of

Dorianism is matched by excessive attention to a renovating "passion." But Basil's will to celebrate "the harmony of soul and body" lacks a location in personal or social life. A process of aesthetic abstraction overtakes his relation with Dorian: "Dorian Gray," he says defensively to Sir Henry, "is merely to me a motive in art. . . . He is simply a suggestion, as I have said, of a new manner. I see him in the curves of certain lines, in the loveliness and the subtleties of certain colors. That is all" (181). As to why Basil does not wish to exhibit the painting that reveals "the secret of my soul" (176), in the manuscript he says, "Where there is merely love, [the world] . . . would see something evil. Where there is spiritual passion, they would suggest something vile" (181). In these passages, the anxious sublimation of homosexual desire in aesthetic form becomes consciously closeting. Dorian's portrait must be kept secret lest its meaning be mediated by the "vile" representation of the Cleveland Street scandal of 1889–1890 in the popular press and by the emerging picture of homosexuality within sexology and criminology.[58] Under these pressures, Basil, contrary to his affirmations, loses the ability to *think Greek* that had been prompted by discussions earlier in the century. The loss is evident in the turn to aesthetic abstraction and, later, to the antinomies of "Christian" morality. This inability negates Hallward's advocacy of "the spirit that is Greek." Congruent with this emptying as well is his double existence, which combines idealization of a young man, socially his superior, plus the undivulged details of Basil's stays in Paris. So much for "the harmony of soul and body."

In *The Picture of Dorian Gray*, masculine desire is presented in the context of Wilde's satire of male culture, especially as it existed at Oxford. Dorian himself is presented as representing an Oxford ideal: "Very young men . . . saw, or fancied that they saw, in Dorian Gray the true realization of a type of which they had often dreamed in Eton or Oxford days, a type that was to combine something of the real culture of the scholar with all the grace and distinction and perfect manner of a citizen of the world. To them he seemed to belong to those whom Dante describes as having sought to 'make themselves perfect by the worship of beauty'" (243). Dorian is also identified with an athletic Greek ideal: after discovering changes in the portrait, he exults that he himself will remain "like the gods of the Greeks . . . , strong, and fleet, and joyous. What did it matter what happened to the colored image on the canvas? He would be safe. That was everything" (227). In a parody of Platonic love, Dorian has fallen for his peers' idolization of his beauty and privilege.[59] Like the young Spartan aristocrats of Pater's essay of two years later, Dorian turns himself into "a perfect work of art" functioning in a world of spectacle.[60] This position has its counterpart in the power that men like Dorian have to abuse others but likewise in the power of other men over them, which makes Dorian paranoid: late in the novel, he becomes "sick with a wild terror of dying. . . . The consciousness of being hunted, snared, tracked down, had begun to dominate him" (153).

Dorian is, in fact, anything but "safe." His danger, including the growing fin de siècle danger of exposure as a homosexual, is one that he shares with his namesake, John Gray, the beautiful, gifted young man of working-class background, whom Wilde befriended after 1889 and probably took, for a time, as his lover.[61] In order to protect his position at the Foreign Office, early in 1892 Gray issued a writ for libel against a newspaper that had reported that he was "said to be the original Dorian of the same name."[62] Gray's career included conversion to Roman Catholicism; a correct but devoted relationship with Mark André Raffalovich, a writer who polemicized on behalf of celibate male homosexuality; and service as a pastor in Edinburgh.

After a long period of silence, in 1922 John Gray published *Vivis*, a little book of poems in an edition of fifty copies. Inserted in the volume on a separate sheet of paper is a vignette, "a drawing of what appears to be a female head, with a mask (a girl's face) tied over the lower half; but when it is turned upside down the picture shows a skull, with the mask, now in reverse, tied over the upper part of the skull. Below the skull is a scroll bearing the words *Non omnia novi*" (literally, "I do not know everything"). Gray's biographer remarks: "Possibly the idea that the drawing is meant to convey is that of careless youth heedless of the four last things— a notion apposite to Gray's own former life."[63] The dual aspect of the image lends it an affinity with the ending of Wilde's novel, which offsets the "exquisite youth and beauty" of the portrait with the "withered, wrinkled, and loathsome . . . visage" of the corpse on the floor (170). In the context of Dorianism, the image suggests the collapse of the sublime association of idealized male flesh with death on behalf of civilization. Here is no flesh, no masculinity, only a travesty of the feminine.

The female mask, face, or body that only partially conceals a death's head is familiar in the iconography of *vanitas*. Morris Meredith Williams, who provided Gray with the drawing, conceived it within a tradition whose erotophobia is specifically misogynistic. Nonetheless, the double image has an apt relation to Gray's disabused view of desire between men. Through Raffalovich's research into the theory of sexual inversion, Gray had access to "third-sex theories" of homosexuality, which "'regarded uranism, or homosexual love, as a congenital abnormality by which a female soul had become united with a male body—*anima muliebris in*

8. Morris Meredith Williams, illustration in John Gray's *Vivis* (St. Dominic's Press, 1922).

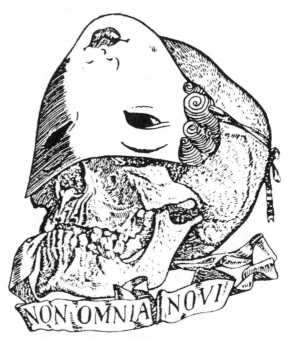

9. The image inverted. "Non omnia novi" ("I do not know everything").

corpore virili inclusa.'"[64] Gray provides a thoroughly ironic version of this metaphysical incongruity, in which the attractions of young male beauty, including his own seductive attractiveness when he was in his early twenties, are a feminine pretense covering moral and physical corruption. More pointed still, the double visage may represent a homosocial/homosexual gaze masked by the feminized mirror image that it proffers to attractive young men. In this reading, the image refers not to Gray's subjectivity (which remains unrepresented) but to the social construction of gender that proffers seductive lures to attractive young men.

Dorianism did not disappear in the new century. In Germany, its appeal continued in *Der Eigene*, a right-wing male homosexual periodical whose circulation reached 150,000 during the Weimar Republic. Promoting a masculinized model of desire between men in the service of Aryan ideals, Adolf Brand, the publisher of the journal, attacked the third-sex theory of homosexuality espoused by his Jewish socialist rival, Magnus Hirschfeld. Benedict Friedländer, a politically conservative, Jewish homosexual likewise argued that "attacks on homosexuals . . . were led by Jews determined to undermine Aryan virility and self-awareness."[65]

In England at the end of the century, the bond between masculine desire and the salvation of the state became inverted. In *L'Affaire Oscar Wilde* (1895), Raffalovich blames Wilde's debacle on national decadence: "La societé anglaise est coupable également."[66] But homosexual polemicists continued to invoke Dorianism. Why? Because it provided a defense of sexual and emotional ties between men. It likewise offered a defense against feminizing representations of men who desired other men. It provided a resonant answer to the difficult question about what utility sexual and emotional ties between men might possess. It validated homosexuals as equal to other men and gave meaning to sacrifice, something that many homosexual men found that their attachments to other men necessitated. Edward Carpenter hated modern war, but he had his own vision of the value of Dorianism. In *The Intermediate Sex* (1908), he writes:

> We have solid work waiting to be done in the patient and life-long building up of new forms of society, new orders of thought, and new institutions of human solidarity—all of which in their genesis must meet with opposition, ridicule, hatred, and even violence. Such campaigns as these—though different in kind from those of the Dorian mountaineers described above—will call for equal hardihood and courage, and will stand in need of a comradeship as true and valiant. And it may indeed be doubted whether the higher heroic and spiritual life of a nation is ever quite possible without the sanction of this attachment in its institutions, adding a new range and scope to the possibilities of love.[67]

Both Carpenter's rhapsody and the panicky image of the masked skull are transformations of the Dorianism of David's splendid painting. The emergence by the early 1890s of male homosexual existence and its representation within contemporary sexology undercut Dorian friendship. The conceptual space, carefully opened for Dorianism within bourgeois culture, narrowed. Despite the ascendancy in the public schools and the older universities of a humanism aligned with a national and imperial ethos, the sublime association of devotion between men with the interests of the state underwent a process of de-idealization that did not erase the connections between friendship and (military) service but which made them increasingly difficult to sustain. Nonetheless, as Carpenter's response shows, the revulsion expressed in the vignette from Gray's book is not the inevitable or the only end to which pederastic models could lead. Pater's mordant view in "Emerald Uthwart" of the social uses to which young male desire could be put and Wilde's satire of the attempt to validate pederastic desire by placing it in service of high culture and self-enclosure within a social elite both imply the need to complete the task of what John Addington Symonds had referred to as *aesthesis* in his *Studies of the Greek Poets*. The work of making desire and relationship between men a mode of ethical action, cultural reflection, and social existence was more important than ever.[68] This project has its own apocalyptic tenor in antagonistic relationship to Dorianism as it is memorialized in David's painting. Even Gray's turn to the priesthood may be interpreted not merely as a lapse into the conventional thinking that Müller had challenged long before but rather as an effort, within the very limited means available after the Wilde trials, to achieve a locus in which the work of *aesthesis* could continue.

3

...

APOCALYPSE AND ANTI-APOCALYPSE IN J. HILLIS MILLER AND WALTER PATER

The Miller-Abrams Debate

The names of Walter Pater and J. Hillis Miller are linked by Miller's invocation in 1976 of Pater as a presiding spirit of allegorical criticism. In this way too, deconstruction became linked with Pater's critical impressionism. Miller, however, subordinates and negates Pater's interest in the cultural construction of masculinity.[1] Miller's defensiveness about issues of masculinity has had significant implications for the cultural politics of deconstruction in the United States; the contest between deconstruction and literary humanism, figured in Miller's debate with M. H. Abrams, is curiously blank about the work of gender in which Abrams is engaged.[2] This stance is one element in Miller's curious restriction of deconstructive operations to literary texts. That the operator of textual analyses in Millerian deconstruction appears to be as unitary as the subject that Abrams installs at the center of Western literary tradition is another.

When Miller became a proponent of deconstruction while teaching at Yale during the early 1970s, he announced his conversion by publishing a critique of Abrams's exposition of literary apocalypse in *Natural Supernaturalism* (1971). Miller emphasizes "the Platonic paradigm" that Abrams finds in works by many romantic writers: the narrative "of a primal unity . . . fragmented and finally . . . brought back to unity again. This sequence is a 'circuitous journey' from creation and fall to the final apocalypse." Abrams emphasizes this structure of apocalyptic narrative as a way of unifying what might otherwise appear to be the disorder of Western history in the nineteenth century. The pattern also functions to produce an integral subject. Abrams minimizes the disruptive effects of Enlightenment thinking on Christian belief and the supersession of Classical norms in romantic ideology by merging all three terms in a reductive, repetitive continuum that he calls tradition. He locates this entity in literary texts and in the coherent human subject to which they are addressed. Abrams is also apocalyptic in a second way: he characterizes the present moment as one of descent into a cultural chaos that stands in stark contrast to the benign unification of which he is a proponent.

Miller opposes to Abrams's circular temporal model a model of time as repetition, a "displacement" or "decentering" that acknowledges differences and incoherence in the construction of individual and group consciousness and history. He finds this sort of model variously in the writings of "Marx, Nietzsche, Freud, and Saussure."[3] In contrast to Abrams's model, Miller's is anti-apocalyptic. Likewise he implicitly criticizes Abrams's tendency to cast the present moment into an apocalyptic narrative in which "tradition" struggles against the "adversary culture" of the 1960s. Given Miller's opposition to Abrams on other grounds, one might expect him to be a defender of cultural proliferation, including the emergence of lesbian and gay rights groups. But Miller has his own way of disavowing the diverse aspects of dissident culture—ironically, by hefting (or displacing, to use his term) the struggles of the late 1960s and early 1970s onto the higher intellectual plane characterized by the names of Marx, Nietzsche, and so on: "These writers, it might be argued, are the true 'adversary culture,' rather than the scurvy crew of Abrams' description who have sought to demolish their life in this world in a desperate search for something new."[4] Miller's position, which in the following years came to characterize much academic deconstruction in the United States, is notably at odds with Derrida's. Derrida has addressed a number of political issues including nuclear deterrence, apartheid, anti-Semitism, and AIDS.[5] The difference between these two theorists needs to be taken into account in any consideration of the possibilities that deconstruction may hold for gay cultural practice.

In some ways, Miller's rerouting of concern is more disturbing than Abrams's stance. Whereas the latter declares his cultural conservatism, Miller puts theory in the service of a high culture that displaces theorists like Marx from cultural politics when that politics is staged from minority subject-positions. Similarly, when Miller defuses the danger of the signifier *Marx* by replacing the term "revolution" with "the more enigmatic concept of repetition," the significance of the comment in relation to the "apocalyptic mood" of the years between 1967 and 1973 must be taken into account.[6] Miller's narrative of the development of critical theory represses other narratives in which Marx, Freud, and Nietzsche have played an important part in the development of oppositional practices among various subordinated groups.

Miller's approach drastically narrows the range of intellectual dissidence. He produces a similar effect by the formal turn that he gives to deconstruction in subsequent essays of the 1970s. For Miller, aporia ceases to be a process of interpretative undecidability and becomes instead localized in the literary or critical text. When Miller observes that "a text never has a single meaning, but is the crossroads of multiple ambiguous meanings," he adapts deconstruction to the reading practices of New Criticism prevalent in English departments in the 1960s.[7] New Criticism celebrated literary form precisely as a reservoir of multiple meanings. Miller transfers to the text the process of interpretation that has, for some time now, been taking place in the messy spaces where different groups nudge against each other in cultural debate. Despite Miller's disagreements with Abrams, then, Millerian deconstruction proves to be inhospitable to cultural heterogeneity. His version of deconstruction ends by reclaiming authority for the literary text as an autonomous site of cultural value.[8]

Miller and Pater

In the course of the 1970s, Miller came to associate rhetorical strategies in the writing of Pater with his own particular formulation of deconstruction.[9] In doing so, Miller ignored or misconstrued the specifically erotic tenor of difference in Pater's writing. Yet male-male desire is as evident a motive in Pater's writing as it is in Winckelmann's, whom Pater in his first major essay proposes as a model of the aesthetic critic. In the last third of the nineteenth century, Walter Pater promoted within the emergent academic field of literary criticism an oppositional mode of reading motivated by an affirmation of sexual and emotional ties between men. He carried this work into studies in painting, sculpture, and architecture; into philosophic essays; and into a genre-crossing, innovative literary form, the imaginary portrait. In his twenties in the 1860s, Pater used the opportunity of writing essays on Winckelmann and on Leonardo da Vinci to begin to theorize a place for perverse sexual self-awareness in cultural formation and critique. When Pater republished the essays in book form in *Studies in the History of the Renaissance* in 1873, he became at once a focus of admiration among young male readers and a target for critics at his university. Between 1875 and 1894, in a continually shifting set of reflections, Pater affirmed desire between men but with increasing attention to the psychological and social means by which homophobia functions. This analysis accentuates his criticism of the norms of manliness that were validated by contemporaries at Oxford such as Arnold, Ruskin, and Benjamin Jowett.

In the 1860s and afterward, education at Oxbridge and the public schools was directed toward producing a cadre of leaders who would devote themselves to the fulfillment of public duty. The formation of this group depended to a large extent on fostering close relations between male students. Whether these bonds became explicitly sexual or not (and they often did), they were sublimated within an ethos of service. The overtly homoerotic bias of Pater's cultural ideal desublimated such intimacy, which played an important part in constructing a relational norm of masculinity at school and in the universities. This norm entrenched bourgeois male privilege in the early 1870s when candidates for positions in the civil service were being required to take competitive exams and when public education was being extended to the population as a whole. Pater's desublimation of high culture threatened to undercut the superiority assured to bourgeois men by their educational routing. Pater's ambiguous position at Oxford, where he functioned as a member of a male elite at the same time that he subtly polemicized on behalf of a form of desire whose overt expression could occur only at the expense of the moral authority of that elite, placed him in a highly self-conscious relation, at once complicitous and antagonistic, to literary expression. When Pater republished his essays in book form in 1873, his colleague Jonathan Wordsworth objected to Pater's publication under the signature of a "Fellow of Brasenose College, Oxford." Wordsworth was not prepared to tolerate the mixing of nonconformity with Oxford discourse.[10]

In *Language and Decadence in the Victorian Fin de Siècle*, Linda Dowling contends that Pater's resistance to the essentialism of Romantic philology makes his writing deconstructive. Although nineteenth-century philology parted from the Christian view that had identified language with a divine, centering, and energizing Logos, the discipline continued to be logocentric insofar as language was identified with human reason itself. The foremost exponent of this view during Pater's lifetime was the comparative philologist and mythographer, Max Müller, who taught at Oxford from 1868 to 1875. Pater's affinities, in contrast, are with Müller's antagonists in the new field of anthropology and with eighteenth-century English epistemology, which, in a revisionary reading of Locke, had acknowledged the arbitrary character of linguistic signs.[11] This rhetorical concept of language matches Pater's sense of its contingent character.

Pater consistently opposes totalizing views of linguistic and other forms of culture. In his essays on Greek mythology, in *Marius the Epicurean* (1885), and in imaginary portraits like "Denys l'Auxerrois" (1886) and "Apollo in Picardy" (1893), his concept of language is material in character, specifically including the relations between language and somatic experience, sexual awareness, and gender-roles. In an early essay, he deplores Samuel Taylor Coleridge's yearning for the absolute and argues instead that "modern thought is distinguished from ancient by its cultivation of the 'relative' spirit. . . . To the modern spirit nothing is, or can be rightly known, except relatively and under conditions.[12] Although Pater grounds this view in contemporary science, especially biology, elsewhere in the essay he draws on the *Symposium* in order to indicate the basis of this proposition in individual experience. For "us," "the Greek spirit, with its engaging naturalness, simple, chastened, debonair, τρυφῆς, ἀβρότητος, χλιδῆς, χαρίτων, ἱμέρου, πόθου, πατήρ, is itself the Sangrail of an endless pilgrimage."[13] The Greek phrase, quoted from the *Symposium* (197D), makes clear that "Greek spirit" is Pater's discreet translation of the term eros.[14] Accordingly, when Pater emphasizes the importance of "know[ing] one's own impression as it really is, to discriminate it, to realise it distinctly," "impression" is in part erotic.[15] Later critics detected in Paterian impressionism a kind of desire that by century's end could be referred to with the new term, *homosexual*. In a hostile review of the Library Edition of the Works (1910), Paul Elmore More objects in particular to the seductive tenor of Paterian interpretation: "Too often his interpretation, when the spell of his manner is broken, will be found essentially perverted."[16] The comment refers both to the canonical text (whose meaning Pater perverts) and to Pater's psychology (which, in More's eyes, *is* perverse). This ad hominem attack contributed significantly to the depreciation of Pater's reputation among modernist writers and critics like T. S. Eliot, I. A. Richards, and F. R. Leavis.[17]

In two essays written in the mid-1970s, Miller contributes to the recovery of Pater while misrepresenting and eventually cliding sexual difference in his work. In "Walter Pater: A Partial Portrait," Miller signs Paterian tradition with the names of a number of men whose homosexuality is well known: "This line [of criticism] leads from certain aspects of Ruskin through Pater and Wilde to Proust, and beyond Proust to Walter Benjamin and to the rhetorical or 'deconstructive' criticism of our own moment in literary criticism." As Miller observes, Pater's criticism depends on ideas of "difference and discontinuity": "Meaning or significance in a personality, in a gem, a song, a painting, a piece of music is always defined by Pater as a force, as the power to make an impression. This power is not single, nor is it a harmonious collocation of energies making a unity. A 'virtue' always results from antagonistic forces, sweetness against strength in the case of Michelangelo, strangeness against the desire for beauty in Leonardo, and so on. The meaning is in neither of the two forces separately, nor in their sum. It arises in the space between them, out of the economy of their difference." Later, more categorically, Miller says that in Pater "meaning" is "constituted by difference."[18] In addition to the mention of Wilde and Proust, the artists to whom Miller refers, Michelangelo and Leonardo, are known to have been subjects of male-male desire. Moreover, the conflations that Miller adduces—of sweetness and strength, of strangeness and the desire for beauty—signify, in Pater, different flavors of homoerotic sensibility.

Having emitted these signals, Miller proceeds to defend deconstruction by dissociating it from *being-homosexual*. Taking as an example Pater's description of a painting of Medusa incorrectly attributed to Leonardo, Miller observes Pater's use of the image to suggest a liminal state in which the expression of wayward desire overcomes the limits of a rigid gender-identification that subsumes the self in masculinist norms, in "the phallus," to use Miller's word.[19] At the same time, he suggests that another sort of male-male desire could capture Leonardo/Pater in phallogocentrism. Miller asks: "Was Pater 'phallogocentric,' frozen like Leonardo himself at a Narcissistic or adolescent homosexual stage?"[20] The implicit answer to this question, which endorses Freud's diagnosis of Leonardo's sexuality, is "yes." The male-male desire to which Miller refers exists within a conventional, that is, heterosexual economy. By specifying this desire as homosexual, Miller associates homosexuality with the logocentrism of conventional academic discourse. Similarly, in the ensuing discussion of the recurrence of Medusa-imagery in *Marius the Epicurean*, Miller leaves Marius unable to resolve either the castration complex or the Oedipus complex despite the fact that Miller might easily argue that Marius, who has "no particular dread of a snake's bite, like one of his companions, who had put his hand into the mouth of an old garden-god and roused there a sluggish viper," overcomes the paralyzing force of these complexes precisely *by letting* the snake bite.[21] Immediately following this passage, Miller shifts to the expressly theoretical portion of his discussion. In the process, Pater's erotic difference is translated into an abstract "incipient theory of signs."[22]

At the end of the essay, Miller reduces meaning in Pater to a play of language whose significance is the indeterminacy of linguistic reference: "His texts lead the critic deeper and deeper into a labyrinth until he confronts a final aporia. This does not mean, however, that the reader must give up from the beginning the attempt to understand Pater. Only by going all the way into the labyrinth, following the thread of a given clue, can the critic reach the blind alley, vacant of any Minotaur, that impasse which is the end point of interpretation."[23] Miller, choosing to satisfy himself with a partial portrait, assimilates Pater to his own theory of critical interpretation. The partiality of the portrait, moreover, resituates Miller's discussion within the academic tradition that he consciously seeks to resist. One should not be surprised, then, that in his usage "difference" does not mean sexual difference—either in the way that the phrase is characteristically used to register the categorization of a feminine Other or in the way that I use it to refer to an awareness of desire not cast in the antitheses of what Monique Wittig refers to as "the straight mind."[24]

The nexus of Ariadne-Theseus-Minotaur-Dionysus-labyrinth is central to "Ariadne's Thread: Repetition and the Narrative Line," perhaps the single most important formulation of Millerian deconstruction. Miller takes as one of three epigraphs to this essay a long passage from "Apollo in Picardy," one of a number of Pater's retellings of the myth of Dionysus. In the passage quoted, Pater describes the collapse of the "long and intricate argument" of "the twelfth volume of a dry enough treatise on mathematics, applied, still with no relaxation of strict method, to astronomy and music." The blocked author of this text is the protagonist, Prior Saint-Jean, whose attraction/repulsion to a latter-day reincarnation of Apollo/Dionysus is the point on which Pater's imaginary portrait turns. Pater draws connections between the phallus (the Prior expects to be rewarded on completion of the work with "well-earned practical reward as superior, with lordship and mitre and ring, of the abbey"), logocentrism (the "method" pursued in the first eleven books), and phallogocentrism (the prior as author). His psychic disintegration is associated both with "new light" and with the birth, in deconstructive terms, of a decentered subject: the twelfth volume "began, or, in perturbed manner, and as with throes of childbirth, seemed the preparation for, an argument of an entirely new and disparate species, such as would demand a new period of life also, if it might be, for its due expansion." The "new period of life" seems to mean both a new historical period, that is, a Renaissance, since the "new light" perceived by the Prior is his anticipation of Copernicus's discovery that the earth moves around the sun, and also a new way of personal living that includes an overtly expressed desire for other males, whether Apollyon, the Apollo/Dionysus figure that the Prior meets during his convalescence at the Grange of Notre-Dame-De-Pratis, or Hyacinth, another Dionysus figure who, on the literal level, is the attractive adolescent who accompanies the Prior on his journey.[25]

The link between the avowal of desire and the idea of history as cultural repetition is characteristic in Pater, who connects both with new knowledge in the natural and social sciences. Adapting from anthropology the idea of culture as a series of recapitulations of earlier phases with a difference, in *Studies in the History of the Renaissance* he devises "an evolutionary scheme showing the transmission of pagan elements under the surface of 'Christian' art from medieval France through Pico of Mirandola into the Renaissance in Italy, then back to the France of du Bellay and thence to the eighteenth and nineteenth centuries."[26] In two pioneering essays, one in *Fraser's Magazine* (in 1872) and the other in *The Fortnightly Review* (in 1873), Andrew Lang, a young literary anthropologist who had come up to Balliol in 1865, attacks Müller's theory of the development of mythology as the corruption of an original solar myth.[27] Drawing instead on the work of Benjamin Tylor, Lang argues the survival of primitive residues: "The lower mythology—the elemental beliefs of the people—do survive beneath a thin covering of Christian conformity."[28] Influenced by these essays and by Lang's earlier articles on the development of French literature, Pater arranges the chapters to account for the phenomenon of the Renaissance in terms of a sequence of survivals and returns of "pagan tradition."[29] This pattern doubles the myth of return summed up in the trope of the young male body red in the grave, which Pater uses on a number of occasions.[30] This image includes the idea that renaissance is possible only in a culture prepared to acknowledge the place in cultural genealogy of desire between men. To these associations, Pater in "Apollo in Picardy" adds mordant observations about desire in male homosocial culture. In homophobic culture, the fantasy of a masculine desire connecting individuals across lines of class—as in the Prior's attraction to Apollyon, whom he takes to be "a serf . . . , a servant of the house, or farm-labourer, perhaps"—necessarily rebounds on itself.[31]

Despite the long epigraph from "Apollo in Picardy," "Ariadne's Thread" includes no discussion of Pater. Instead, taking another epigraph, this time from Elizabeth Gaskell's *Cranford*, as his point of departure, Miller analyzes the myth of the labyrinth in strictly heterosexual terms. In "Walter Pater," Miller recognizes that the recurrence of the radiant figures of Denys and Apollyon embodies alienation in antagonistic, medieval environments: "The tragedy of all these figures is in the incompatibility between the meanings they carry and the material conditions within which they are forced to embody them." Homophobia, however, is one condition that goes unnamed. Misreading the significance of the trope of the "new body," Miller contends that Pater decorporealizes the body in a set of fugitive traces.[32] But, as Jeffrey Wallen has pointed out, the situation is more complex than Miller allows. Pater repeatedly invokes the word "embodiment" to refer to the work of art: the "sensible embodiment" of "thought" remains an ideal goal of art.[33] Although Pater just as regularly registers the "discrepancy between meaning and its incarnation," this ideal remains.[34] Similarly, Pater repeatedly invokes the idea of a cultural renewal in which the human body will be recognized as an object of desire without neurotic anxiety.[35]

Pater's double attitude helps account for key concepts in his critical theory. In the first place, difference is intrinsic to his position as one schooled in a "normal" masculine outlook with which he finds himself to be at odds. This awareness inflects a revisionist view of literary figures such as Plato while fueling skepticism about logocentric interpretations of language and tradition. Pater was altogether aware of the anxieties about desire and the body inherent in such traditions as Neoplatonic interpretations of the *Dialogues*. His descendental interpretations of writers like Plato and Hegel were part of a polemical project to revalidate desire, especially between males. This project implies a shifting set of relations among new discourses, emergent communities, and hegemonic masculinity. When Pater, in the chapter in Marius in which he describes the ritual of the Mass in the primitive church, remarks that "there were noticeable, among those assembled, great varieties of rank, of age, of personal type," he is not invoking a nostalgic sense of community.[36] He is describing an egalitarian ideal at odds with the social stratification of "Christian" Britain in the late nineteenth century. When he speaks in "The Minor 'Peace of the Church'" of the "rehabilitation of peaceful labour" in the figure of Christ and "of the ideal of woman, of the family, of industry, of man's work in life" in the image of the Holy Family, he declares his affiliation with the feminists, laborers, and socialists who worked for legislative reforms in the 1880s.[37] These passages and others place him in that stream of late Victorian liberalism that was drawn toward social democratic politics.[38] Yet he attacks the formation of masculinity within Victorian liberalism which both legitimated resistance to the claims of the Irish, industrial laborers, and women after passage of the Second Reform Bill in 1867 and underwrote the role that young, well-educated men would be called on to play in administering the Empire.

After the Indian Mutiny of 1857, Utilitarian and Evangelical rationales for British expansion abroad lost a good deal of their persuasive power. Instead, subject peoples were categorized as racial degenerates. The upshot, as Karl Marx predicted in articles written for the *New York Daily Tribune*, was "a more repressive dominion."[39] When in a lecture delivered at Oxford six years later, Matthew Arnold extenuated the persecution of Christians during the reign of Marcus Aurelius on the grounds that "Christianity appeared something anti-civil and anti-social, which the State had the faculty to judge and the duty to suppress," he prepared his young listeners to acquiesce in the suppression of subordinated groups whose existence "appeared" to be at odds with State interests.[40] For his part, writing in the overtly imperial Britain of the 1880s, Pater criticizes conventional gender-roles and the institutions that propagate them. In the chapter "Manly Amusement," at the end of volume 1 of *Marius the Epicurean*, he uses a scene of gladiatorial combat to attack ideas of masculine self-worth that depend on aggression and physical brutality. Yet more significant, he criticizes the Stoicism of the emperor, Marcus Aurelius, which authorizes his complicity with the spectacle. Arnold and others typically invoke Aurelius's philosophy as a guide for young men. In underlining the confusion of high mindedness, *raison d'état*, and privilege in Aurelius's tolerance of abuses of power, Pater comments on the moral confusion of his contemporaries at Oxford.

In his position as both a privileged and a subordinated male, Pater was well versed in what is today referred to as hegemonic masculinity. Challenging social-role models of masculinity, John Lee has used the phrase to mean "not . . . 'the male role' but . . . a particular variety of masculinity to which others—among them young and effeminate as well as homosexual men—are subordinated. It is particular groups of men, not men in general, who are oppressed within patriarchal sexual relations, and whose situations are related in different ways to the overall logic of the subordination of women to men. A consideration of homosexuality thus provides the beginnings of a dynamic conception of masculinity as a structure of social relations."[41] Despite the basis of Lee's analysis in contemporary sociology, the statement has implications for a study of nineteenth-century English literary culture. First of all, although Lee emphasizes the central importance to masculinity of the subordination of women, he also adduces the significance for masculinity of the subordination of working-class men, men of color, boys, and homosexuals. In this way, he indicates symmetries between the structure of male-female relations, on the one hand, and male relations, on the other. Without underplaying the fact that male homosexuals at times occupy the hegemonic male position with regard to women, children, and some other males, the structural parallel that Lee adduces indicates the basis in experience of Pater's critique of Oxonian masculinity. In other words, although terms like "homosexual" or "homosexual existence" need to be used with care in order to avoid anachronism, the relational structure described by Lee provoked resistance in 1885 as it continues to do today.[42]

In the pointedly titled "Manly Amusement," Pater draws the specific connection between the games and a relational understanding of masculinity by observing that the emperor has organized them in order to celebrate the engagement of his daughter "to a swinish but influential general."[43] Besides touching on the unequal status of men and women in marriage, Pater locates Marcus Aurelius in relation to the debate within the Victorian middle class over appropriate masculine behavior. In this context and in contrast to Arnold's portrayal of the emperor as "so beautiful a moralist," Pater's emperor embodies the sacrifice of moral sensitivity, bodily well-being, and emotional affect which Arnold's listeners were expected to be prepared to make in the service of God and Empire.[44]

In *Marius* Pater supplements his critique of Roman/British logocentrism with an approach, at once rhetorical and material, to the Logos in the chapter "The Will as Vision." Although Dowling and others argue that Pater abandoned earlier, theologically based views of congruence between self and meaning, on the one hand, and self and verbal expression, on the other, some current commentators argue that a nostalgic pursuit of the authorizing Word motivates his writing. Following another Yale critic, Harold Bloom, Daniel O'Hara contends that in "The Will as Vision" "Pater expresses . . . a sublime experience of the presence of a divine spirit, a creative Logos, pervading nature."[45] Yet this assertion misses the rhetorical character of the experience of Pater's protagonist as he meditates "in an olive-garden."[46] In a paragraph that begins with a recollection of Marius's two most important friendships, with Flavian and Cornelius, Marius casts his apprehension of divine presence in terms of an analogy with the experience of friendship: he imagines the reality of a "*Creator . . .* even as one builds up from act and word and expression of the friend actually visible at one's side, an ideal of the spirit within him." The analogy points not to an antithesis—of the friend's physical expressivity versus his "spirit," for instance—but to the basis in bodily awareness of a sense of noumenal presence. The paragraph begins and ends with the experience of male friendship, though friendship of a special character in this novel, in which Pater polemically opposes hegemonic masculinity.

Marius's turn at the end of the chapter away from the afternoon's epiphany and back to everyday life indicates the primary importance in Pater/Marius's view of improving the time. Marius wonders: "Must not all that remained of life be but a search for the equivalent of that Ideal, among so-called actual things—a gathering together of every trace or token of it, which his actual experience might present?" The weight of emphasis in the quotation is not on the fugitive character of material actuality but on the need to find equivalences in mundane life for one's desires, and apprehensions. Both sides of the equivalence remain within the range of human experience. Marius's search is complex: he attempts to overcome self-alienation, including alienation from the body; he searches lifelong for an intimate male relationship; he seeks a community infused, to use anachronistic terms, with democratic and communitarian values. He looks toward "the 'new city,'" "some celestial New Rome" brought within scope of the temporal imagination.[47]

Paterian Apocalypse

Marius's allusion to the descent of "the holy city" (Rev. 21.2) at the end of the Apocalypse is a reminder of how caught up the early Christian

Church was in the hope of the descent on "a new earth" (Rev. 21.1) of Christ's kingdom. In the second half of the novel Pater uses the intersection of Marius's search for the perfect friend with the apocalypticism of the Christian community as to interrogate apocalyptic and anti-apocalyptic aspects of narrative structure. In contrast to Miller, in *Marius* these tendencies are intimately associated with Marius's shy, tender, celibate love of the Christian soldier, Cornelius. In contrast to Abrams's synthesizing use of apocalyptic pattern, Pater was particularly interested in how individual and group trauma are implicated in narrative structure. Likewise, he was aware how seductive the appeal of martyrdom could be for members of a despised minority, who hope against hope that their suffering can bring closer the promised hour of vindication.[48] As Cathy Caruth has argued, the history of a minority group can be written only in relation to the history of other groups, subordinated and dominant. Moreover, the collective history of such a group is discontinuous because it is marked by catastrophe. These catastrophes can be accessed only in the form of trauma, a consciousness effect in which some aspects of memory become available only at the price of the loss of other aspects of experience. "Trauma evokes the difficult truth of a history that is constituted by the very incomprehensibility of its occurrence."[49]

At the end of *Marius*, Pater imagines how one part of Christian history came to be constituted. Marius's history crosses an incident in the process by which the Christians invented a history for themselves. After an earthquake, a group of Christians are rounded up by local townspeople, who blame them for the disaster. Marius is seized not because he is a Christian but because he is traveling with Cornelius, the Christian legionary who is his "more than brother!"[50] After purchasing Cornelius's freedom, Marius dies of an illness that he contracts while on a forced march. In the very last words of the novel, Pater reports that the Christians constitute these events as a narrative of martyrdom within their own history, "holding his death, according to their generous view in this matter, to have been of the nature of a martyrdom; and martyrdom, as the church had always said, a kind of sacrament with plenary grace."[51] In this context, the adjective "generous" is ironic since the construction of Marius as Christian martyr can occur only at the expense of the construction of Marius as a man who dies for love of another man. Hence, for another minority group, constituted in part by the passage in Parliament of antihomosexual legislation in 1885, the fictive enrollment of Marius in the martyrology means the traumatic loss of his memory to another history, that of men who love each other. Within a fictional frame, Pater redresses this loss by reclaiming Marius's devotion to Cornelius. This act provides the end of the novel with an additional, partial apocalyptic frame, in which Marius's permanently deferred love can be imagined, within the rhetoric of Christian apocalypse, as the love of the "the holy city," of "a bride adorned for her husband" (Rev. 21.2). In terms of this schema, Cornelius becomes a figure of Christ, the Lamb, whose imminent descent is proclaimed at the end of the Apocalypse.[52] "And God will wipe away every tear from their eyes. And death shall be no more; neither shall there be mourning" (Rev. 21.4). The implicit mystic union of Marius/Cornelius translates into the most extravagant terms the romantic fantasies of late Victorian, morally conservative, Christian homosexuals.

The most significant deconstructive reading of Pater since Miller's is Jonathan Loesberg's book *Aestheticism and Deconstruction: Pater, Derrida, and De Man* (1991). Loesberg emphasizes Pater's framing of questions of religious belief within aesthetic terms that validate religious experience without resolving questions of belief. He describes this suspension of judgment as a mode of resistance on the part of Pater to dogmatic assurance, whether based on religious or positivist grounds: "We can thus see Marius' ambiguous death as precisely the aesthetic construction of an experience of the religious, for the narrator and the reader, that remains aesthetically inclusive rather than exclusively Christian."[53] Once again, what begins as a deconstructive gesture ends by establishing a new consensus. Loesberg's "we" of critic, narrator, and reader excludes the connection between the construction of Marius as saint and the historical trauma of a love between men that remains perennially without habitation. Transforming Marius's biography into the life of a martyr, the Christians achieve an apocalyptic end. But this ending installs Marius in Christian history only at the price of repressing his actual uncertainty. Individual and group trauma among Christians is overcome by the expedient of repressing his agnosticism. Thus writing Christian history requires the repression of another history: the history of sexual and emotional ties between men, in which Marius's "decision against himself, in favour of Cornelius,"[54] is a significant (albeit fictional) incident. The motivating factor of Marius's love of his Christian friend is negated at one level so that it can be conserved on the higher level of religious truth. In this play of crossing motives and representations, Pater demonstrates how minority history is made.

This relationship between two possible narratives of individual and group history does not exhaust Pater's interest in apocalyptic narrative. Marius's reference to a New Rome, a phrase that was subsequently invoked in the name of the succession of the Roman papacy to the authority of the Old Rome, was liable to be received with irony at post-Tractarian Oxford. Pater contrasts the "minor" peace of the church, which he celebrates, to that other "Peace of the church, commonly so called, under

Constantine."[55] Similarly, the renewed persecution that occurs shortly after Marius's introduction to the Christian community negates the moment of the minor peace in a catastrophe that destroys the careful balance of cultural forces that Marius admired in the Christian community at Rome. Pater draws both moments into an ongoing pattern of historical recurrence. In other words, apocalypse in the novel occurs in the plural and in material contexts such as the epidemic of plague, during which Flavian, Marius's earlier beloved, dies. Current commentators believe that a number of factors, including a devastating outbreak of plague in A.D. 165, contributed to the belief widespread in the Empire that civilization was in decline.[56] Pater frames Christian apocalypse in *Marius* within this other temporal narrative of decadence. By including the conditions under which that narrative comes to be constituted, he emphasizes the rhetorical character of both sorts of constructs.

In the context of the 1880s, Marius's apocalyptic language echoes the sentiments of Socialist reformers such as Carpenter and his friends at Millthorpe. Similarly, the persecution that overtakes Marius and Cornelius at the end of the novel augurs the renewed persecution of male "friends" that would issue from the Labouchère amendment. In the two major romantic involvements of Marius's life, with Flavian during his school days and with Cornelius, Pater provides a type of the history of subjects of male-male desire as he experienced it from his twenties at Oxford in the 1860s to his friendships with High Church Anglicans in London in the 1870s and afterward. Along with other young aesthetes such as A. C. Swinburne and Simeon Solomon, Pater found the 1860s to be years of remarkable cultural expansion. The arrest of Solomon on a morals charge in a London washroom in 1873 marked the end of this period. Subsequently, Pater came increasingly in contact with men who espoused a chaste or celibate ideal and took part in Anglican ritual and community life in London.[57] In *Marius*, he writes in sympathetic response to their particular combination of homoeroticism, religion, and social service.[58] In the 1880s context of social purity agitation by a wide range of women's groups and others, he attempts to conciliate the position of these men with that of middle-class feminists. Hence his emphasis on the prominence of women and children among the Christians at Rome during the minor peace.

Apocalypse in the novel, whether it refers to disasters like the plague or to the intermittent peace and persecution experienced by Christians or to the waxing and waning of dissidence in contemporary Britain, is a partial frame intersected by others, such as the decadence, and by the ebb and flow of a wide range of politics. Because a critic like O'Hara fails to see the politics of class, race, sex, and gender which affiliate Pater with members of groups subjected to hegemonic masculinity, he glides over Pater's interest in the sublunary equivalents of Marius's "vision" in the olive orchard. Instead, O'Hara complains that: "Pater in the end falls prey to his own beautiful idealizations, becomes *victimized by his impossible dreams,* and so appears as the perfect object of attack, awash in the sea of *his own fantastic impotence.* For when one asks what idea of society and of the individual's relation to society does this vision of the creator reinforce, one finds that the answer involves a rationalization, exquisitely phrased, of *the need to capitulate* to the structures of power at work in the world whatever the historical epoch."[59] Ascribing to Pater a logocentrism that he consciously resisted, O'Hara also imposes on him the stereotype of the fin-de-siècle aesthete (i.e., homosexual), fiddling while Rome burns. One could scarcely worse misread Marius/Pater's endorsement of "Christianity in its humanity, or even in its humanism, in its generous hopefulness, for man, its common sense, and alacrity of cheerful service, its sympathy with all creatures, its appreciation of beauty and daylight,"[60] an endorsement that, we should remember, is based on Marius's attachment to his "half-known friend."[61]

In the Labyrinth

If a new form of male friendship provided one counter to the ideological construction of masculinity in Victorian high culture, Pater's material approach to cultural artifacts provided another. For example, in the figures of interpretation that he deploys in a variety of texts—"the lover of strange souls" who tries to define "Leonardo's genius," or the "I" who pieces together the fragmentary remains of Denys' existence in "Denys l'Auxerrois"[62]—Pater attempts to theorize difference as a motive of cultural production. In the theory of *Anders-streben,* Pater argues that the non-self-identical structure of the subject is necessary to cultural production. Pater proposes this view in the essay "The School of Giorgione," published in a journal in 1877 and not added to the *The Renaissance* until the third edition in 1888. Specifically, Pater identifies music as "the object of the great *Anders-streben* of all art, of all that is artistic, or partakes of artistic qualities."[63] More generally, he uses the term to refer to the tendency for work in *any* medium to exceed its "own limitations" in the search for greater expressiveness:

> Although each art has thus its own specific order of impressions, and an untranslatable charm, while a just apprehension of the ultimate differences of the arts is the beginning of aesthetic criticism; yet it is noticeable that, in its special mode of handling its given material, each art

> may be observed to pass into the condition of some other art, by what German critics term an *Anders-streben*—a partial alienation from its own limitations, through which the arts are able, not indeed to supply the place of each other, but reciprocally to lend each other new forces.[64]

As Miller has observed, *Anders-streben* refers further to language and critical impression: "The moment, it turns out, though unique, is not single. Each 'impression' is in fact 'infinitely divisible.' . . . It is divisible because it is self-divided, an *Andersstreben* [*sic*], or striving to be other than itself."[65] In art, "alienation" or what Miller refers to as self-division is implicit in the very limits of the medium itself.

Anders-streben also locates the producer or receiver of the work of art as a subject of desire limited by the conditions of material existence. In the nineteenth century, music was often regarded as the medium par excellence of excess and passion, usually between a man and a woman. But music has a further valence in a revisionary masculine tradition, where it is associated—by both Shelley and Pater—with the rebellious flute-player Marsyas. In the prospectus that Leonard Smithers issued in 1893 at the time of the original publication of *Teleny*, a pornographic novel written by a number of men in Wilde's circle, Smithers refers to "the subtle influence of music and the musician in connection with perverted sexuality."[66] This specifically male homosexual connotation is elaborated in the polemical writing of Carpenter, who remarks: "As to music, this is certainly the art which in its subtlety and tenderness—and perhaps a certain inclination to indulge in emotion—lies nearest to the Urning nature."[67] Present in Pater's conception but missing from Carpenter's is the idea of alienation that checks this tendency.

In his essay on Pater, Miller refers to the myth of Ariadne and Dionysus in the passage cited earlier, in which he says that Pater's "texts lead the critic deeper and deeper into a labyrinth until he confronts a final aporia. . . . Only by going all the way into the labyrinth, following the thread of a given clue, can the critic reach the blind alley, vacant of any Minotaur, that impasse which is the end point of interpretation."[68] In the myth, the hero Theseus is saved by the love of a young woman, Ariadne. He is saved *from* being devoured by a monster, half man/half beast at the center of the labyrinth. In Miller's abbreviated version, the Minotaur is not encountered; rather, following Ariadne's (in context, Pater's) thread, the critic learns that the monster does not exist; he is a figment provoked by nameless anxieties. At the center of the labyrinth is an aporia. In "Ariadne's Thread," Miller uses the myth of Theseus and Ariadne as a figure of deconstruction generally. Commenting on this essay in the course of a discussion in which she attempts to locate "the relations between deconstruction and feminism as practiced in the United States," Nancy K. Miller has argued that Hillis Miller erases feminine/feminist difference by conflating Ariadne's thread with his own critical practice. The same point could be made about the elision of homosexual difference in his translation of Pater into a deconstructor. The male heterosexual subject position from which Miller writes requires the elision of both sorts of difference. Nancy Miller describes how contradictions in the position produce these effects: "The masculist critic uses Ariadne to negotiate his encounter with the woman, perhaps in himself, the monstrous self the male critic might meet at the heart of the maze of heterosexuality."[69]

Reading the myth as Hillis Miller presents it, I notice that a woman's love spares the hero the risk of encountering a male/monster that recalls the demonic representations of men sexually involved with other men that have long characterized Western culture. In "Walter Pater," it is not a woman but the *feminized* homosexual who enables the hero to avoid confrontation. Accordingly, Miller is free to leave nominally unanswered the question whether Pater like Leonardo is "frozen" at an "adolescent homosexual stage." In the psychological economy of O'Hara's essay, Pater's "impotence" enables a contrasting display of vigor on O'Hara's part. It is necessary to O'Hara's argument to ignore Pater's complex politics, since otherwise the categories of seriousness, political relevance, and masculine self-assertion would be mingled with a weak, that is, a subliminally homosexual approach. In Miller, Pater, domesticated as an Ariadne-*manqué*, becomes useful to the male deconstructionist, who, now able to thread the maze, can show that the monster does not, after all, exist. The Minotaur is an aporia. At this moment, the process of subordination and elision serves yet another function in enabling an implicit fantasy of release from the bonds of conventional masculinity. Yet the setting aside of male homosexual difference has a number of unforeseen consequences. For one thing, if the specificities and self-divisions of gender and sexuality are to be excluded, then what exists within aporia? Does it become a "blind alley?" In "Ariadne's Thread," the sexual mingling described in the opening interpretation of the myth is superseded, in the turn to theory, by a statement of "nine areas of linear terminology" in terms of a strictly literary taxonomy.[70]

At the end of Miller's essay, gender returns in the form of expressly male anxieties when Miller moves to the third text from which he has drawn the epigraphs, Elizabeth Gaskell's *Cranford*. This final section deals with fears of genealogical extinction since, in Cranford, an "effeminate or effeminizing doubling" threatens to lower the birth rate to zero.[71] Miller wittily invokes these anxieties, conjured by a female writer, in order to dispel them, but this attempt miscarries because of the absence of other differences. Instead, what is reinscribed is continuing anxiety about the legitimate exercise of cultural authority within an alienated male intellectual elite. In its refusals, gaps, and reversals, therefore, Miller's writing signals the importance of those who, like Pater, have tried to write masculinity differently. In that process, deconstructive criticism has a significant part to play—as it does, for example, in recent work by gay critics like Lee Edelman and Alexander García-Düttmann. To play that part, however, requires an approach that recognizes both linguistic contingencies and continual analysis of the assumptions of hegemonic masculinity within the academic practice of deconstruction itself.

Since the onset of AIDS in the early 1980s, Miller has belatedly come to recognize that writing masculinity differently is a significant project within contemporary literary studies. In the context of a position paper on emergent cultural studies in the United States, Miller acknowledges the place of minority formations in articulating the new discipline. He refers to "new forms of consolidation and solidarity, for example, among women, or gays or lesbians, or Asian-Americans, forms that will work as means of giving power to such marginalized groups without falling back into some form of thinking in terms of self and other, us and them, or in terms of some pre-existing unity and right to power."[72] Although the contrast that Miller draws between "giving power" and a "right to power" is question-begging—since it occludes precisely the effort to affect the field of power relations so that new relations become possible—the coming to visibility of minorities in his thinking is a modest positive sign. Miller continues to believe that work from minority positions requires the corrective ministrations of his particular version of critical theory. But as Pater's writing long ago demonstrated, work informed by difference is capable of continually resisting itself as well as the truths of gender and other politics that negate it.

4

...

E. M. FORSTER
AT THE END

In an uncanny fashion, the decade following 1885 framed the history of emergent homosexuality in doubly apocalyptic terms. On the one hand, the rapid growth of social relations and cultural production justifies calling the early 1890s a period of homosexual renaissance. But the reconciliation of Christian, social democratic, and homosexual outlooks that Pater attempts in *Marius the Epicurean* was negated already in 1885 by passage of the Labouchère amendment, with its wide-ranging, antihomosexual provisions. Once enacted, the amendment was a time bomb, in place for detonation at an unspecified moment when it promised to do massive damage. When it did go off in 1895, it ruined more than Oscar Wilde. It devastated hope and destroyed affiliation.

In this chapter, I consider the case of E. M. Forster as symptomatic of the effects of the Wilde trials. Forster's first published short story, "Albergo Empedocle," is a temporal allegory of the end of the effort to reimagine masculinity, a task that nineteenth-century men had conducted in excavating the Greek and Roman pasts. Forster, who was in his mid-teens during Wilde's trials, appears to have been permanently affected. Young men like John Gray, Aubrey Beardsley, and Alfred Douglas, who were in their late teens or early to mid-twenties between 1890 and 1894, experienced moral and practical support from other homosexuals when they questioned hegemonic values. After he entered Cambridge, Forster too found friendship and encouragement among homosexuals such as Oscar Browning, G. Lowes Dickinson, and others. While an undergraduate at King's College, he became romantically entangled with H. O. Meredith. But Meredith was at least nominally straight, and sexual fulfillment eluded Forster for many years. Not until he fell in love with a young man named Mohammed el Adl while in Alexandria during World War I did Forster become sexually experienced.

In the meantime, he enjoyed friendships with homosexual men and supportive women while simultaneously undergoing a series of intense, sexually frustrated relationships with heterosexual or bisexual men. While no definitive answer is available why Forster's homosexuality was for so long blocked at the site of the genitals, the end of relatively open homosexual self-expression in 1895 posed major difficulties in his personal life and in the career that unfolded for him during the first decade of the new century as an ironic observer of the tragicomedy of English upper-middle-class life and manners.

"Albergo Empedocle" was suitable for publication in one of the homosexual magazines that had appeared at Oxford and London early in the decade. After 1895 these magazines had vanished or had changed their editorial policies. Wilde had made writing for a double audience the height of chic, but the glamor disappeared after male homosexuality had been stigmatized in the most public fashion. Male heterosexual writers also lost the opportunity to assess gender norms critically.[1] The relatively public opportunities for socializing and collaboration that male homosexuals had briefly enjoyed ceased to exist. As a young homosexual writer with a keen eye for the details of bourgeois domestic life, Forster found himself without a suitable social or publishing context. That he overcame these limits in a string of successful novels, climaxing in the publication of *Howards End* in 1910, was a triumph that could not be sustained indefinitely. Forster expresses the situation as early as a diary entry of 16 June 1911. Shortly after the success of *Howards End* and at a time when he was in his early thirties, he writes: "Weariness of the only subject that I both can and may treat—the love of men for women & vice versa."[2]

Even when Forster in his fiction resolutely focuses on male-female relations, they have as a limiting term the dangers posed by excessive investments between men. The threat of what Victorian sexologists defined as sexual inversion actively shapes the representation of conventional sexuality in Forster's writing, and this fact is already true in "Albergo Empedocle." In referring to this novel situation, which pertains not only to Forster's difficulties but to his social milieu, I use the term *the heterosexual contract*, by which I mean the prescribed investment of young men in relations with women whose main significance is their relation to social (re)production.[3] This contract, which defines both male-female relations and the male relations that frame them, marks a significant change from the male homosocial construction of sexuality prevalent in the mid-Victorian period. The contract demands a "forgetting" of desire between men that Forster figures at the literal level through the use of amnesia. As for young women, in their roles as fiancées or wives, they must sacrifice the slightest suggestion of a female difference that might exist outside the limits of the phallogocentric order.[4]

The new context has implications for the structure of Forster's fiction, in particular for the function of irony with respect to the reader as an excluded third term, who is, nonetheless, implicated in the text by how desire is structured between a narrator and narratee.[5] Ross Chambers argues that oppositional writing depends primarily on irony, a trope that can be put into operation only in the presence of a reader, who is the necessary third term. Chambers distinguishes two kinds of irony in oppositional writing: an irony of negation, which negates values of the dominant culture to whose members the text is in the first instance addressed; and an irony of appropriation, whereby the text suggests different desires to a reader or group of readers in opposition, wittingly or unwittingly, to the values of the dominant group.[6] Remaining for the most part within the limits of reader-response theory, Chambers does not exploit the possibility that structural irony affords the calling into existence of as yet indeterminate social groupings. "Albergo Empedocle," although addressed to conventional readers of *Temple Bar*, the journal in which it first appeared, appeals to a second set of readers who share Forster's need both to express and to dissemble a special interest in male intimacy.

This latter group are in an oppositional relation to the heterosexual contract along with its affiliations of class, rank, and nationality—even if, like Harold, the protagonist of the story, they aren't quite aware of the fact. In "Albergo Empedocle," male-male desire places one at the margin of the heterosexual contract but not altogether outside it.[7] This positioning at the margin is necessary if the processes of group-formation are to occur but also opens possibilities of self-deception and failure in personal relations that neither Harold nor Tommy, the framing narrator of the story, escapes.

The significance of the setting of Forster's story amid Greek ruins on Sicily brings to mind the end during the 1890s of the debates, dating from the late Enlightenment, of the significance of intimacy between males in the institution of pederasty as it had existed in different forms at ancient Athens and Sparta. While Forster as a boy was recoiling from the philistine atmosphere of Tonbridge School, Victorian philology entered a final phase as Walter Pater and Wilde, between 1890 and 1892, continued ironically to undercut the uses to which Greek models were conventionally put in elite education. Even when Greek studies were used to serve the political, social, and economic purposes of male elites, philology performed a useful function in foregrounding the connection between male intimacy and cultural and social production. Because they were part of conventional education, such ties were critiqued by writers like Pater and Wilde. However, the debates had compelled homosexual polemicists to theorize connections between masculine desire and positive outcomes in cultural and social relations, and the fact that Forster's generation was forced to abandon this project had negative consequences for the process of transforming Great Britain into a fully democratic state.[8]

In "Albergo Empedocle" Forster responds to both of these endings by drawing on tropes of metempsychosis and amnesia. On a visit with his bride-to-be and her parents to Sicily, Harold dreams that he has lived before as a Greek at Girgenti, the site of the former city of Acragas, a major commercial and cultural center during the Age of Pericles. The experience seems to suggest that although it may no longer be possible to *think Greek*, it is still possible to *become Greek*. This rapture, however, can be achieved only at the cost of disconnection from normal existence; in other words, only when it has become impossible to envisage a hermeneutics of Greek love, does the protagonist overleap the work of intellection by assuming for himself a metaphoric identification with the Other. This projection is precipitated by the refusal of Mildred, Harold's fiancée, and her family to comprehend the possibility of being-different. Harold is pushed into a breakdown and has to be repatriated by force to that other island, Great Britain, the counter to Sicily in the story. There he becomes the permanent ward of a mental hospital: "Long before Harold reached the asylum his speech had become absolutely unintelligible: indeed by the time he arrived at it, he hardly ever uttered a sound of any kind" (62).

Under the pressure of rejection by others, metempsychosis becomes an identification that captures the subject within a virtually complete solipsism. The recovery of a prior existence is incompatible with modern life because "we" (that is, we late Victorians) are amnesiacs. "We" have forgotten what it means to think Greek—even though as late as the early 1890s writers were showing us how to do so.[9] Accordingly, while philology retains the grammar and syntax of ancient Greek, in Forster's rhetoric it has lost the capacity of enunciation. Only Tommy, whose avowals of "love" for Harold equivocally frame the story, shares his friend's belief: "I firmly believe that he has been a Greek—nay, that he is a Greek, drawn by recollection back into his previous life. He cannot understand our speech because we have lost his pronunciation" (62). Tommy, however, does not speak Harold's language either or, rather, he can speak it only with the language of the body, the most equivocal of utterances, in the kiss that he receives from Harold at the end of the story. The role that Tommy plays needs to be regarded warily since his witness leaves Harold fixed in place as the subject of an existence almost totally estranged from "ours" and onto which, in view of Harold's muteness, Tommy is free to project what he will. Yet his fidelity to a love that cannot be voiced in return is the one space that Forster finds for expressing desire between men.

The extremity of Harold's situation suggests yet one more ending, this time generic, implied in Forster's short story; and that is the end of realist narrative, particularly in the novel, as a story in which two male rivals struggle for possession of a woman.[10] When Forster uses male-homosocial triangulation, he uses it differently, to show that at least in his fiction, the mediation of desire between men in a female object has ceased to constitute the terms of normal sexuality. Writing from a tacitly homosexual subject-position, Forster frames relations between men and women with an eye to desire between men. This framing poses the possibility of another narrative trajectory to some readers while presenting male-female relations not so much as normal but as representative of the institution of heterosexuality. In this context, Forster describes the implications for female subjectivity of the position of women as "wife" or "woman" within this order. This representation, particularly in Mildred, contributes to the critique of marriage but operates as well to limit Forster's awareness of how female subjectivities can exist in resistance to the formation of gender. Forster demonstrates the cost to women of their positioning within heterosexuality but at the expense of failing to respond to their capacity to differ from their prescribed roles.

In "Albergo Empedocle," the triangle of Harold, Mildred, and Tommy focuses on Harold. Despite the fact that Tommy and Harold's mutual if asymmetrical desires for each other set the interpretive horizons of the story, after Harold's experience Mildred reveals another, more forceful triangle at work: that of herself, her future husband, and her father, Sir Edwin. Mildred takes the following view of Harold's experience: "Worn out," Harold "had fallen asleep, and . . . had indulged in a fit of imagination on awaking. She had fallen in with it, and they had encouraged each other to fresh deeds of folly. All was clear. And how was she to hide it from her father?" (55). As the family expedition indicates, Harold is marrying not just Mildred but also her family. In return, the contract guarantees Mildred a fixed place in the scheme of things.

As Eve Kosofsky Sedgwick has shown in her discussion of Charles Dickens's *Our Mutual Friend* (1864–1865), woman's work in the triangle, as it functions in mid-Victorian fiction, is to save the male from his own indecisive and unrecognized desires.[11] Harold conforms to this script when he insists that Mildred validate his dream by kissing him with passion, something previously absent in their relations (57). His demand for her knowing acceptance belongs yet more properly to a moment late in male homosocial existence when, as Sedgwick shows, this time by way of her reading of "The Beast in the Jungle," a short story by Henry James also published in 1903, woman as "friend" serves the function of cherishing the secret of John Marcher, a man so deeply closeted that he forgets that he has told her his "secret."[12] Sedgwick argues that Bartram's function as "friend" is precisely to serve as the repository of Marcher's secret. Like a number of late Victorian wives who married men attracted to other men,[13] Mildred's ambivalent relation to her status as woman makes her initially prepared to undertake this exacting role but only on the condition that she too become Greek—by which she means that within her role as wife she occupy the place of an imaginary Other to Harold and thereby become more nearly his equal. When she decides that supporting Harold will, to the contrary, require self-sacrifice on her part while reinforcing her subordination as woman and her exclusion from "Greek" culture, she turns on him with remarkable vehemence. As for Harold, he is innocent of what his secret might be or why it needs to be a secret at all (50–51). His incomprehension signals that the male-homosocial role of woman as the friend or wife who keeps a man's secret does not in this story provide an effective bound to errant desires. Harold's Greek experience moves him outside the terms of the heterosexual contract. What he needs are interlocutors who can share his memories.

A Roman Ending

"Albergo Empedocle" begins with a letter that seems to set in place the sort of male homosocial triangulation that is a familiar aspect of realist narrative in Victorian fiction. As described by Harold, however, the situation sounds not quite right:

> We've just come from Pompeii. On the whole it's decidedly no go and very tiring. What with the smells and the beggars and the mosquitoes we're rather off Naples altogether, and we've changed our plans and are going to Sicily. The guidebooks say you can run through it in no time; only four places you have to go to, and very little in them. That suits us to a T. Pompeii and the awful Museum here have fairly killed us—except of course Mildred, and perhaps Sir Edwin.
>
> Now why don't you come too? I know you're keen on Sicily, and we all would like it. You would be able to spread yourself no end with your archaeology. For once in my life I should have to listen while you jaw. You'd enjoy discussing temples, gods, etc., with Mildred. She's taught me a lot, but of course it's no fun for her, talking to us. Send a wire; I'll stand the cost. Start at once and we'll wait for you. The Peaslakes say the same, especially Mildred.
>
> My not sleeping at night, and my headaches are all right now, thanks very much. As for the blues, I haven't had any since I've been engaged, and don't intend to. So don't worry any more.
>
> Yours,
> Harold (36)

It is fairly evident that Harold's dissatisfaction with traveling expresses an underlying awareness that the engagement mentioned at the end of the letter is a mistake. The prenuptial tour is, in reality, a series of detours that "go" nowhere and whose predetermined stops on the way have "very little" in them, except, that is, for threatening Harold with annihilation. The "awful museum" at Pompeii, with its domestic detritus dug up from volcanic ash, connotes marriage, the family, philistine culture, and the burdens of imperium. In other words, Pompeii is a subliminal reminder of the life-destroying responsibilities that Harold is about to assume. For his part, he would rather be on another trip, one that would "suit" him "to a T"—that is, to a *T/Tommy.*

In this light, it is not surprising to find Harold resisting his fiancée in her role of cicerone. As Tommy writes a bit later: "Mildred . . . was the fount of information. It was she who generally held the Baedeker and explained it. She had been expecting her continental scramble for several years, and had read a fair amount of books for it, which a good memory often enabled her to reproduce" (37). The key word here is memory, figured in the Baedeker, which connotes repetition. Memory in this sense only appears to "scramble" since it knows where it's headed, having learned its object by rote before meeting it. In contrast to this work of memory is the belief, held by Empedocles who once lived at Acragas, in "the transmigration of souls" (41), a mode of being that enables one to be constituted as wholly other.

Early on in the story, Mildred defends Harold's capacity for imagination against her father, who doubts that Harold has any. As well, it is Mildred who sets matters in motion by telling Harold en route to Girgenti that "today you must imagine you are a Greek" (42). Yet Mildred's capacity for sympathy is put cruelly to the test when Harold experiences his prior existence at Acragas. His continuing psychic stability depends on her sharing this belief with him; with no sense of exaggeration, he says to her: "I might have died if you hadn't believed me" (50). And Mildred does try. "Oh, Harold," she says, "I too may remember. . . . Oh, Harold! I am remembering! . . . In the wonderful youth of Greece did I speak to you and know you and love you. We walked through the marble streets, we led solemn sacrifices, I armed you for the battle, I welcomed you from the victory. The centuries have parted us, but not for ever. Harold, I too have lived at Acragas!" (53) Without her guidebook, however, she fails. She can become Greek only by translating Greece and Greek love into a parody of suburban bliss. Her difference, which accommodates no difference, is fake, as she says later: "pure imagination, the result of sentimental excitement" (54). Harold's sleep, however, has converted him into a truth-sayer. In response to her claim to have lived at Acragas, he quietly responds: "'No, Mildred darling, you have not'" (53).

The reader shortly learns that, contrary to his report to Tommy, headaches and insomnia do continue to trouble Harold. Mildred shows no awareness of these symptoms of bodily and spiritual *dis*-ease. To her as to her father, Harold might just as well be a piece of classical statuary. His external deportment conforms to the observation of an educator like Benjamin Jowett that

> You may look at a Greek statue and be struck with the flexure of the limbs, the majestic folds of the drapery, the simplicity, the strength. And yet scarcely any topics arise in the mind of the uncritical [viewer]. . . . The highest art is colourless like water, it has been said; it is a surface without prominences or irregularities over which the eye wanders impressed by the beauty of the whole with nothing to detain it at a particular point. . . . It is a smooth surface over which the hand may pass without interruption, but the curious work lies beneath the surface: the effect only is seen from without. The finer the workmanship the more completely is the art concealed.[14]

This remark is, if not colored, then shadowed by the preterition that draws attention to while denying the fact that Greek "limbs" may draw "the eye" (and "the hand") to a "particular point," a point which redirects attention from a surface without openings to "the curious work" accessible only from the inside. Precisely Harold's presentation of "a surface without prominences or irregularities" makes him a suitable candidate as son-in-law, almost too suitable. Sir Edwin Peaslake remarks: "Of course I'm very fond of him, he's a thoroughly nice fellow, honest as the day, and he's good-looking and well-made—I value all that extremely—but after all brains are something. He is so slow—so lamentably slow—at catching one's meaning" (44).

In Sicily, however, Harold betrays a disturbing propensity to imagine that he is "someone else," a "dodge" (39) he confesses that he occasionally resorts to when he has trouble falling asleep—or when he has "the blues" (40). When Sir Edwin discovers this capacity, he is shocked: "It is never safe to play tricks with the brain," he admonishes. "I must say I'm astonished: you of all people!" (40). It's even worse after Harold's dream when Sir Edwin demands that unless the young man acknowledge that he has been deluded, the marriage will not take place. What is troubling ("queer" in Sir Edwin's usage) is Harold's ability to change when he encounters something or someone different.

As the mention of Sir Edwin in Harold's letter indicates, Harold's contract is only incidentally with Mildred even as it is only incidental that she has something to say about the Greek temples at Girgenti: she can repeat what she has read. Similarly, in the role of wife and mother, she will repeat the genealogy of the Peaslakes. The corporate character of the engagement is implicitly extended in the brief reference at the opening to another ending, the destruction of Herculaneum and Pompeii as a result of an eruption of Vesuvius in A.D. 79. Pompeii signifies the analogy between English and Roman culture both in the static density of existence as recovered from the ashes in archaeological digs and in the characteristic twinning of Roman and British imperium in nineteenth-century English thought.[15] The sense of closure impressed on Harold during his visit to "the awful Museum" helps set the stage for the crisis at Girgenti.

On the train from Palermo, Harold's view of Sicily comments ironically on England's economic and political position at the end of the century: "They had hardly crossed the watershed of the island. It was the country of the mines, barren and immense, absolutely destitute of grass or trees, producing nothing but cakes of sallow sulphur, which were stacked on the platform of every wayside station. Human beings were scanty, and they were stunted and dry, mere withered vestiges of men. And far below at the bottom of the yellow waste was the moving living sea, which embraced Sicily when she was green and delicate and young, and embraces her now, when she is brown and withered and dying" (42). This vision suggests the actual as opposed to the putative effects of Empire since Sicily's denudation is a result of centuries of foreign invasion and domination. Tommy/Forster's outburst contrasts, however, to the commentary of the tenth edition of *The Encyclopaedia Britannica* (1902), which blandly remarks on the systematic transfer of capital from Sicily to the north after the unification of Italy:

> Like all southern Italy, Sicily in 1860 was poor, notwithstanding the possession of notable reserves of monetary capital. On the completion of Italian unity part of this pecuniary capital was absorbed by the sudden increase of taxation, and a much greater part was employed by private individuals in the purchase of lands formerly belonging to the suppressed religious corporations. . . . Both the revenues acquired by taxation and the proceeds of the land sales were almost entirely spent by the State in northern Italy, where the new Government, for administrative and military reasons, had been obliged to establish its principal organizations, and consequently its great centres of economic consumption. (9:618)

The Peaslakes identify with Sicily's conquerors. After the small upset that occurs when Sir Edwin learns about Harold's "dodge," Mildred restores quiet by returning to the guidebook: she "passed on to the terrible sack of Acragas by the Romans. Whereat their faces relaxed, and they regained their accustomed spirits" (41).[16]

Tommy's "keen" interest in Sicilian archaeology, however, associates

10. Caspar David Friedrich, *The Temple of Juno at Agrigentum*, ca. 1828–1830. Courtesy Museum für Kunst und Kulturgeschichte, Dortmund, Germany.

him with the world, both pastoral and civic, of *Greek* Sicily, which appears to offer in Acragas a model of colonization far different from the Italian, Roman, or English. Harold's letter betokens the wish to recover this existence in company with Tommy (even if the wish can only be uttered in negation and displaced onto Mildred). In Tommy's absence the possibility of recovery is open to Harold only in something like the form of his experience at Girgenti, where he falls asleep in the afternoon sun between the legs of a toppled colossal statue of Atlas and awakes convinced that in an earlier life he has lived as a citizen of Acragas.

> [There] were two fallen columns, lying close together, and the space that separated them had been silted up and was covered with flowers. On it, as on a bed, lay Harold, fast asleep, his cheek pressed against the hot stone of one of the columns, and his breath swaying a little blue iris that had rooted in one of its cracks. . . .
>
> Sleep has little in common with death, to which men have compared it. Harold's limbs lay in utter relaxation, but he was tingling with life, glorying in the bounty of the earth and the warmth of the sun, and the little blue flower bent and fluttered like a tree in a gale. The light beat upon his eyelids and the grass leaves tickled his hair, but he slept on,

and the lines faded out of his face as he grasped the greatest gift that the animal life can offer. (47–48)

Mildred frames the scene as a tourist should: "He looked so picturesque, and she herself, sitting on the stone watching him, must look picturesque too. She knew that there was no one to look at her, but from her mind the idea of a spectator was never absent for a moment. It was the price she had paid for becoming cultivated" (47).

By 1903, high culture, including Greek culture, had been thoroughly commodified for the consumption and adornment of members of Mildred's class. Exotic locales provided the props for situating members of this group in preformulated ways. Mildred responds to such a scene as a masculinist observer would. Her gaze is from the position of one who is always already an object within such a scene. This framing excludes the possibility that instead of responding in a "cultivated" way Mildred might be changed by contact with "animal life" or by a pastoral existence that combines both spontaneous and cultivated responses. Hence the metonymic function of the guidebook, whose mapping determines before one leaves home what knowledge will or will not be acquired while abroad.[17]

For a middle- or upper-class male homosexual, Greek culture could be commodified in another way in the form of sexual tourism—whether the object of desire remained phantasmic as it did for Forster on his Italian and Greek tours of 1902 and 1903 or whether it was acquired in more practicable ways. When Baron von Gloeden, for instance, photographed young Sicilian peasants in the ungarb of ancient youth, the discrepancy between sign and signifier indicated the inability of representation to suture the difference between material and imaginary reality. Nonetheless, these images, with the blessing of local Sicilians, drew homosexuals to the villa at Taormina from which von Gloeden sold his postcards.[18] Forster pitches the attraction in another register. In "Albergo Empedocle," Greek culture provides the opportunity of imagining a "better love," as presumably it does for Tommy, whose interest in Sicily is described as that not of a tourist but of an archaeologist. Yet even when resolutely scientific or highminded, trips like Forster's visit to Girgenti in 1902 exist within a structure of erotic fantasy that is marked by class and ethnic snobbery. Forster/Harold/Tommy's aspiration to a better love is distinguishable but not dissociable from the other meanings of fin-de-siècle tourism. For these men, absorption in Greek culture, though oppositional in Chambers's use of the word, signified economic and national distinction.

Against these significations, Forster buttresses the oppositional meaning of Harold's experience through intertextual reference to polemical texts of the homosexual renaissance of a few years before. Mildred's gaze at Harold recalls that of the Prior at the sleeping figure of Apollo/Apollyon in Pater's "Apollo in Picardy," an imaginary portrait of 1893.[19] In the story, Pater uses the setting of a monastic community in order to analyze the psychological effects of homophobia on a male homosocial subject. The blue iris recalls the hyacinths that blossom after the murder, probably at the hands of the Prior, of his young companion, Hyacinth. Harold's habit of looking out the window of the asylum recalls the Prior's similar practice after he is judged to be insane and placed under house arrest. "Gazing . . . daily for many hours, he would mistake mere blue distance, when that was visible, for blue flowers, for hyacinths, and wept at the sight."[20] In Forster's less ironic text, we simply don't know what Harold sees. The references to Pater, however, provide textual means of overcoming the limiting terms of the "spectator" envisaged by Mildred.

Sweet Nothings

At the end of "Albergo Empedocle," the narrator observes:

> Most certainly he is not unhappy. His own thoughts are sweet to him, and he looks out of the window hour after hour and sees things in the sky and sea that we have forgotten. But of his fellow men he seems utterly unconscious. He never speaks to us, nor hears us when we speak. He does not know that we exist.
>
> So at least I thought till my last visit. I am the only one who still goes to see him; the others have given it up. Last time, when I entered the room, he got up and kissed me on the cheek. I think he knows that I understand him and love him: at all events it comforts me to think so. (63)

Just as the story begins with a missive from Harold to Tommy, it ends with another, with Harold's chaste kiss. In a story in which the reader has learned something of the semiotics of kissing, this kiss is a bodily sign of Greek love in contrast both to the proffered kiss of conscious desire that Mildred rejects at Girgenti and to the "decorous peck" (50) that had earlier sealed her engagement. In a world that has become amnesiac by resolutely turning away from *thinking Greek*—and Tommy includes himself among the "we" who have forgotten—Tommy can at best be only nearly sure what the language of the body means when, in the final words of the story, he says: "I think he knows that I understand and love him: at all events it comforts me to think so" (63). Tommy needs comfort because, though his absence from Sicily was necessary, it meant that he was not at hand at Harold's moment of truth. Accordingly, Tommy has missed, perhaps for good, his own chance to reenter Greek subjectivity.

By adhering to the Christian counsel to visit the sick, Tommy does, however, give witness to his love for Harold. Indeed, in Tommy's telling, his love frames the story even though at the start that love appears to have been baffled and remains so throughout. Harold, Tommy confides, is "the man I love most in the world" (37). Yet the role of witness and the confidence with which Tommy uses the verb are odd in view of the ignorance that usually attends love in this story. In addition, by proffering this knowledge to the reader as though it were fairly straightforward, Tommy posits a line of shared cognition between Harold, himself, and the reader, despite the fact that the story is structured in such a way as to leave such a possibility in suspension. At no time do Harold and Tommy clearly understand love in the same way. Instead, the assumption of intelligibility on Tommy's part depends on a reading effect. In the experience of readers of the story, there may exist relations that will complete Tommy and Harold's untold, unconsummated "love." Tommy makes a utopian appeal to a reader who has recovered the ability to *think Greek*, who understands touch, and who has enough imagination to project a world in which it would make sense to say as Harold does: "I was better, I saw better, heard better, thought better. . . . I loved very differently. . . . Yes, I loved better too" (51, 52). By this appeal, Tommy calls into being a reader of the future who may be described as the subject of a gay erotics. Moving beyond the frame of the heterosexual contract, the text implies the potential existence of cultural and social spaces in which men will be able to voice and to enact their mutual sexual and emotional bonds.

At this point, the ends that accompany Forster's hesitant beginnings as a writer help explain the discrepancy between hope and contingencies. Forster, who was born on New Years Day 1879, was sixteen years old during the Wilde trials of 1895. As "a little cissy" aware of the distances, including distances of desire, between himself and others his age, Forster was both appalled and instructed by the punishment meted out to Wilde, the only homosexual of his class who seemed able simultaneously to appeal to newly emergent groups, including male homosexual and lesbian ones; sharply to satirize the powers that be; yet to continue to enjoy entry and success in the worlds both of middlebrow and highbrow culture.[21] Two years later, when Forster left Tonbridge School to enter King's College, he found a place at which the conditions for a life of Greek harmony still seemed to exist: "Body and spirit, reason and emotion, work and play, architecture and scenery, laughter and seriousness, life and art—these pairs which are elsewhere contrasted were there fused into one. People and books reinforced one another, intelligence joined hands with affection, speculation became a passion, and discussion was made profound by love."[22]

Forster achieved this sense of wholeness especially as a result of being selected for membership in the Apostles, the Cambridge undergraduate society of which Alfred Tennyson and Arthur Henry Hallam had been early members and which achieved new distinction at the turn of the century through the membership of men like Bertrand Russell, Alfred North Whitehead, Lytton Strachey, Leonard Woolf, and John Maynard Keynes.[23] Moreover, the line into this group was affective: Forster was sponsored for membership by H. O. ("Hom") Meredith, a handsome, bright, athletic, sexually confused young man, with whom Forster fell in love. While arguments in defense of male homosexuality were put forward at the weekly meetings, members kept quiet about their sexual involvements; and Forster and Meredith's intimacies were confined to "kisses and embraces."[24]

In a biography of Forster, Francis King comments that "Meredith, a basically heterosexual man, probably took the physical lead, either out of kindness or out of curiosity, but Forster was the one who was in love."[25] King's condescension notwithstanding, Meredith appears to have signed the heterosexual contract with difficulty. Shortly after he and Forster became friends, Meredith became engaged to Caroline Graveson, then "had a nervous breakdown."[26] In 1906, Meredith wrote to Keynes from Manchester: "I think I am dead really now. . . . Or perhaps I should say I realise now what was plain to others two years ago. I come to life temporarily when I meet Forster." Furbank remarks: "Forster, as was his habit in friendship, made vigorous efforts to rouse Meredith out of his apathy. They would go for long walks, endlessly discussing Meredith's problems, or sometimes walking in total silence while he brooded."[27] In this relationship, Forster appears to have played the role of "Tommy."

The homosexual members of the Apostles or, later, Bloomsbury lived in a country in which they were vulnerable to disgrace, blackmail, and legalized persecution. Under the relatively new terms of the Labouchère amendment, the prohibition of "gross indecency" brought a far wider range of acts between men—including kissing—within the net of the law. Indeed, even those Saturday night deliberations about the nobility of male love were potentially liable to prosecution. Within these circumstances, Forster, referring to himself as a homosexual, uses the term "minority." Returning from a trip to Greece in 1904, he describes himself as though he were part of a barren Mediterranean landscape: "I'd better eat my soul for I certainly shan't have it. I'm going to be a minority if not a solitary, and I'd best make copy out of my position. There is nothing contemptible or cynical in this. I too have sweet waters though I shall never drink them. So I can understand the drought of others, though they will not understand my abstinence."[28] For Forster in 1904, being a minority meant living privately and celibately. Faced with this sort of isolation, it is not surprising that the insulation of groups like the Apostles increased or that homosexual involvements came to appear to outsiders to be a part of a "cult."[29]

Forster's decision not to reprint "Albergo Empedocle" during his lifetime is in keeping with the extreme sense of apartness expressed in the preceding quotation. Yet it is a part of the continuing interest of this story that it calls into existence the members of a minority *group*. This structure depends in turn on contingencies: on the existence of a homosexual radical culture before 1895, on its subsequent suppression, and on the continuing effects of the work of gender in Victorian Greek studies. Even when it was no longer possible to contest the meaning of masculinity within philological inquiry, the efforts of writers like Pater, Wilde, and others continued to lend fortitude to men like Forster.

Forster is often thought of as a man with two careers: the first climaxed with the publication of *A Passage to India* in 1924, after which he ceased to publish new fiction. The second career is a posthumous one as a writer of gay short stories and the novel *Maurice* (1970). The two parts of Forster's career, however, and the frustration of his work as a novelist after 1924 were conditioned by the institution of heterosexuality, which enforces in literature either conventional sexuality or a complex relationship to specifically homosexual desire. In this sense, Forster had not two careers but one marked by continual compromise and resistance.

In projecting hope beyond the end of hope, Forster at the very outset of his career took a postapocalyptic stance. Given this positioning, it is altogether appropriate that he destined for posthumous publication the gay writing that he eventually produced. In this way, though continually marked by the events of 1895, Forster ensured that he would become the contemporary of the first generation of gay activists to live after sex between men was partially decriminalized by the Sexual Offenses Act of 1967. Forster's contemporaneity with gay liberation proved to be an unsettling, even unwelcome phenomenon.[30] But it provides a continuing testimony to the traumatic origin of male homosexual identity.

TWO

FIN DE MILLENNIUM

(Overleaf) 11. Stephen Andrews, *The Death of Abel Cry Me a River,* 1990. Photo by Isaac Applebaum. Courtesy Garnet Press Gallery, Toronto.

5

···

FRAMING WILLIAM BURROUGHS: FROM FRANK KERMODE TO DAVID CRONENBERG

Coming Home

Part Two of this book comes to rest with two texts produced in the first wave of gay literary responses to AIDS. In Chapter 7 I consider "An Oracle" (1986), the first piece of fiction by Edmund White in which he addresses AIDS. In Chapter 8 I end, where in Chapter 1 I began, in London of the 1980s. In *The Swimming-Pool Library* (1988), Alan Hollinghurst develops a double temporal focus remarkably akin to the one that Neil Bartlett uses in *Who Was That Man?* Although the past that Hollinghurst presents is that of the Oxford Wits of the 1920s, Lord Nantwich's fascination with the 1880s connects the past in Hollinghurst's novel with the late Victorian milieu to which Bartlett resorts in attempting to come to terms with a crisis in contemporary gay existence.[1]

The opening chapters of Part Two continue to examine the intersection of sexual politics in elite male academic culture with the critique of humanism in poststructuralist theory in the United States. Because these struggles occur around the vexed term, *postmodernism*, that word is an important one for these chapters. In Chapter 6 I focus on the antagonistic stance toward Andy Warhol that Fredric Jameson adopts in his highly influential 1984 essay, "Postmodernism, or The Cultural Logic of Late Capitalism." Jameson argues that postmodern sensibility is characterized by what he terms the hysterical sublime. Hysteria in this instance, however, is masculine, constituted in terms of an ecstatic sense of the dissolution of the male ego in bodily sensation that is matched by an equally intense revulsion from men who enjoy sexual and emotional ties to other men. This double bind is thoroughly implicated in Jameson's lament over the loss of (masculine) agency under the economic regime of late capitalism.

Andreas Huyssen's definition of postmodernism provides a useful point of departure. "Starting from the *Selbtsverständnis* of the postmodern as it has shaped various discourses since the 1960's," Huyssen describes postmodernism as "a slowly emerging cultural transformation in Western societies, a change in sensibility."[2] Expert cartographer of postmodernism that he is, however, Huyssen errs when he argues that poststructuralism became significant in American postmodernism only in the late 1970s. He overlooks the debate about apocalypse that began early in the decade between M. H. Abrams and J. Hillis Miller which was inflected by Miller's gradual shift to a deconstructive stance. He also overlooks the debate in the late 1960s between Abrams and Paul de Man which implicated deconstruction in American reaction against both critical theory and postmodernism. And by opening a gap between postmodern art in the United States during the 1960s and "French poststructuralism," he assumes that the cultural production of artists such as Andy Warhol and Jack Smith was untheorized,[3] but if cultural production can do the work of theory, then a strong case can be made for the theoretical coherence and purposiveness of Warhol's projects. Implicitly rejecting the modernist aesthetic that informs New York action painting, Warhol drew on his training at Carnegie Tech in European avant-garde tradition to make innovative art from a marginal subject position that was characterized by several subordinated identifications.

Huyssen postdates the importance of sexual politics, especially in relation to gay cultural practices, in the opening arguments about postmodernism. While emphasizing the impact of movement politics in the 1970s, he radically underestimates the significance of the gay cultural politics that Susan Sontag notes in her classic essay on camp. The two strands of "modern sensibility" which Sontag isolates ("Jewish moral seriousness and homosexual aestheticism and irony") and which were especially associated with high culture emanating from New York City were not only present during the 1960s but were also increasingly in conflict, as they continued to be, with greater vehemence, during the Reagan-Bush years.[4]

Similarly, when Huyssen describes the "counter-culture," he tends to register a widening range of difference within hegemonic discourse. For example, the proliferation that Leslie Fiedler celebrates in his essay, "The New Mutants" (1965), focused, as his title suggests, on transformations of the species rather than on the formation of new individual and group identities. According to Fiedler, the myth characteristic of what he terms postmodern fiction

> is quite simply the myth of the end of man, of the transcendence or transformation of the human—a vision quite different from that of the extinction of our species by the Bomb, which seems stereotype rather

than archetype and consequently the source of editorials rather than poems. More fruitful artistically is the prospect of the radical transformation (under the impact of advanced technology and the transfer of traditional human functions to machines) or *homo sapiens* into something else: the emergence—to use the language of Science Fiction itself—of "mutants" among us.[5]

Interpreting this shift in the most general terms possible, Fiedler says of "the new irrationalists": "For them the true rallying cry is, 'Let id prevail over ego, impulse over order,' or—in negative terms—'Freud is a fink!'"[6]

Yet when Abrams and Frank Kermode respond to the attack on "humanism," they take the author of *Naked Lunch* to be the exponent of disorder. In Chapter 5 I explore the construction of masculinity implied by the panicked invocation of William Burroughs as a sign of the collapse of Western civilization. Burroughs's writing is thoroughly apocalyptic, but narrative structure in *Queer*, the autobiographical fiction that he wrote in the 1950s and withheld from publication until 1985, takes the particular form of queer apocalypse. In queer apocalypse, an errant "I" stumbles to exotic locales in search of an elusive, ultimate intoxication. This subject is condemned to psychic and physical disintegration since, disidentified from the oedipal contract, he lacks as well any alternative psychological or social structure in relation to which he might constitute himself.[7] Although this absence is usually represented in terms of a hopeless dependence on a straight-identified object of desire, what is missing is not a norm of the male couple but norms of sociality in relation to which male couples and coupling might become significant. David Cronenberg's 1991 film of *Naked Lunch* draws on fictional, biographical, and autobiographical texts in order to conflate Burroughs with his fictions. The result indicates that queer difference is quite recuperable within modernist paradigms in contemporary filmmaking.

Culture Clash

The early 1990s marked the return of William Burroughs as an icon within high culture and the mass media. This renewed attention occurred as a result of the release of the critically well received film, *Naked Lunch*, directed by the Canadian filmmaker David Cronenberg. In writing the script, Cronenberg fashioned a postmodern metafiction that combines aspects of Burroughs's autobiographical writing, including *Queer*; Ted Morgan's biography, *Literary Outlaw: The Life and Times of William S. Burroughs* (1988); and *Naked Lunch*. The result is a carefully controlled, psychologically coherent narrative in which Cronenberg conflates

12. Peter Weller as Bill Lee in David Cronenberg's film of *Naked Lunch*. Photo by Attila Dory and Brian Hamill. Courtesy Alliance Releasing, Toronto; Twentieth Century-Fox, Los Angeles.

Burroughs with Bill Lee, the protagonist of *Queer* and *Naked Lunch*. The closure that Cronenberg effects in this way paradoxically renders the thematic of the film not postmodernist but modernist. He produces a mythic figure of the artist in revolt with which he and the young men who admire his films can identify. But Cronenberg's apocalypse is very different from the formal and thematic apocalypse of Burroughs's fiction.

Rereading Kermode's critical analysis of apocalypse, I was surprised to discover that the Burroughs of *Naked Lunch* plays a brief but important role in *The Sense of an Ending*. Kermode uses Burroughs as the exemplar of the postmodern fiction that received widespread media attention in 1960s. Kermode ignores novelists like Ralph Ellison, John Barth, Joseph Heller, and Thomas Pynchon, whom Robert Alter in 1966 attacked for the "apocalyptic postures" of their fiction.[8] Instead Kermode focuses on Burroughs, whose association with drug addiction and homosexuality put him beyond the pale. Identifying Burroughs's work with what Kermode refers to as "*avant-garde* writing," Kermode describes "the language of his books" as "the language of an ending world."[9] Against this backdrop of cultural disintegration, Kermode carries on an urgent defense of what he refers to in contrast as "traditionalist modernism." By choosing *Ulysses* as his exemplary text, Kermode positions himself as a leading proponent of a modernism that by becoming institutionalized within undergraduate curricula in anglophone universities, had truly become "traditionalist." In this chapter, I oppose queer apocalypse in Burroughs's writings to the modernist apocalypse in which Cronenberg frames him. I trace as well episodes in the institutional history of literary criticism in the United States in which "Burroughs" and, more generally, postmodernist fiction and poststructuralist theory figure in a critical metanarrative, homophobically charged, of reaction against cultural innovation. When Kermode describes the lineage in which Burroughs writes as one that "destroys the indispensable and relevant past,"[10] apocalypse becomes a set of metaphors that shape Kermode's own historical and critical analysis.

Burroughs's textuality acquires further significance in relation to the contest over the legal definition of pornography that centered on *Naked Lunch* in the mid-1960s. In this context, *Naked Lunch* is validated within liberal discourse as an exemplary instance of juridically defined free speech. This discursive siting is a motivating element in Cronenberg's long involvement with Burroughs. As for Kermode, by enlisting *Ulysses* against "*avant-garde* writing," he draws for support on a text, at one time excoriated for its literary experimentation, that was involved in a major obscenity ruling in a U.S. court in 1933.[11] In the renewed struggles of the 1960s, Kermode places himself on the side of freedom of literary expression in order to limit the range of acceptable expression not on legal but on cultural grounds.[12]

The crises of the 1960s prompted the development of a neoconservative cultural critique that climaxed during the second Reagan administration. Literary humanists, many of whom had formerly been liberals, reacted against "avant-garde" practice and other forms of cultural dissidence, some of which challenged the universities in which these men taught. Whether liberal or conservative, many were associated in their critical writing and teaching with the modernist classics. The debate between "modernism" and "postmodernism" was waged on other bases too, including resistance to the incursion of poststructuralist theory from abroad, particularly France. What is easily forgotten today is the sexualized rhetoric and apocalyptic narrative within which these arguments were carried on. In light of this discursive history, subsequent episodes in cultural politics, such as the decision taken early in the Bush presidential campaign of 1992 to target male homosexuals, become more comprehensible.[13]

In *Natural Supernaturalism: Tradition and Revolution in Romantic Literature* (1971), M. H. Abrams translates the current debates into an argument about literary periodization. Abrams differentiates "romanticism" from "modernism" in a way that corresponds with the modernist/ postmodernist, humanist/poststructuralist oppositions of contemporary polemic. It is this context that made the consequent argument between Abrams and J. Hillis Miller so highly charged. Apocalyptic pattern can be transferred into critical discourse as a framing narrative. This is the case with Abrams, who deploys an apocalyptic metanarrative in his clashes with Miller, de Man, and other of the so-called Yale Critics.

Abrams articulates his readings of English romantic poetry within a narrative of fallen and restored consciousness. In this construct, displaced from Christian belief, an original sense of being at one with oneself and nature is succeeded by a period of divided self-awareness and alienation from the external world. Abrams contends that romantic poems restore to the lyric persona a sense of unity with self and "the order of the living universe."[14] When Abrams first put forward this narrative in the 1950s in an influential book, *The Mirror and the Lamp*, it underlined the ethical seriousness of literary studies. In that decade of cold war struggle, literary criticism acquired a level of prestige hitherto unknown in the United States.

Though the terms, texts, and dates are different, in *Natural Supernaturalism* Abrams's dyad of "romanticism" and "modernism" carries the same phobic charge that Kermode attaches to what he terms "anti-traditionalist modernism."[15] Abrams contrasts a catastrophic narrative of the "end" of culture to the millennialist vision that he ascribes to romanticism. In the ensuing clash, he makes clear his identification with the romantics' attempt to adopt "the traditional persona of the poet-prophet" in order "to speak with an authoritative public voice" at a time of "crisis of civilization and consciousness": "I decided to end *Natural Supernaturalism* by identifying, in my chosen authors, those Romantic positives which deliberately reaffirmed the elementary values of the Western past, and to present these values in a way directly addressed to our own age of anxiety and of incipient despair of our inherited civilization."[16]

Abrams's text expresses what Derrida refers to as a "unity of the apocalyptic tone" that results in monotonous iteration of the apocalyptic pattern of redeemed selfhood.[17] The experience of an original state of unity "between self and nature" is followed by a solipsistic fall, which is followed in turn by a "personal secular redemption" that issues in an experience of restored unity.[18] This pattern provides by implicit analogy a model of social and cultural unification.

Abrams represents late 1960s culture in contrast as a time of catastrophic decline. Although he limits his specific reference to literature and the visual arts, critical culture, especially emergent deconstruction, is implicitly targeted, as is a wide range of cultural dissidence that at the time threatened the unity of tone of a wide range of institutions, including the Department of Defense, the Democratic party, and elite East and West Coast universities such as Cornell, where Abrams taught. By the late 1960s, gay liberation had also emerged as a significant element within this dissidence. Deploying a gnostic apocalyptic narrative in which the forces of Life are poised against the forces of Eros *à rebours*, Abrams writes:

> Salient in our own time is a kind of literary Manichaeism—secular versions of the radical *contemptus mundi et vitae* of heretical Christian dualism—whose manifestations in literature extend back through Mallarmé and other French Symbolists to Rimbaud and Baudelaire. A number of our writers and artists have turned away, in revulsion or despair, not only from the culture of Western humanism but from the biological conditions of life itself, and from all life-affirming values. They devote themselves to a new Byzantinism, which T. E. Hulme explicitly opposed to the Romantic celebration of life and admiringly defined as an art which, in its geometrized abstractness, is "entirely independent of vital things," expresses "disgust with the trivial and accidental characteristics of living shapes," and so possesses the supreme virtue of being "anti-vital," "non-humanistic," and "world-rejecting." Alternatively, the new Manichaeans project a vision of vileness, or else the blank nothingness of life, and if they celebrate Eros, it is often an Eros *à rebours*—perverse, hence sterile and life-negating.[19]

Abrams's disparagement of those who revolt against "the biological conditions of life itself" is a not very covert allusion to subjects of male-male desire—such as Rimbaud, mentioned by Abrams, and Beat writers, including Burroughs, attacked by Kermode.

The passage occurs in a context in which Abrams responds to recent critiques of the poetry of William Wordsworth that negate Abrams's earlier emphasis on the "integral unity of thought and feeling"[20] in Wordsworth's aesthetic. Although Abrams directs his comments toward these critics, the implicit target of his remarks is de Man. In an important essay, "The Rhetoric of Temporality" (1969), de Man critiques Abrams's argument about the unification of consciousness with language and nature by means of the romantic symbol.[21] In the second part of the essay, where he discusses romantic irony in Baudelaire, de Man repudiates "the inherent violence" of normal sociality while defending the decision to fashion an ironic fiction of personal madness even if, in doing so, the artist risks the loss of sanity.[22] Abrams's stricture on Baudelaire in the passage cited above glances at the prominent place of Baudelaire in the ethic of de Man's essay. In singling out French Aestheticism and Decadence for criticism, Abrams tars with a single brush both the proponents of French

poststructuralism and the Beats. Irony as validated by de Man is antipa-
thetic both to Abrams's injunction to "qualified hope" and to the norm of
"consonance" that Kermode identifies with traditionalist modernism.[23]

Sexual Politics and *The Sense of an Ending*

Kermode's career and ideological stance are symptomatic of changes in
higher education in the United States and Great Britain following World
War II. In the United States, the G.I. bill dramatically increased opportunities for former members of the armed services to enroll in colleges
and universities. In Britain, change occurred more slowly. Passage of
the (Butler) Education Act in 1944 promised "Free Secondary Education for All." But this goal was achieved only by a compromise that resulted in a class-segregated model that preserved the traditional public
schools.[24] Following publication in 1963 of the Robbins Report on higher
education, the government embarked on a major effort to convert uni-
versity-level education from "a minority's privilege" into "a universal
right."[25] Democratization did not include transforming the organization
and curricula of universities. As John Sutherland has argued, university
expansion conserved "the traditional nature of the British university
(above all its small size, autonomy, pastoral relationships between staff
and student, liberal Newmanesque ethos, and close tutorial teaching
method)."[26] Through secondary and higher education and institutions
such as the Arts Council (1945) and the BBC Third Programme (1946), a
much wider portion of the British populace enjoyed access to high culture. But culture also assimilated lower-middle and working-class citizens to middle-class values. In the universities, the study of English
literature served an important function in consolidating a consensus that
validated conventional culture while affirming efforts to democratize British society. By the 1960s, "EngLit" had become the central humanistic
course of study. But lags in curricular and administrative reform under-
mined the centrality of literature as a locus of culture and as a way of
inculcating civility among upwardly mobile students. The new demo-
graphic mix undercut the very consensus on which government financing
of increased access to higher education depended.

Kermode's peripatetic career, which brought him to many universities
in England and the United States, is an index of the expansion of personal
and professional opportunities that took place at this time. Sutherland
argues that Kermode played a "crucial" role in widening the critical and
theoretical range of English studies from the late 1950s to the 1970s.[27]
By the time he presented the lectures at Bryn Mawr College that were to
appear one year later in book form as *The Sense of an Ending* (1967),

cultural dissidence among students and members of minority groups in Britain and the United States had become a disturbing phenomenon. Within this context, the politics of Kermode's book are complex. In the dawning battle between modernists and postmodernists, he provides a moderate defense of literary modernism against what Leslie Fiedler and Ihab Hassan were beginning to celebrate as postmodernism.[28] Kermode defends the autonomy of literature against the politics of both academic conservatives and radicals. But in making his own political intervention, he depends on the very principles of aesthetic form that he defends. In his argument, modernist literary form, especially in the novel, validates the norms that he and other liberal academics have traditionally found in literature.

In *The Sense of an Ending*, Kermode focuses on the paradigms that human beings invent to give meaning to what would otherwise be "purely successive, disorganized time." Apocalypses or "fictions of the End" distinguish *saeculum* or ordinary chronicity from a sense of time that "ends, transforms, and is concordant." Between these two times occurs a third, a "period of Transition," in which the character of the End, whether millennial or catastrophic, is determined or revealed. Kermode argues that although predictions of the End are continually being made, they are counterbalanced just as frequently by what he refers to as a "clerkly scepticism," reminding the faithful "that arithmetical predictions of the End are bound to be disconfirmed." When scepticism fails, apocalyptic paradigms degenerate into what Kermode refers to as "myths," explanatory fictions whose hypothetical character has been ignored or forgotten. To illustrate this point, he contrasts the use of mythic form in high-modernist poetry to the right-wing political mythmaking that occurs in the *obiter dicta* of modernists such as Wyndham Lewis, D. H. Lawrence, William Butler Yeats, Ezra Pound, and T. S. Eliot.[29]

Kermode finds in apocalyptic thinking "clues to the ways in which fictions, whose ends are consonant with origins, and in concord, however unexpected, with their precedents, satisfy our needs." Despite his criticism of the extreme right-wing political views expressed by a number of male modernist writers, Kermode revalidates "traditionalist modernism" as exemplified by *Ulysses*. According to Kermode, narrative form in Joyce's novel acknowledges both the inconsecutive character of daily existence and the impulse to organize human experience in myth. Joyce deploys both mythic and random temporal structures in *Ulysses*. In this way, he avoids the Scylla of irrational belief, on the one hand, and the Charybdis of *chronos*, mere "passing" or "waiting time," on the other. He achieves this end by means of aesthetic *form*, which serves a further function in Kermode's argument by providing a fictive model of order in a world that suffers from being either too organized or not organized enough. "Alone" among the "great works" of traditionalist modernism, *Ulysses* "studies and develops the tension between paradigm and reality, asserts the resistance of fact to fiction, human freedom and unpredictability against the plot. Joyce chooses a Day; it is a crisis ironically treated. The day is full of randomness. There are coincidences, meetings that have point, and coincidences which do not. We might ask whether one of the merits of the book is not its *lack* of mythologizing." In this composite form, partly realist, partly mythic, Joyce is able to contain the full range of existence.[30]

Kermode interprets *Ulysses* as fashioning a norm of realism appropriate to modern life. In doing so, he reasserts the traditional idea that aesthetic *form* can have a regulative cultural significance. This affirmation is doubled by an implicit analogy between literary form and the forms of bureaucratic rationalism in the modern industrial state. In the 1960s, liberal intellectuals were confident that these forms could be used to protect "human freedom" from the effects of political mythmaking on both the Left and the Right, from the consequences of random events, and from the destabilizing effects of the social reforms that they fostered. Yet even within the limits of cultural politics, Kermode's use of *Ulysses* begs the question of the extent to which *literary* fictions can serve to satisfy a general need within culture for a sense of order. Kermode overvalues the capability of aesthetic form to give a sense of consonance to human existence. He makes this commitment at the expense of "clerkly scepticism" when, as in the passage quoted above, he falls into blank assertions about what is "reality" and "fact." Kermode's analysis of apocalyptic pattern should preclude his forgetting that "reality" is shot through with fictive and mythic structures and that "fact" acquires significance within narratives.

Kermode's critique of mythical thinking is further directed against two of the leading critical theorists of the decade, Northrop Frye, who, in the words of Jan Gorak, proffers a "myth of an undissociated past," and Marshall McLuhan, who provides a "myth of an undissociated future."[31] Both myths are apocalyptic. Invoking "clerkly scepticism," Kermode dismisses the Frye of *A Natural Perspective* as "the critic of regress towards myth and ritual, writing regressive criticism about plays he finds to be regressive."[32] Kermode invokes the norm of reality/realism against myth as it structures critical discourse. Kermode would have found particularly disturbing Frye's description of apocalypse in *Anatomy of Criticism* (1957).[33] Frye concludes his theory of symbols with a discussion of what he refers to as the anagogic or universal phase of symbolic meaning.[34] In this phase, representational elements are organized within literary form to express untrammeled human desire. In Frye's words:

> When we pass into anagogy, nature becomes not the container, but the thing contained, and the archetypal universal symbols, the city, the garden, the quest, the marriage, are no longer the desirable forms that man constructs inside nature, but are themselves the forms of nature. Nature is now inside the mind of an infinite man who builds his cities out of the Milky Way. This is not reality, but it is the conceivable or imaginative limit of desire, which is infinite, eternal, and hence apocalyptic. By an apocalypse I mean primarily the imaginative conception of the whole of nature as the content of an infinite and eternal living body which, if not human, is closer to being human than to being inanimate. [35]

Frye's tracking of desire to its "conceivable or imaginative limit" is in sharp distinction to Kermode's endorsement of aesthetic form as a reality principle governed by compromise between sense-making and sense-resisting aspects of representation. Although Frye reminds his readers of the "hypothetical" relation between imaginative modeling and the external world, Kermode ignores this insistence.[36] In relation to 1960s youth culture, Frye's utterance was liable to be construed as an endorsement of the most extravagant fantasies of liberated desire. That a basis for such delusions could be found in the work of a leading theorist, who drew his critical citations from the most revered texts of the English canon, made his position that much more unacceptable to some.

Kermode expresses his most serious misgivings over the tendency in "adversary culture" to subvert the very possibility of producing consonant fictions of contemporaneity. Locating such work in the line of "anti-traditionalist modernism" or Dada, he names as current practitioners American writers of the Beat Generation such as Jack Kerouac, Allen Ginsberg, and Burroughs.[37] In making this criticism, Kermode resists American incursions into British culture as well as the dissidence among blacks, students, antiwar demonstrators, feminists, and gays, which threatened liberal consensus in the United States during the years following Lyndon Johnson's election to the White House in 1964. Kermode's attack on Burroughs in particular may be contrasted to "a symptomatic occasion" held at the Albert Hall in London in June 1965, where "a reading of Beat and Underground poetry for 6,000 people" occurred "in an atmosphere . . . of 'pot, impromptu solo acid dances, of incredible barbaric colour, of face and body painting, of flowers and flowers and flowers, of common dreaminess in which all was permissive and benign.'"[38]

Kermode opposes academic or "traditionalist" modernism to emergent postmodernism. In his view, postmodern culture (which he describes as "*avant-garde*" or "anti-traditionalist") is marked by apocalyptic illusions, the demise of literary form, and the glorification of substance abuse. To this litany, he adds obsession with sexual perversity. He finds all the elements of this bizarre concatenation in "Burroughs," whose work he appears to know primarily by way of Ihab Hassan's essay "The Subtracting Machine": "His is the literature of withdrawal, and his interpreters speak of his hatred for life, his junk nihilism, his treatment of the body as a corpse full of cravings. The language of his books is the language of an ending world, its aim, as Ihab Hassan says, is 'self-abolition.' *The Naked Lunch* is a kind of satura, without formal design, unified only by the persistence in its satirical fantasies of outrage and obscenity."[39] Kermode may fail to cite the title of *Naked Lunch* accurately, but that does not stop him from objecting to Burroughs's subversion of narrative by means of the "cut up method" in writing.[40] He likewise objects to Burroughs's prophecy of "the cold apocalypse of the race." Recoiling from Burroughs and falling into the critical embrace of Wyndham Lewis, Kermode cites approvingly Lewis's analogous censure of Marcel Proust's "cheap pastry of stuffy and sadic romance," his "sweet and viscous sentimentalism." "Imagine Lewis on the cult of orgasm, or on Allen Ginsberg," exclaims Kermode.[41]

Although the homophobia of these references is, if anything, even more evident today than when they were first written, Kermode's antipathy is ostensibly directed against Burroughs's antihumanism. In his writing, Burroughs attacks the rhetorics of domestic and public responsibility which he sees as a prime constituent of identity. Like Wilde before him, Burroughs says: "To speak is to lie." He focuses attention on language (or the Word) as the chief instrument in the hands of the powers to which, in his fiction, he refers as the Novia Guard: "Picture the guard as an invisible tapeworm attached to word centers in the brain on color intensity beams. The Head Guards are captives of word-fallout only live in word and image of the host." In a favored metaphor uncannily prescient of the specter of HIV infection, Burroughs projects human subjection in terms of a universal viral incursion.[42] This invasion can be dispelled only by undoing the verbal codes that constitute consciousness and identity. "Rub out your stupid word," says Burroughs. "Rub out separation word 'They' 'We' 'I' 'You' 'The!' Rub out word 'The' forever. . . . Go back to Silence. Keep Silence. K. S. K.S. . . . From Silence re-write the message that is you."[43] Only by an imaginative escape from discourse, only by entry into silence can cultural prescriptions be derailed.[44] Burroughs's critique of the linguistic construction of subjectivity is congruent with the critique of the subject under way in structuralist and poststructuralist theory in the 1960s, including writing by Foucault and Derrida.[45] Writing in mid-decade, Kermode found Burroughs's position unacceptable because it invalidated the authority of the interpretative community in which Kermode played a modestly oppositional role. He complains that Burroughs's writing ignores the need to address "a public of a certain kind, a public which cannot visualize the conditions which might obtain after its own extinction."[46] Yet by challenging Burroughs, Kermode's anxiety betrays him into projecting the very end of the culture beyond which he and others "cannot visualize."

Apocalyptic Burroughs

Like the Derrida of *The Post Card*, Burroughs has long been preoccupied with the "reality engineering" made possible by twentieth-century technology. This concept has an important locus in the development of American commercial culture from the 1920s to the present. Burroughs's analysis of the construction of identity depends on what Michael R. Solomon and Basil G. Englis have referred to as "the conventional communications model" used in traditional marketing strategy. In this model communication is represented in terms of "a message transmitted from a source to a receiver via some medium."[47]

In *Queer*, the autobiographical fiction that Burroughs wrote in Mexico shortly after accidentally killing his wife, transmission is often represented as having the unified tone described by Derrida. The meaning of the message is determined by the prescribed identities of sender and receiver. Burroughs uses metaphors of consumption (of junk and sex, especially homosexual) to describe the subject under control. These metaphors refer to the engineering of consent in the market economy as well as in command economies such as the USSR.[48] According to Burroughs, control is "one-way telepathy" whereby the agents of those with a monopoly of knowledge and technology dominate the general population. "I have a theory," says Lee, that "the Mayan priests developed a form of one-way telepathy to con the peasants into doing all the work." In *Queer*, power is exercised within the context of the cold war. Reporting on a magazine article that he has read, Lee says: "The Russians are using Yage [a consciousness-altering drug] in experiments on slave labor. It seems they want to induce states of automatic obedience and ultimately, of course, thought control. The basic con. No build-up, no spiel, no routine, just move in on someone's psyche and give orders."[49] The most inward aspects of consciousness are subject to manipulation: "Automatic obedience, synthetic schizophrenia, mass-produced to order. That is the Russian dream, and America is not far behind. The bureaucrats of both countries want the same thing: Control. The superego, the controlling agency, gone cancerous and berserk. Incidentally, there is a connection between schizophrenia and telepathy. Schizos are very telepathically sensitive, but are strictly receivers. Dig the tie-in?" (91). Invoking U.S.-Soviet conflict, Burroughs extends the reference of "control" to the social conformity that characterized U.S. culture in the 1950s.

Burroughs writes in a genre of dualistic apocalypse that posits the possibility of a cosmic conflict between the powers of the Angel of Darkness and of the Sons of Light. He represents material existence as a set of signs that conceal/reveal malign powers that can take possession of the human mind. His favored image of such signs are hieroglyphs: "In 1939, I became interested in Egyptian hieroglyphics and went out to see someone in the department of Egyptology at the University of Chicago. And something was screaming in my ear: 'YOU DON'T BELONG HERE!' Yes, the hieroglyphics provided one key to the mechanism of possession. Like a virus, the possessing entity must find a port of entry." Burroughs insists on the possibility of demonic possession: "My concept of possession is closer to the medieval model than to modern psychological explanations, with their dogmatic insistence that such manifestations must come from within and never, never, never from without. (As if there were some clear-cut difference between inner and outer.) I mean a definite possessing entity" (xix–xx, xix). The point of this mythology is not Burroughs's belief in it. If the reader were meant to be *convinced* of Burroughs's belief in this myth, then it would become just one more "con," one more way of foreclosing questions of agency and representation. Rather, the model puts in question the reduction of signs to their referents and the reliance within humanist ideology on binary pairs such as inner/outer. There is no interiority reserved from manipulation. Hence the emphasis on signs as hieroglyphs that contain coded instructions of which receivers are unaware. Because hieroglyphs were traditionally taken to signify the secret knowledge of an Egyptian priestly elite, they are metaphors of control. But as material signs, hieroglyphs are liable to reversible, plural, and contradictory significations. The hieroglyph can program, but in the process of reception it can be recontextualized.

Burroughs sees Freudian analysis as yet another mode of technology. Accordingly, he resists the psychoanalytic explanations of homosexuality that passed for scientific knowledge in the United Stated during the 1950s. But he also lacks a concept of minority sexual identity. And he lacks an erotics, which might provide a locus at which ethical and social relations could be developed. In short, he has no readily available way in which to validate desire for sexual and emotional ties with other men.

Homosexual activity becomes literally hieroglyphic late in the novel. Traveling in Ecuador, Burroughs comes across "ancient Chimu pottery, where salt shakers and water pitchers were nameless obscenities: two men on all fours engaged in sodomy formed the handle for the top of a kitchen pot" (94–95). Burroughs has no knowledge of the cultural context in which these objects were produced.[50] Instead, in a moment of symbolization that Cronenberg later literalizes in the most extravagant special effect of his film, Lee asks: "What happens when there is no limit? What is the fate of The Land Where Anything Goes? Men changing into huge centipedes . . . centipedes besieging the houses . . . a man tied to a couch and a centipede ten feet long rearing up over him. Is this literal? Did some hideous metamorphosis occur? What is the meaning of the centipede symbol?" (95). In this passage, symbol acquires universal significance; in Frye's terms, it is anagogic. Symbols in this mode become representational elements within an apocalyptic narrative that describes "the conceivable or imaginative limit of desire." But Frye's "infinite and eternal living body" of desire is in Burroughs a waking nightmare.

Burroughs's commentary on hieroglyphics is yet more unsettling in that he adduces it in addressing the anxiety he continues to experience over having accidentally killed his wife in the early 1950s. Burroughs contends that his inability to construe this act within conventional ethical terms motivated his turn to writing: "I am forced to the appalling conclusion that I would never have become a writer but for Joan's death, and to a realization of the extent to which this event has motivated and formulated my writing. I live with the constant threat of possession, and a constant need to escape from possession, from Control. So the death of Joan brought me in contact with the invader, the Ugly Spirit, and maneuvered me into a lifelong struggle, in which I have had no choice except to write my way out" (xxii). Burroughs distinguishes a number of different relations between writer and text. First, writing can provide a means of mastering prior experience through verisimilar representation. He describes the autobiographical fiction of his first novel, *Junky* (1953), in these terms. Second, writing can be a process that produces an "I." Burroughs says: "While it was I who wrote *Junky*, I feel that I was being written in *Queer*." Such a process can be useful, even necessary, when the subject experiences itself as unintegral. In terms of apocalyptic thinking, writing can provide a means of staving off or recovering from "possession." "I was also taking pains to ensure further writing . . . : writing as inoculation. As soon as something is written, it loses the power of surprise, just as a virus loses its advantage when a weakened virus has created alerted antibodies" (xiv).

As I mention above, Burroughs writes in a genre of gnostic apocalypse that projects a shadowing world of malign significance. The obverse of the genre is the quest for illumination. In *Queer*, this apocalyptic quest is figured by the fictionalized account of a South American journey in search of yage. While living in Mexico City, Burroughs undertook such a search together with a young straight-identified man with whom he was infatuated. In the novel and in Morgan's biography, this man goes by the pseudonym Eugene Allerton. In the novel, Lee and Allerton are unable to locate the hallucinogen. The book shifts into yet a third apocalyptic mode when the pair arrive at the town of Puyo: "Dead end. And Puyo can serve as a model of the Place of Dead Roads" (xvii). Puyo fails to be either Heaven or Hell; hence, arrival there is anti-apocalyptic. So then is the narrative of *Queer* generally. *Queer* is a novel about Lee's attempt to achieve "contact" with Allerton (2). Yet Lee has chosen as the object of intimacy a straight-identified man. In this choice, Burroughs/"Lee" negates the conventional narrative trajectory that ends in marriage. But he also perversely confirms it by placing himself in the position of the "woman" who frustratedly yearns for a man. This path, like the search for yage, is headed nowhere. As if in acknowledgment of that fact, between the end of chapter 9 and the beginning of the epilogue, Allerton simply disappears from the book. There is no account of his departure. He is simply gone.

In the introduction to *Queer*, Burroughs describes the writing of the book as a "performance" played out to a chosen audience of one, in which a painfully dispersed "I" devises rhetorical routines to "mask, to cover a shocking disintegration." This pattern becomes the definitive one in Burroughs's fiction, especially *Naked Lunch*, his "vision of the post-Bomb society," which is comprised literally of a set of performances or "routines," though with the difference that they are no longer directed to a single addressee from among Burroughs's acquaintance (xv).[51] The motive of this textual performance is not to achieve self-integration but rather to achieve "contact or recognition, like a photon emerging from the haze of insubstantiality to leave an indelible record" (xvi). The photon leaves a trace.

Burroughs's abandonment of notions of integral or even heteronomous selves in favor of a metaphor of the self as trace invites the analysis not of an individual consciousness but of queer culture in the postwar years. Although the theory of possession can be read as providing a convenient way to transfer responsibility for Joan Burroughs's death onto some alien thing, his account has parallels with the experience of many subjects of same-sex desire. Anxieties about control make sense in relation to dominant structures of gender and sexuality that are phobic about contamination occurring across genders and that define same-sex desire as outside the realm of the human. The tendency to introject this view of same-sex desire is exacerbated in hip and Beat culture by the absence of public modes of expression that could have provided alternative narratives of personal experience. Yet the intersection of perverse sexual behavior with bohemian existence in the 1940s and 1950s contributed to the development of gay male politics. The historian John D'Emilio has argued that rubbing shoulders with the Beats, "gays could perceive themselves as nonconformists rather than deviates, as rebels against stultifying norms rather than immature, unstable personalities."[52] Nonetheless, there is a tendency, both in gay social history and other accounts, to play down the significance of the homosexual hipster between 1945 and the advent of Jack Smith and Andy Warhol and early 1960s.[53] Reading Burroughs provides an opportunity to begin to rewrite the relations of desire in "hip" culture.

Burroughs, *c'est moi*

When he wrote the screenplay for the film version of *Naked Lunch* (1991), which he also directed, David Cronenberg effaced the history to which I have just referred by framing the novel within a heterosexual reading of Burroughs's biography. This misrepresentation demonstrates anew how the narratives in which queer existence is represented subordinate being-queer to the truths of heterosexual culture.[54] Cronenberg's transferential investment in Burroughs is useful for examining the ideological function of key concepts within literary humanism such as aesthetic form, closure, and authorial control. Cronenberg's framing of Burroughs, moreover, indicates how metaphoric substitutions in fictional narrative can allay cultural anxieties at a particular time and place. The insistence on control in thematic and formal terms, the emphatic closure of the script, and the decision to coalesce biography and fictional text into a unified allegory of the creative process make the film, for all its "special effects" and "difficult" material, an exercise in what Kermode refers to as traditionalist modernism.

Cronenberg has long had a reputation as a director who exercises an unusual degree of control by writing his own scripts and by financing his films outside the usual channels. The latter has been made possible by public funding and favorable tax legislation in Canada and by the development of technical resources for filmmaking in Toronto, where *Naked Lunch*, including the scenes set in Tangiers, was shot. Cronenberg draws on Toronto's financial resources and production facilities to adapt genres more usually associated with low budget, exploitation films made in Hollywood.[55] His northern location has enabled him to resist pressures to mainstream his work, even after the release of conventionally financed, commercially successful films like *The Fly*. In this way, he has managed the cross between high and low culture that is usually associated with postmodern art.

In addition to affinities with Pop Art, Cronenberg from the start has shown a strong attraction to the work of the Beats, especially Burroughs, who came to prominence with the publication of *Naked Lunch*, first in Europe in 1959 and then in the United States three years later. From the beginning, Cronenberg's films have shown marked affinities with Burroughs's outlook. Like Burroughs, Cronenberg is obsessed with bodily metamorphoses produced by mysterious invasive organisms. His scripts, like Burroughs's novels, are dominated by conspiratorial institutions. Both are also preoccupied with a play of "masculine" and "feminine" difference within masculinity that threatens the stability of the ego, though in one case the masculinity is homosexual and in the other it is heterosexual. These obsessions have also proved to be attuned to the hysteria around AIDS in the mid-1980s. Cronenberg's most successful commercial release to date, *The Fly*, appeared at the height of "AIDS paranoia" in 1986.[56] In a characteristic gesture, Cronenberg has distanced the film from that moment: "The AIDS connection is very superficial. I see it [*The Fly*] as talking about mortality, about our vulnerability, and the tragedy of human loss." Despite the universal rhetoric of this response, the editor of a collection of commentaries by Cronenberg notes that the context in which the film was released inevitably links it with AIDS.[57]

Cronenberg's career has long been implicated in the increasingly overt struggle between gay artists and the remnant of the alienated East Coast male intellectual elite who once dominated liberal thinking in the United States.[58] The rightward shift of this group has resulted in the emergence of Jewish neoconservative journalists, such as Hilton Kramer, who have long been outspoken antagonists of postmodern art. Cronenberg has eschewed this position, as he also has the views of Jewish "hawks" on national security issues and the defense of high culture by academic polemicists such as Allan Bloom. *Naked Lunch* was released during the course of a continuing crisis generated by outraged conservative and Christian responses to the funding of a Robert Mapplethorpe exhibition by the National Endowment for the Arts.[59] Cronenberg includes in the film a prolonged shot of a sculpture in a pawnshop window. The figure is of a nude male hanging suspended by his arms with a Mugwump on his back. Foreshadowing a scene of sexual assault that occurs near the end of the film, the figure refers secondarily to an image that has been exploited by political and religious fundamentalists in the recent moral panic, namely, Andres Serrano's *Piss Christ* (1987), a photograph of a wood-and-plastic crucifix immersed in urine. In public appearances ac-

13. Andres Serrano, *Piss Christ*, 1987. Cibachrome photograph of a wood-and-plastic crucifix immersed in urine. Courtesy of the artist and Paula Cooper Gallery, New York City.

companying the release of *Naked Lunch*, Cronenberg has strongly opposed current antipornography moves, whether emanating from the Supreme Court of Canada, from right-wing bigots like Patrick Buchanan and Jesse Helms in the United States, or from feminists like Andrea Dworkin and Catherine MacKinnon.[60] In these interventions, Cronenberg always speaks within the terms of a general humanism. Despite this fact, his commitments have significant connections with cultural politics as it involves sexual and ethnic minorities.

Cronenberg's relationship to the politics of sexual representation in American culture has a defining significance for his position as a Toronto artist who is also Jewish. True to the liberalism of American and Canadian Jewish intellectuals of the 1960s, Cronenberg has consistently linked his choice of subject matter with the assertion of freedom of speech. His decision to film *Naked Lunch* was motivated as much by the special significance of this novel in the development of American juris- prudence as it was by cathexis with Burroughs. The obscenity trials that followed publication of *Naked Lunch* in the United States in 1962 exon- erated the book and clarified the Brennan Doctrine, new at the time, which held that a book could be declared legally obscene only if it was "utterly without redeeming social importance. The portrayal of sex in art, literature, and scientific works is not in itself sufficient reason to deny material the constitutional protection of freedom of speech and press."[61] The decision taken by the Massachusetts Supreme Court on 7 July 1966 made Burroughs's novel the benchmark for what is and is not legally ob- scene in the United States. In view of continuing efforts today, by political and moral conservatives and by some feminists, to widen the definition of obscenity, renewed attention to the novel is specifically political.[62]

Since visual representations are especially vulnerable to political at- tack, Cronenberg put himself at risk by making the film, but he limited that risk in a number of ways. For instance, whenever he treats homo- sexual relations directly, he does so with comic disgust. In the one scene of anal penetration, the active partner metamorphoses into a huge centi- pede-like creature that fuses with its passive victim. Thus Cronenberg overstamps sexual violation with his own signature as a master of special effects. Because Bill Lee, the male protagonist, reacts to the scene with horrified revulsion, and because the technological display distances the viewer from the action, the young, heterosexual male Cronenberg "fan" can experience the thrill of sexual danger from the secure vantage of Bill Lee's reaction and the control of special effects.[63]

The representation of male homosexual difference in the film substi- tutes for the representation of ethnic difference, especially Jewish ethnic difference. This particular substitution is grounded in the history of rep- resenting minorities. Writers like George Mosse and Sander Gilman argue that anti-Semitic prejudice has long included accusations of effeminacy and sexual perversity. The stigmatized body of the members of this ethnic group has been used as a surface on which sexual meanings can be writ- ten over "racial" ones.[64] The prosecution and imprisonment of Oscar Wilde, for instance, provided opportunities for Jewish artists and intellec- tuals of the fin de siècle to identify *with* an innovative artist who had been subjected to attack by members of the philistine majority. At the same time, men like Karl Kraus and Gustav Mahler were able to identify *against* sexual aspects of "Wilde" that resembled those routinely pro- jected on despised subgroups among Jews. In the aftermath of the Wilde trials, this double movement permitted assimilated "German" Jews to

identify with advanced artistic and intellectual positions while simultaneously resisting Aryan chauvinism and distancing themselves from
association with recent Jewish migrants from Eastern Europe.[65] Cronenberg's fixation on Burroughs works similarly. He identifies with Burroughs
as an artistic iconoclast in revolt against the commercial and political
pieties of American culture at the same time that he dissociates himself
from the "womanly" Burroughs who is a sexual pervert. In the process,
Cronenberg asserts his superiority to bigotry while defending himself and
other Jews against derogatory stereotypes.

By assimilating himself to an idealized version of the best aspects of
American and anglophone Canadian liberalism, Cronenberg disavows affiliation with minority subject-positions.[66] For example, in *Cronenberg on
Cronenberg*, he attacks the doctrine of "political correctness." "Bullshit"
is his word for any attempt, from feminist, gay or other positions, to censor
a script during the production process.[67] Although I agree with Cronenberg's stance on censorship, I suspect that the aggressiveness of his reaction registers a recoil from minority identification that is necessary in
order to enable him to identify with anglophone culture's best self. Cronenberg, who speaks of his "fusion" with Burroughs, has repeatedly identified his repertory of imagery with the aesthetic articulation of the
symbolic in Burroughs's writing.[68] At times, Cronenberg recognizes that
his Burroughs is a translated one: "I was forced . . . to fuse my own sensibility with Burroughs and create a third thing that neither he nor I would
have done on his own. It's like the Rubaiyat of Omar Khayyam." But there
are moments in writing the script when the fusion is complete: "When I
transcribed word for word a sentence of description of the giant centipede,
and then continued on with the next sentence to describe the scene in
what I felt was a sentence Burroughs himself could have written, that was
a fusion. I . . . almost felt for a moment, 'Well, if Burroughs dies, I'll write
his next book.'"[69] The final comment recalls a "cynical joke" that Freud
recounts in the course of discussing what he refers to as "the law of ambivalence of feeling" that individuals experience in relation to their inti-
mates. In Freud's telling, a husband remarks to his wife: "If one of us two
dies, I shall move to Paris."[70] Cronenberg's joke indicates how intensely
ambivalent his connection with Burroughs is.

Fusion, which is an instance of accentuated transference and counter-
transference, paradoxically gives Cronenberg a way to master his imaginary investment in Burroughs,[71] not only because what is unique in
Burroughs is rewritten under the signature, "Cronenberg," but also
through the shaping of the script and by means of the technology of film.
Cronenberg combines details from the biography of Burroughs, particularly the shooting of his wife, which occurs twice, at the beginning and at

14. Judy Davis plays a double role in David Cronenberg's *Naked Lunch* as wife to Bill Lee/Burroughs and as Jane Bowles, Burroughs's friend in Tangiers. Photo by Attila Dory and Brian Hamill. Courtesy Alliance Releasing, Toronto; Twentieth Century-Fox, Los Angeles.

the end of the film, with surreal elements adapted from the fiction such as the Mugwumps. The combination, which fuses fact, fiction, and motive in "Burroughs," produces a reversible, metonymic chain of cause and effect between "art" and "life," but the chain is very much that of Cronenberg's script.

Although Burroughs does see his life after the killing of his wife as a series of efforts to gain control over the significances of that extreme act, Cronenberg represents Burroughs's relationship to the shooting as one of repetition. In other words, "shooting" Joan in life and in obsessive rerun is an example of the sort of acting out to which the psychoanalyst draws attention in the course of an analysis.[72] At the end of the film, Burroughs receives permission to continue to practice his "art" only after he kills his wife (once more). "Shooting" is a term used more in relation to filming than to writing, with the result that the shooting of Joan operates as a switch point for representing processes having to do primarily with Cronenberg. Burroughs shot once; Cronenberg "shoots" twice. Moreover, it is Cronenberg who casts Judy Davis to play the parts both of Joan Lee and Joan Frost (the latter character a translation of Burroughs's Jewish friend in Tangiers, Jane Bowles). This conflation heterosexualizes and anglicizes the narrative while, in the predictable manner of a psychological thriller, it drains both women of specificity, converting them into Woman or Mother.[73]

Soon after Bill Lee becomes addicted to the black powder, his Clark-Nova typewriter, metamorphosed into an insect with a talking asshole, tells him to type "homosexuality" because homosexuality is a good cover for an "agent." Lee starts typing. The transaction suggests that perversity is discursively produced, an act of writing that is a being-written. Yet agency of the sort that most interested the Beats and that they drew on in *à rebours* tradition is also involved: the typist makes a deliberate choice to take on him or herself the burden of perversity. This commitment attracts Cronenberg to Burroughs, but the ability for homosexuality to exceed its discursive boundaries requires the setting of a contractual limit. Hence Cronenberg, in a line virtually the same as one of Lee/Burroughs's in the film, says: "I'm not afraid of the homosexuality, but it's not innate in me."[74] Yet at times Cronenberg uses the camera subjectively, seeing through Lee's eyes, with the result that he identifies the (implicitly straight male) viewer's emotional reactions with Lee's—especially in the scene of sexual introjection. The identification of Lee with young straight male viewers is further underwritten by Cronenberg's choice in casting Peter Weller, an actor best known for his roles as the cyborg protagonist of *RoboCop* and *RoboCop 2*. The shared viewpoint works to confirm the actor, the character, the viewer, and the writer-director in a sense of difference that is still normal enough to recoil from male-male sex. The murder of Kiki conflates sodomy, sexual assault, and murder—a set of conventional associations in the heterosexual imaginary that resonates with the intensified anxieties about "unsafe sex" that have attended AIDS. By intensifying this affect in a scene in which the literal referents are not to AIDS, Cronenberg types the effect even more indelibly onto the white surface of the viewer's consciousness.

It is also pertinent that a Moroccan is the object of this violence, a specificity negated by Cronenberg's insistence when interviewed that the entire action of the film occurs in New York. Similarly, the "Arabian" and "African" character of Fadela, the object of Joan Frost's cathexis, is erased when she turns out to be, *in effect*, a white man. Jewish cathexis in Arabs is a point that is both expressed and erased in *Naked Lunch*. Converted into Davis/Frost, the Bowles character ceases to be Jewish.[75] Kiki, the young Moroccan, is played by Joseph Scorsiani. The conflation of southern European with Moroccan ethnicity reinscribes the traditional racist dichotomy between Northern Europeans and "Orientals," a divide that apparently begins at Locarno. When Oriental or Jewish referents surface in the film, they are unflattering. In the bug powder shop, the dispenser, who apparently eats the stuff, is an East Asian. The owner is A. J.

15. Monique Mercure as Fadela in David Cronenberg's *Naked Lunch*. Photo by Attila Dory and Brian Hamill. Courtesy Alliance Releasing, Toronto; Twentieth Century-Fox, Los Angeles.

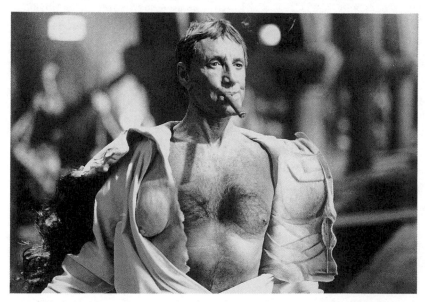

16. But what is Roy Scheider doing in a female body suit? Roy Scheider as Fadela/Dr. Benway in David Cronenberg's *Naked Lunch*. Photo by Attila Dory and Brian Hamill. Courtesy Alliance Releasing, Toronto; Twentieth Century-Fox, Los Angeles.

Cohen. In a scene early in the film that is set in the shop, Lee sits as far as possible from the exterminators, who are eating lunch. The men look like inmates of a concentration camp.

Typewriting and hallucinating (sometimes the two processes fuse) are scenes that conform to the orthodox model of psychoanalytic practice in which the (male) analyst's subjectivity is not engaged during the analytic process. Transferred to the film, the paradigm absolves Cronenberg (and the viewer) from implication in Burroughs's deviance despite the acknowledged exploitation of transference.[76] A have-your-cake-and-eat-it-too approach is also evident in the Freudian metanarratives in which Cronenberg somewhat sententiously couches his project. Accepting "the Freudian dictum that civilization is repression," he argues for the liberating effect of artistic desublimation in work like his own. At the same time, the location of perversity in specifically *aesthetic* discourse absolves Cronenberg of "social responsibility" while likewise abstracting homosexuality into a generalized linguistic transgression.[77] Even the choice of homosexuality as the privileged sign of transgression is Freudian. In the Dora case, for instance, Freud remarks: "I have never yet gone through a single psychoanalysis of a man or a woman without having to take into account a very considerable current of homosexuality."[78] Comments like this one, which he repeats in the postscript at the end of the case, can be read as signaling an obsessive interest in (male) homosexuality, an interest involved in Freud's friendship with Wilhelm Fliess.[79] But these comments can be read just as plausibly in another way. When homosexuality is used as a generic index of psychological unease, it ceases to have significance in relation to a set of social forms. Precisely this effacement of the social reference of homosexuality makes it possible to use the term to signify many other referents.

In an interview in the gay press, Cronenberg describes the "talking asshole" not as the loquacious site of sodomy but as "the one underneath, from the dark place, who says stuff that nobody wants to hear but will not be denied and they can shove candles up and all that stuff, but still it's going to be heard."[80] Cronenberg describes *Naked Lunch* as a "coming out" movie, but, as usually occurs when adapted by heterosexuals, the phrase is recontextualized: Cronenberg comes out—*as a writer*, which is hardly the same thing. One cannot be imprisoned, lose one's job, one's medical insurance, one's spousal benefits, or one's visitation rights for coming out as a writer. Furthermore, Cronenberg's "take" on Burroughs/Lee's perversity naturalizes Burroughs's homosexuality by psychologizing it. The social significance of sexual perversity is left, at best, implicit. Thus, a timely opportunity is lost to analyze queer culture among the

Beats in relation to the very different queer culture that has developed since lesbians and gay men constituted visible subcultures. The displacement of social motives and effects to psychological ones is routine in Hollywood production; and in this respect, despite *auteur*-ial aggrandizement, *Naked Lunch* is as much subject to de facto control as are other commercial films.

The effacement of sexual and gender difference in *Naked Lunch* is a reminder of how de-historicizing Cronenberg's approach is. In an interview published in a Toronto gay newspaper, Cronenberg asks rhetorically about the shooting of Burroughs's wife: "Is he killing the heterosexual part of himself to realize himself? Is he killing the female part of himself, or is he killing the creative part?"[81] The answer to these questions is no: he is killing Joan Vollmer, who shortly before this incident had left Mexico City to file for a divorce in Cuernavaca.[82] In Cronenberg's questions, this woman, her history and situation, are translated into the metaphor of an internalized femininity. Cronenberg's interest is in "the woman within" the man. Female difference is significant insofar as it refers to an Other within. Similarly, in one of the film's effects, Joan Frost's Moroccan "dominatrix," Fadela, rips off a plastic body suit to disclose underneath Dr. Benway, the chief executive officer of Interzone Inc.[83] So much for lesbian difference, represented here as a delusive projection of desire toward the simulacrum of a female body that conceals a "real man" underneath. Similarly, in the scene of anal rape, Cloquet's metamorphosis functions as a sign of Cronenberg since the production of such effects is typical of his work. This moment of demonstrated technical mastery is also the moment, as Danny O'Quinn has argued, when a metanarrative of "control" subsumes all the differences and perversities (of gender, sex, race, art-making, crime, and drugs) thus far registered.[84] After the visit to Cloquet, Lee is in position to become Benway's chief "agent"/pusher. At the end of the film, he leaves in a van for Annexia (which Cronenberg identifies with "Canada" in one interview)[85] together with Frost, then shoots her when the border guards demand to see an example of his writing.

One could multiply the number of times in the film that referents disappear into artistic phantasmagoria. Cronenberg, for instance, argues that Tangiers, the colonial setting of much of the film's action and all its homosexual sex, is a wholly imaginary place: "One understands by the end of the film that Lee never really leaves New York City."[86] This effacement of the material conditions in which Burroughs lived, wrote, and shot his wife is necessary to produce the myth of the artist in which Cronenberg/ "Burroughs" is lodged and to constitute that myth as reality. Nonetheless, both in *Queer* and in the appended introduction (1985), Burroughs gives the name of "Mexico" to "The Land Where Anything Goes." It is to Mexico that he fled with his wife and two children in order to avoid prosecution for possession of heroin and marijuana in the United States. And it was in Mexico, where, according to his report, women were radically devalued and in Mexico City, at the time "the murder capital of the world," that he says "the accidental shooting of my wife, Joan," occurred (v, 20, vii, xvi). The framing myth of addiction and control that gives the film its political allegory, though it has referents in Burroughs's experience and writing, is a portentous simulacrum that blocks the sorts of analysis of race, class, and gender relations that Burroughs's biography and fiction might prompt. Gender relations are not always violent. Sex (including homosex) is not always addictive, nor are drugs. What, then, are the conditions of violence and abuse?

Cronenberg's "fusion" with Burroughs/Lee is apocalyptic in the catastrophic sense that Derrida finds in male homosocial tradition, where a precursor is made to say what a younger man wants him to say. The script is also apocalyptic in the more familiar sense of retelling the modernist artistic myth of the Dionysian male artist who needs to undergo a kind of death in order to be born into artistic creativity.[87] But the film is not apocalyptic in the sense of opening new possibilities of meaning by unsettling the norms of representation.

Oliver Stone's *JFK*, released shortly before *Naked Lunch*, shares with it a number of attitudes: a sense of apocalyptic menace, a predilection for conspiracy theories, the projection of an enemy within—named by President Eisenhower in a clip at the beginning as "the military-industrial complex." Like Cronenberg, Stone also takes an unflattering view of homosexual snobs and lowlifes, whom he contrasts to the home-loving though increasingly obsessive New Orleans district attorney Jim Garrison, played by Kevin Costner. Gay reviewers have attacked Stone and Garrison for "making gays the scapegoats" of the Kennedy assassination, a plausible complaint since the one person ever to stand trial for his alleged share in a conspiracy to kill the president is Clay Shaw, who is portrayed in the film as a prominent New Orleans businessman and homosexual.[88] Garrison's wife (Sissy Spacek) accuses him of hounding Shaw because of his homosexuality. Yet homosexuality in Stone's film functions as an unstable signifier. The break in the case is provided by Willie O'Keefe, a gay hustler and prison convict. True, he turns out to be a right-wing wacko; but he is also a Teiresias-figure, the person, both woman and man, who can unravel the secret of corruption stalking the land. In one scene, Lee Harvey Oswald, the assassin-who-is-not-one, masquerades as the queer he-may-or-may-not-be. A defrocked priest, eventually murdered, is the only one among the conspirators who shows signs of remorse.

He and Garrison's wife become passion bearers, who carry the emotional stigmata of Garrison/Costner's effort to find out the truth about the shooting. (The autopsy scene, the most shocking in the film, is a gruesome parody of the laying to rest of the sacrificed leader.) All these types have a place in the history of homosexual representation, but in *JFK* they exceed these limits. No single gendered or sexual position sets the standard of normative subjectivity in this film, nor can any particular position be quarantined from infection. Similarly, the cutting of *JFK*, the repetition and mixing of documentary with fictional footage, in 8mm, 16mm, and 35mm, color and black and white, splices together the pieces of Stone's conspiracy theory at the price of showing the viewer that crucial evidence is lost and that no single narrative of the assassination can be believed with confidence. In this way, the film negates the desire for apocalyptic closure that appears to motivate it.

In contrast, Cronenberg's screenplay mixes biography, autobiography, conventional story, and hallucinatory narrative in a seamless whole that turns out to be the familiar narrative of the artist who sacrifices life (read wife or inamorata) to art and whose art becomes his life. In this sense, Cronenberg takes Burroughs's defamiliarizing representation of routines of addiction and control and refamiliarizes them. The narrative fuses Burroughs and Cronenberg with the romantic stereotype of the artist as antihero that the Beats drew from the nineteenth-century tradition of Poe and Baudelaire, Rimbaud and Verlaine. In this aesthetic discourse, art becomes the regulative norm that validates the extremity of Burroughs's experience while justifying Cronenberg's choice of subject matter. Now that postmodernism is the mode, Burroughs, the academy's onetime anarchist nemesis, has become the patron saint of Soho and the East Village. Asserting that *Naked Lunch* is "the first truly postmodern literary text," Gary Indiana makes Burroughs not only the source of the New Narrative but a leading progenitor of virtually all postmodern cultural practice with the exception of architecture. Converted into an icon, what remains unaddressed is the significance of Burroughs's queerness to the history of sexual minorities.[89] In his introductory remarks to *Everything Is Permitted*, Burroughs emphasizes Cronenberg's decision to approach "homosexuality as a somewhat unwelcome accident of circumstance and plot." Not wearily but dryly, Burroughs observes: "Probably he simply did not, as an artist, find that aspect of 'Lee' to be significant to the story he wanted to tell in the film."[90] Yes, precisely.

6

...

ABSENT BODIES / ABSENT SUBJECTS: THE POLITICAL UNCONSCIOUS OF POSTMODERNISM

Fredric Jameson's career spans the period in the 1960s when he and other leading American intellectuals shifted from a modernist to a postmodernist stance and from a preoccupation with structuralism to an interest in poststructuralist theory. His subsequent writing carries with it residues of the struggles over the construction of masculine gender and sexualities explored in Chapter 5.[1] Jameson's critique of Andy Warhol in the 1984 essay that became the opening chapter of *Postmodernism, or The Cultural Logic of Late Capitalism* (1991) recalls onslaughts on Warhol by art critics of the 1960s like Hilton Kramer, who since then has become a leading neoconservative commentator but who, two decades ago, was a liberal. Kramer complained about Warhol's ties with "the world of high-fashion publicity, with its corps of professional faddists, its canny retailers, its worship of fame, money, and scandal, and its indispensable alliances with homosexual bohemia."[2] Jameson adds to this sort of disdain for Warhol a rhetorical excess that conveys contemporary anxieties about AIDS, contagion, and mortality which inflect a text in which they are nowhere explicitly specified.

Since Jameson's particular evocation of sublime affect is the leading contribution that he has made to postmodern sensibility, the unacknowledged implication of male-male desire in what he refers to as the hysterical sublime sexualizes that sensibility in powerful and disturbing ways. Like Lyotard, Jameson emphasizes how the capacity to know exceeds the capacity to represent knowledge in late capitalist culture. According to Lyotard, this asymmetry results in the dominance of sublime affect within postmodern representation.[3] Lyotard finds a basis for hope in this mode of the sublime since "emphasis can be placed on the power of the faculty to conceive" rather than on the limits of presentation.[4] Jameson's *postmodern* position, however, is paradoxically cast in the mode of the *modernist* sublime, which, in Lyotard's view, responds to the new situation with nostalgia for lost totalities.[5] For Jameson, who writes as a Marxist, nostalgia is directed toward the possibility of mapping a route to general social transformation. Since, as a postmodern writer, however, he is skeptical in the extreme about such a possibility, sublime affect in his work produces a postmodern apocalyptic that negates the possibility of Marxian apocalypse.[6]

In the history of the East Coast intellectual elite outlined in *No Respect*, Andrew Ross emphasizes the significance of the "cultural economy" of camp in the development of postmodernism during the 1960s. Ross argues that camp "challenged, and, in some cases, helped to overturn legitimate definitions of taste and sexuality."[7] The opening chapter of Jameson's *Postmodernism, or The Cultural Logic of Late Capitalism*, which was published in slightly different form in the *New Left Review* in 1984, intervenes on both sides in this contest. On the one hand, in his aggressiveness toward Andy Warhol, Jameson attempts to protect advanced cultural practice from homosexual contamination; on the other hand, in giving "a camp or 'hysterical' sublime" a central position among his analytic terms, Jameson attempts to adapt the subversive energies of camp to his own purposes.[8] This double effort is a classically sublimating one insofar as Jameson attempts to *conserve* the innovative and critical aspects of pop culture, which is strongly associated with Warhol's signature, while *negating* the gay significations of Warhol.[9]

The experience of the postmodern sublime provides a substitute for another apocalypse within the Marxian tradition in which Jameson situates himself. As the title of the book indicates, Jameson draws his highly schematic view of the structure of capitalism from Ernest Mandel's *Late Capitalism*. Yet Jameson also implicitly critiques the vision of universal transformation with which Mandel's book ends. In other words, despite Jameson's insistence that radical politics must be based on class consciousness (331; see also 318–331), his view is consonant with the current consensus among avant-garde intellectuals in the United States that Marx's view of "(the proletarian) class as subject of history" fails to provide an adequate basis for theorizing and practicing radical politics.[10] Furthermore, the psychological "thickness" of Jameson's postmodern subject subverts any attempt that might be made to represent the proletarian subject as a transparent signifier of historical truth. In Jameson's essay, gendered representations refer to a sensation of bodily absence that is both cause and effect of a perceived loss of agency by the postmodern subject. This absence may be construed as the loss of *self-presence*, by which I mean a consciousness of self generated by ability to act that includes awareness of bodily contour and movement. Although absence is obviously related to a loss of confidence that history has a class subject, it is just as strongly related to a crisis within the construction of masculinity.

In *Postmodernism*, Jameson represents absence by means of a number of shoe-images, especially pictorial images by van Gogh and Andy Warhol. He analyzes the sensation in theoretical terms in section 4 of the essay, titled "The Hysterical Sublime" in the *NLR* version (32).[11] According to Jameson, the "camp or 'hysterical' sublime" is a "euphoria" experienced within postmodern spaces that are "felt as incompatible with the representation of the body. The world . . . momentarily loses its depth and threatens to become a glossy skin, a stereoscopic illusion, a rush of filmic images without density. But is this now a terrifying or an exhilarating experience?" (32, 34). Later, in an unfolding metanarrative, the experience is situated within Jameson's feeling of being lost in the "hyper-crowd" (40) of registrants at the annual meeting of the Modern Language Association held at the Bonaventure Hotel in Los Angeles in 1982. He observes: "So I come finally to my principal point here, that this latest mutation in space—postmodern hyperspace—has finally succeeded in transcending the capacities of the individual human body to locate itself" (44). In a bodily code, this "principal point" is the telos toward which the essay moves. In what follows, which in another code *should be* the goal of the essay, namely, the restoration of self-presence in a newly reformulated politics, Jameson finds himself stymied. He is unable to affirm the capacities of representation, agency, or subject-formation that he believes to be necessary for the recovery of a radical politics.

The work of reconstituting the subject, which I take to be the most significant work of Jameson's text, is performed by a narrative of the loss and recovery of agency. The turns of this narrative are so evident that Jameson can scarcely be unaware of them—however much he may fail to recognize the work of gender being performed. The failure of such recognition helps account for the double bind with which the essay ends. Jameson shows no ability to analyze the transcoding between theoretical concerns and anxieties about gender and sexuality that occurs in the text. And yet, in ending, he seconds Louis Althusser's assertion that the postmodern subject must be gendered. Nonetheless, Jameson leaves unaddressed the attendant need to give due consideration to "the dimension of the Lacanian Symbolic itself" (54).

Jameson's metanarrative has a context in the struggles over the meaning of masculine existence that have engaged various groups, including feminists and gay men, for the past quarter century. One of the key figures in that context is Andy Warhol, whom Jameson describes as "the central figure in contemporary visual art" (8). The appropriation of camp taste by pop art in the early 1960s was part of a conflict that took place between newly assertive gay men in avant-garde culture and other members of the American, East Coast male elite; whether Jewish, liberal, or, as in Jameson's case, on the political left.[12] Critical attacks marked by homophobia were part of the campaign.[13] Although Jameson sometimes takes a "Gee whiz" stance in celebrating "utopian" aspects within "even the most degraded type of mass culture," he shows no such indulgence to Warhol.[14] This refusal resembles the blankness of Jameson's response to feminist postmodernism.[15] In the essay as it appears in revised form in the book, Jameson has added a quotation from a single such writer, namely Linda Hutcheon. The citation is negative, and Jameson misspells her name (22). This gaffe, together with his general insensitivity to the contributions of feminists to postmodernist theory and practice, indicates what Cornel West has described as the failure of Jameson's writing to "address modes of political praxis in its own academic setting."[16] Regarding Warhol, Jameson writes as though he were oblivious of the criticisms that Rudolf Arnheim, Kramer, and other critics leveled against gay pop artists such as Warhol, Jasper Johns, and Robert Rauschenberg.

Craig Owens has connected issues of representation in critical theory, including Jameson's, with the idea of theory-as-phallus, that is, the idea of theory as a gendered site that requires the exclusion of feminist theory/practice from the discourse of straight-identified male theory.[17] Attention to feminine/feminist difference would lead inevitably to the gender-analysis of male theory itself, which is a powerful reason for theorists like Jameson to ignore feminist work.[18] Hence, too, their customary tendency to marginalize and denigrate gay cultural practices. Nevertheless, a less defensive consideration of Warhol could show how, within his own terms, he addresses the questions of representation, agency, and the subject which have been so troubling for theory. Entering high culture from an acknowledged position of cultural deficit—as an awkward, effeminate young man, as a boy from a coal mining town, and as a Roman Catholic of Slovak lineage—Warhol carried on his own subversions of gender and other institutional formations. Paradoxically, he turned his position as an *un*subject into one that expresses agency and sociality while renovating art and simultaneously engaging in a thorough critique of the fashioning of subjects and communities through cultural representation.

No Deposit . . .

Jameson ends the opening chapter by presaging the return of the subject. This return, however, appears to be as much distant as yearned for. Jameson writes:

> The new political art (if it is possible at all) will have to hold to the truth of postmodernism, that is to say, to its fundamental object—the world space of multinational capital—at the same time at which it achieves a breakthrough to some as yet unimaginable new mode of representing this last, in which we may again begin to grasp our positioning as individual and collective subjects and regain a capacity to act and struggle which is at present neutralized by our spatial as well as our social confusion. The political form of postmodernism, if there ever is any, will have as its vocation the invention and projection of a global cognitive mapping, on a social as well as a spatial scale. (54)

The utopian promise of a regained agency is troubled by its very desperation. Not once but twice Jameson puts in doubt the possibilities of representation and presence that he invokes. As well he confesses to a "confusion," both "spatial" and "social," regarding issues of representation.

Jameson insists that political action requires at least the conceivability of making representations of the real world. In the course of the essay, however, he argues that in the most recent moment of capitalism, that of multinational capital with its attendant nuclear and electronic technologies, "the truth" becomes, in effect, unrepresentable. Accordingly, the function of ideology, in the Althusserian sense of "articulating" scientific knowledge in relation to "the experience of daily life," is at present not possible at all (53). Still, Jameson remains wedded to an iconic model of representation even when he phrases the issue as the need "to think the impossible totality of the contemporary world system" (38).[19]

The paradox he expresses could be used to articulate approaches to individual and collective agency that do not depend on positing a need for totalizing representations. In postmodern culture, moreover, global theories like that of Mandel on the three stages of capitalism since 1800, which Jameson adopts, can become counterproductive. Instead of enabling the transformation of reality, they can exacerbate an already pervasive paranoia by raising it to the level of abstract thought. Jameson observes: "Insofar as the theorist wins . . . by constructing an increasingly closed and terrifying machine, to that very degree he loses, since the critical capacity of his work is thereby paralyzed, and the impulses of negation and revolt, not to speak of those of social transformation, are increasingly perceived as vain and trivial in the face of the model itself" (5–6). Jameson himself exaggerates this tendency by translating Mandel's argument from its historic specificities into a reductive typology.

Both the image of the machine and that of the "global cognitive mapping" (54) of a postmodern political practice are at odds with another view of contemporary culture that Jameson includes in an earlier essay. In "Reification and Utopia in Mass Culture" (1979), he observes: "The only authentic cultural production today has seemed to be that which can draw on the collective experience of marginal pockets of the social life of the world system: black literature and blues, British working-class rock, women's literature, gay literature, the *roman québécois*, the literature of the Third World."[20] This observation, if pursued, could offer a way out of desperation, paranoia, and impasse by means of a politics practiced at micropolitical levels and between shifting coalitions of individuals and groups. Although this approach too depends on theory, it does not depend on claustrophobic theoretical machines.[21] Moreover, the suggestion is very much in accord with those offered by a number of other North American analysts of postmodernism.[22] But Jameson remains skeptical of a politics of difference which he fears might reflect mere "stylistic and discursive heterogeneity without a norm" (17).

If the advantages of a decentered politics are obvious and if examples of agency are already evident, why not take advantage of these openings? Here the centrality of the hysterical sublime to Jameson's experience of postmodernism is highly relevant. The simultaneous celebration and denigration of the hysterical sublime figures both attraction to and repulsion from the dissolution of the bounds of the male subject. This condition needs to be refused because it undoes precisely those conventions of a stable masculinity that Jameson depends on in order to be able to represent himself as a subject and agent. But the attractiveness of the hysterical sublime prevents Jameson (and, in his view, the postmodern subject) from relinquishing the sensation. Hence a double bind.

Color It Sepia

Jameson introduces the male body in the opening chapter of *Postmodernism*. It appears as an informing trope in displaced fashion as a fetish object: as the shoes of a peasant woman as presented by Martin Heidegger in a well-known commentary on Vincent van Gogh's painting *Old Shoes with Laces* (1886). In his essay, "The Origin of the Work of Art," Heideg-

17. Vincent van Gogh, *Old Shoes with Laces*, 1886. Rijksmuseum Vincent van Gogh, Amsterdam. Courtesy Art Resource, New York.

ger interprets the painting as expressing a totality of which the shoes are the incarnating sign:

> There is nothing surrounding this pair of peasant shoes in or to which they might belong, only an undefined space. There are not even clods from the soil of the field or the path through it sticking to them, which might at least hint at their employment. A pair of peasant shoes and nothing more. And yet.
>
> From the dark opening of the worn insides of the shoes the toilsome tread of the worker stands forth. In the stiffly solid heaviness of the shoes there is the accumulated tenacity of her slow trudge through the far-spreading and ever-uniform furrows of the field, swept by a raw wind. On the leather there lies the dampness and saturation of the soil. Under the soles there slides the loneliness of the field-path as the evening declines. In the shoes there vibrates the silent call of the earth, its quiet gift of the ripening corn and its enigmatic self-refusal in the fallow desolation of the wintry field. This equipment is pervaded by uncomplaining anxiety about the certainty of bread, the wordless joy of having once more withstood want, the trembling before the advent of birth and shivering at the surrounding menace of death. This equipment belongs

to the *earth* and it is protected in the *world* of the peasant woman. From out of this protected belonging the equipment itself rises to its resting-in-self.[23]

In Heidegger's analysis the depiction of an object refers to a totality that becomes comprehensible through a double act of interpretation, first by the artist, then by the critic. In this way, representation of an object becomes the rhetorical figure of an accessible truth. Heidegger continues:

> What happens here? What is at work in the work? Van Gogh's painting is the disclosure of what the equipment, the pair of peasant shoes, *is* in truth. This entity emerges into the unconcealment of its being. The Greeks called the unconcealment of entities ἀλήθεια. We say "truth" and think little enough in using this word. If there occurs in the work a disclosure of that which *is* in that, what, and how it is, then there is here an occurring, a happening of truth at work.
>
> In the work of art the truth of what *is* has set itself to work. "To set" means here: to bring to a stand. Something that *is*, a pair of peasant shoes, comes to stand in the work in the light of its being.[24]

Jameson supplements this reading with his own, to which I will return in a moment. He remarks that Heidegger's interpretation has "a satisfying plausibility" (8), an equivocal phrase that masks both skepticism and envy of the ease with which Heidegger moves from a painting to a world-picture.

The production of this picture depends on how gender functions in the passage. To Heidegger it is important that the shoes are a woman's and that the land that she treads is female: "In the shoes there vibrates the silent call of the earth, its quiet gift of the ripening corn and its enigmatic self-refusal in the fallow desolation of the wintry field." Jameson indicates his awareness of the gender-coding obliquely by noting that, in commenting on the passage, Jacques Derrida has referred to the shoes as "a heterosexual pair, which allows neither for perversion nor for fetishization" (8). Yet Jameson errs, since Derrida's text, "Restitutions of the Truth in Pointing [*pointure*]," is a "'polylogue' (for *n* + I—female—voices)," in which no single statement can be said to express Derrida's own view. Moreover, Derrida refers to the shoes as bisexual not heterosexual.[25] They are both vulval, with "the dark opening of the worn insides," and phallic, "the equipment itself rises to its resting-in-self."

Jameson describes Heidegger's analysis in implicitly gendered and sexualized terms. It translates "the meaningless materiality of the body and nature" into "the meaning-endowment of history and of the social" (7). He does make the "earth" yield cultural meaning. By drawing attention to the male work of cultural production, Jameson indicates signs of a competitive gender-anxiety in the quotation. Heidegger cites female *re*-productivity twice, both as the earth that bears a "gift" and as the woman who gives birth, while simultaneously demonstrating through his writing the higher-because-intellectual productivity of the male couple of artist and mediating theorist who together generate the *"world."* [26] Artist and critic give birth to the work of art as an interpretive act and thereby transcend the female bodies of land and woman.

In addition to Heidegger's reading, Jameson offers his own, which sublates Heidegger's heterosexual obsessiveness by rising to a yet more abstract level of theory. Where Heidegger emphasizes the totality of peasant existence, Jameson concentrates on the painting as a sign of artistic self-awareness in Mandel's first stage of capitalist development. According to Mandel, between 1848 and the 1890s, technology was dominated by "machine production of steam-driven motors." [27] The division of labor characteristic of this stage is mirrored in the opticality of van Gogh's painting. Emphasizing this sensate aspect of artistic production, Jameson isolates it from metaphors of copulation and birthing while preparing the ground for his argument that art becomes increasingly sensational in the late twentieth century, and sensation, restricted and reduced to the visual, becomes more abstract both ipso facto and as an allegorical sign of the artist at work under an intensified division of labor. Jameson's interpretation exaggerates the abstraction of the van Gogh by neglecting its tactile qualities, which mesh with its optical ones, and by stressing its function as a sign of Mandel's totalizing view. These displacements yield utopian results; the painting becomes "a Utopian gesture, an act of compensation which ends up producing a whole new Utopian realm of the senses, or at least of that supreme sense—sight, the visual, the eye—which it now reconstitutes for us as a semi-autonomous space in its own right—part of some new division of labour in the body of capital, some new fragmentation of the emergent sensorium which replicates the specializations and divisions of capitalist life at the same time that it seeks in precisely such fragmentation a desperate Utopian compensation for them" (7). Nonetheless, the work of theory in this passage, which moves in the direction of postmodern "space," occurs at the expense of body. Jameson dissociates the painting from the bodily work of making that is evident in the painting. This sublimating process also occurs in Jameson's use of the word "body," which is displaced from an individual human being to "the body of capital."

It is characteristic of the level of abstraction in the chapter that the painting of shoes by van Gogh that Jameson reproduces is not the same one that Heidegger discusses. Moreover, as Meyer Schapiro has pointed out, Heidegger's reading is adrift. Having tracked down which painting, of a possible eight, Heidegger had in mind, Schapiro argues that the shoes are not a peasant's nor are they a woman's. Rather, the painting appears to be of a pair of shoes that van Gogh wore while in Paris in 1886–1887. To Schapiro, this connection suggests that the painting is an exercise in meditative attention to what Schapiro regards as "the personal and physiognomic in the shoes."[28]

Canvassing the debate between these two writers, Derrida observes that although Schapiro criticizes Heidegger for projecting reference onto the image, Schapiro ignores his own projection of van Gogh's presence into the painting. Moreover, Derrida makes a convincing case that in characterizing the owner of the shoes as "an artist . . . , a man of the town and city," and—later—"a brooding, self-observant drifter," Schapiro identifies image and maker with his own self-image as an aesthetic, urbane European, in exile in New York City.[29] By translating van Gogh from his own self-conception as a peasant-artist into a prototype of the alienated modern artist, Jameson repeats the gestures of appropriation—of artifact and artist—that Derrida questions in Heidegger and Schapiro's accounts of the painting.[30] Jameson's reading effaces the painting both as a set of bodily gestures and as a mode of personal meditation. To that extent, the attenuation of the subject is Jameson's projection.

Photographic Negatives

Jameson next proceeds to contrast van Gogh's shoes to the series Diamond Dust Shoes by Andy Warhol. As in the discussion of Heidegger/van Gogh, the particular image in question is of little interest to Jameson, nor is he interested in the transformation of the image that Warhol achieves by using a photographic negative, a transformation that underscores the fact that the image is no "real" or "true" representation. Jameson does not specify which painting in the series he refers to; rather, his concern is with the works as a category. Jameson argues that the image[j], which is based on a photographic negative of rows of women's dress shoes, converts shoes into fetish objects that lack both affect and meaning as signifiers of a totalizable truth.[31] Or rather, their resistance to interpretation is precisely what characterizes them as signifiers of postmodern culture. Jameson, moreover, argues that they construct no subject-position for the viewer: "Nothing in this painting organizes even a minimal place for the viewer" (8), an observation that continues the process of evacuating the subject already under way in Jameson's reinterpretation of van Gogh's painting.

18. Gallery interior. From the advertisement for the Achenbach Kunsthandel, Frankfurt, Germany, that appeared in the summer 1989 issue of *Arts Magazine*. Courtesy Achenbach Kunsthandel, Düsseldorf, Frankfurt, Munich.

Jameson responds to the painting with an excess of affect oddly without counterpart in his analysis of van Gogh. "Here . . . we have a random collection of dead objects, hanging together on the canvas like so many turnips, as shorn of their earlier life-world as the pile of shoes left over from Auschwitz or the remainders and tokens of some incomprehensible and tragic fire in a packed dancehall" (8). The "we" of these lines clearly feels itself to be the object of emotional violence. Moreover, it does occupy a subject-position, namely, as subject of what Jameson will later term the hysterical sublime. The inscription of Warhol's image into Jameson's critical discourse, complete with its own cathected subject, is an act of translation, remarkable for the aggressiveness with which it effaces Warhol's careful efforts to resist the projection of emotional affect onto representations.

In a recent exhibition at the Achenbach Gallery in Frankfurt, Germany, a black-and-white painting in this series was hung next to a multiple-image portrait of Marilyn Monroe. At a 90-degree angle was hung a single-image, silkscreened portrait of Elizabeth Taylor similar to ones made by Warhol in 1963. In front of the painting of shoes is a stack of Warhol's simulated Campbell's Tomato Juice boxes. In this setting the fetishized character of Warhol's imagery and its metonymic relation both to "commodity" and to "woman" is altogether evident. Two sets of displacements, however, tend to demonstrate that these objects are commodity fetishes. First are displacements in the technical processes whereby the images are made: for instance, the use of preexisting photographic images and the intervention of the silkscreen process between them and the images of Liz and Marilyn that appear on the canvas. The silkscreen process leaves signs of choices made by the fabricators of the images, who are probably persons other than Warhol himself.[32] In the shoe painting, use of a negative image demonstrates the mechanical, phased process whereby photographic simulacra of reality are fashioned.

The second set of displacements has to do with the type and repetition of the objects represented in the shoe picture. Though this aspect is characteristic of the world of advertising and of Warhol's commercial images of shoes drawn in the 1950s,[33] the number of shoes draws attention away from particular objects to the general category of "shoes," to their status as commodity objects and as representations of American class-values, aspirations, and investments.[34] Juxtaposed with images of Liz and Marilyn, both the objects that are human and those that are inanimate tend to be flattened on one horizon of commodity-use, replication, advertisement, circulation, availability, redundancy, and disposability.[35] This mode of presentation emphasizes the prescribed character of the fetish object as well as of the gaze of the subject. The sense of displacement of the subject that troubles Jameson and apparently triggers his response operates for Warhol as part of an analytic process that resists the viewer's tendency to invest himself (or herself) in the images as fetishes. In other words, Warhol constructs not a neurotic effect but an alienation effect.[36]

Warhol's attention to this range of issues places the series of shoe images within the terrain of conceptual art. This observation is consistent with Jameson's contention that the relation between artist and work of art has become increasingly abstract and disembodied in the late twentieth century.[37] Nonetheless, Warhol is present to these works in a number of ways. For one, he has chosen to produce his paintings in a high-art tradition that provides an alternative to the tradition that emphasizes art as a uniquely personal mode of expression. In the late 1940s, Warhol was enrolled in the program in Pictorial Design at Carnegie Tech in Pittsburgh. There he came under the influence of ideas promulgated by Laszlo Moholy-Nagy at the New Bauhaus or Institute of Design in Chicago. Moholy's book, *Vision in Motion* (1947), which includes images of photographic negatives, was "the most influential text in American art education of the period." In the book, Moholy writes: "People believe that they should demand hand execution as an inseparable part of the genesis

19. The dust jacket of Fredric Jameson's *Postmodernism; or, The Cultural Logic of Late Capitalism* (Durham: Duke University Press, 1991). Courtesy Andy Warhol Foundation.

of a work of art. In fact, in comparison with the inventive *mental* process of the genesis of a work, the question of its execution is important only in so far as it must be mastered to the limits. The manner, however, whether personal or by assignment of labor, whether manual or mechanical, is irrelevant." In adapting this approach to image making, Warhol later devised the idea of artistic signature as trademark, not the trademark of an authorial style, handling, or mythic iconography but the literal trademark of consumer products or star-images, images that convert an individual into a trademark of himself or herself. Displacing himself as subject in this way, Warhol has *become* a subject, so that when we see an image of a coke bottle or of Liz, we read not "Coca-Cola" or "Elizabeth Taylor" but "Warhol."[38]

Jameson appropriates this process when he chooses one of the Diamond Dust Shoes as the cover image on the dust jacket of *Postmodernism*. The image of the Warhol painting refers as much to the author's name as to the title of the book. In this way and together with Jameson's by now well known critique of these images, Diamond Dust Shoes becomes the trademark of "Jameson," theorist of postmodernism. Such mimicry might be considered the sincerest form of flattery despite Jameson's expressed skepticism about the effectiveness of such moves as a mode of analysis of artistic and commercial production (9). Yet, as I have argued, Jameson's translation of Warhol elides precisely the approach that the painter developed from his original position of cultural deficit. Born and raised outside the parameters of elite culture, Warhol made that disadvantage work to his credit and in the process redefined the meaning of high culture in the United States. Jameson also underestimates the status of Warhol's paintings as individual works of art. The silk-screen process results in unique registers of images that "stop time," demanding that the viewer stop and look closely even if the trademark character of the image invites a look-at-a-gulp. Although Jameson does mention the prominence of shoes in Warhol's commercial work, he ignores the series of shoe-portraits of celebrities which Warhol exhibited in 1956 and which were included in the Frankfurt installation. It is probable that Warhol was familiar with comments in Sigmund Freud's study of Leonardo that connect male homosexuals with shoe fetishism.[39] Freud argues: "Fetishistic reverence for a woman's foot and shoe appears to take the foot merely as a substitutive symbol for the woman's penis which was once revered and later missed."[40] Warhol responded to this suggestion by using shoe images in ways that both acknowledge and ironize their fetishistic significance within psychoanalytic theory. Among the collages of the mid-1950s, for instance, he includes a tribute to Christine Jorgensen which comments on the fetishistic aspect of transsexuality.[41] Jorgensen is a Danish transsexual famous for being the first to undergo a sex-change. Jorgensen made use of medical technology to turn his body into the "substitutive symbol" of a woman. No more appropriate "symbol" of Jorgensen could be found than a shoe fetish, which also symbolizes the loss of something that never existed in the first place.

Both the Diamond Dust Shoes and the earlier shoe portraits use camp style and subject matter to register Warhol's resistance to masculinist approaches to artmaking. The shoe portraits flaunt their refusal of the aesthetic of Abstract Expressionism that dominated New York painting during the 1950s.[42] At the time, Warhol also attempted unsuccessfully to arrange an exhibition at the Tanger Gallery of the images that are still misleadingly referred to as his "private 'boy drawings.'"[43] As Bradford R.

Collins has commented: "The submission was refused, of course: in the context of the conservative social attitudes of the decade and the masculine atmosphere of Abstract Expressionism, such subject matter was unacceptable."[44]

The Hysterical Sublime

Jameson frequently makes use of Freudian analytical technique—as, for instance, when he refers to "a kind of return of the repressed in *Diamond Dust Shoes*, a strange compensatory decorative exhilaration" (10). However, the phrase, "return of the repressed," better refers to Jameson's text than to Warhol or to the Diamond Dust Shoes. Far from attempting to conceal his "swish," Warhol very much performed it. As Mandy Merck demonstrates, the series is a kind of homage to drag queens who purchase oversized high heel shoes at the curbside display tables in Manhattan's garment district from which Warhol often purchased large numbers of shoes.[45] Gay reference is evident in particular works of art, in his collaborations with other individuals, in group projects, and in the "alternately glacially ironic and self-distancing but also aggressively 'deviant' and exhibitionistic milieu of New York pop culture of the '60s, a culture that first centered around [Jack] Smith but soon shifted to Warhol."[46] In these activities, Warhol and others adapted gay camp taste in art that was at once hip, commercial, and a mode of high culture.

In Jameson's text "intentional repression" triggers "the mechanism of conversion" that produces the affect of the hysterical sublime.[47] Continuing from the passage cited above, Jameson contrasts to the glint of diamond dust on the surface of Warhol's paintings "the august premonitory eye flashes of Rilke's archaic Greek torso which warns the bourgeois subject to change *his* life: nothing of that sort here, in the gratuitous frivolity of this final decorative overlay" (10).[48] Jameson invokes Rilke's Apollo in order to draw a nostalgic contrast between what Hal Foster has referred to as "transgressive strategy and utopian desire" in modernist art and what Jameson sees as apocalyptic euphoria in Warhol.[49] Yet the surprising introduction of Apollo at this point suggests that Jameson is engaged in his own process of fetishizing the paintings. He compares their glinting surfaces with the "light" shining from Apollo's skin—I say "skin" because the torso of Apollo referred to in the poem is headless: "If there weren't light, / . . . its skin wouldn't gleam like the fur of a wild animal, / and the body wouldn't send out light from every edge / as a star does." The conversion is double. The painting image is converted (by *Jameson*) into a (male) fetish-object. But it also becomes the target of phobic anxieties about the gleaming surface of the male body.[50]

Just as Heidegger in responding to the van Gogh shoes indulges in a sort of fetishism that "reduces history to nature,"[51] Jameson indulges in another kind of fetishism, one that reduces history to aesthetics. Not only is sexual and emotional attraction between men repressed so also is the particular "transgressive strategy and utopian desire" involved in the politics of gay liberation at the end of the 1960s and early in the 1970s. This moment of political affirmation is one referent of the Apollo-figure. Apollo is traditionally an androgynous figure, whose gender-crossing connotes the attempt that first-wave gay theorists like Dennis Altman made to imagine a desire that would undo the construction of gender.[52] The commodification of gay existence during the 1970s followed by the onset of AIDS abruptly checked such hopes. Other references in Jameson's comments on *Diamond Dust Shoes*—the "tragic fire in a packed dancehall" and "Auschwitz"—refer in displaced fashion to other moments in recent social history: the gay discotheques of the 1970s, the sexual euphoria that some gays found in that decade, and the catastrophic losses to AIDS in the years following.[53] Jameson's reference to the "deathly quality" (9) of the Warhol shoes particularly resonates in the context of the new crisis.

About "euphoria," not just Warhol's or that of other gays but even more so that associated with the "intensities" of postmodern urban space (29), Jameson is ambivalent. Describing the experience of being inside the Bonaventure Hotel, he speaks of the loss of a sense of bodily integrity in the "hypercrowd" (40) that throngs the spatially confusing public spaces. "You are in this hyperspace up to your eyes and your body; and if it seemed [to you] before that suppression of depth I spoke of in postmodern painting or literature would necessarily be difficult to achieve in architecture itself, perhaps [you may now be willing to see] this bewildering immersion as the formal equivalent in the new medium."[54] The sensation of "bewildering immersion" is the ultimate condition of the postmodern subject. Jameson uses his experience in the Bonaventure as a metaphor for the central condition of postmodernism, the state of the hysterical sublime, "incompatible with the representation of the body" (34): "The sublime was for Burke an experience bordering on terror, the fitful glimpse, in astonishment, stupor and awe, of what was so enormous as to crush human life altogether: a description then refined by Kant to include the question of representation itself—so that the object of the sublime becomes now not only a matter of sheer power and of the physical incommensurability of the human organism with Nature but also of the limits of figuration and the incapacity of the human mind to give representation to such enormous forces" (34).

At this moment, when the power to represent either the body or the world is lost, Jameson explicitly introduces the topic of homosexuality by describing this state as "a camp or 'hysterical' sublime" (77). In Susan Sontag's "Notes on 'Camp,'" which Jameson mentions, Sontag argues that "homosexuals, by and large, constitute the vanguard—and the most articulate audience—of Camp." Further, she contends: "Jews and homosexuals are the outstanding creative minorities in contemporary urban culture. . . . The two pioneering forces of modern sensibility are Jewish moral seriousness and homosexual aestheticism and irony."[55] The condition of the hysterical sublime is dystopian in the extreme; yet Jameson has argued that theorists need to seize on those aspects of postmodern culture which however debased, occluded or confused, permit some expression to "intolerable, unrealizable, properly imperishable desires."[56] Thus he also characterizes the Bonaventure as a "complacent and entertaining (although bewildering) leisure-time space" (44). The question arises, then, what about camp's associations with specifically gay culture? What "imperishable desires" belong to men who have sex with other men? Is Jameson somehow signaling that sexual and emotional ties between men also have a part in utopian experience and aspiration?

Let Us Now Praise Famous Men

Jameson's ambivalence about the hysterical sublime underlines the need in critical theory specifically to address questions about male relations and the male body, its felt needs and fantasies. Jameson contends that postmodern culture is characterized by "the waning of affect," the disappearance of the depth model, and the loss of a historical sense (11–12, 18–21).[57] Yet at times Warhol installs a gay subject at the center of postmodern culture without sacrificing either affect or a sense of history. In contradicting Jameson's account of Warhol and postmodern culture, I do not mean to suggest that Warhol solves in some conclusive way the problems that Jameson poses. Nonetheless, many of Warhol's activities do provide solutions within particular contexts, although other producers need to keep working out new and different if equally provisional ones.

Let Us Now Praise Famous Men (1963) is one of at least five works done by Warhol early in the 1960s that combines images by fellow pop artist Robert Rauschenberg with what look like snapshots from the Rauschenberg family album. The best known of these images, in the third row from the top of the painting, is a family portrait taken in 1926 at Port Arthur, Texas, where Rauschenberg's father dug postholes for the local power and light company.[58] The image anticipates the photographs that Walker Evans took for James Agee's *Let Us Now Praise Famous Men*, a "documentary report of the late 1930s about three tenant farmer families in the

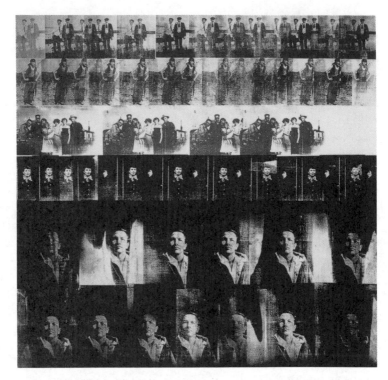

20. Andy Warhol, *Let Us Now Praise Famous Men*, 1963. Courtesy Michael D. Abrams.

southern United States." Nan Rosenthal reports that when the project was complete, the report was rejected for publication by the journal that had commissioned it because it "was insufficiently patronizing toward its subject." After publication, it fell out of view until it was reprinted in 1960. In 1962, a photograph of the Bud Woods family group included in the volume was shown at an exhibition of rural photography from the depression years at the Museum of Modern Art. Although the Rauschenberg group is not destitute, they are sufficiently ordinary to make comprehensible Rauschenberg's quip about "being 'poor white trash.'" In the version in the Michael D. Abrams collection, the repeated silkscreen images of the photograph have been printed in a sepia-colored ink that signifies temporal distance, evoking nostalgia. Yet, as I have indicated, the immediate art-context of the use of this image is one of the recovery of work that had originally been ignored because it made readers uncomfortably aware of the indignities suffered by other Americans.[59]

The use of sepia and the repeating image demonstrate the codification of the image within a sign system in which what actually once was be-

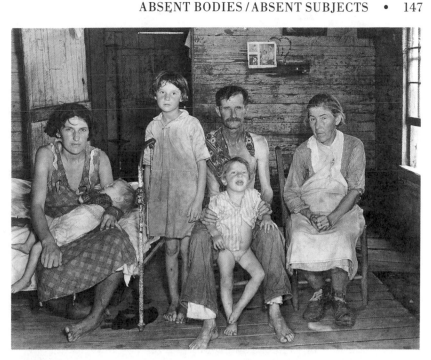

21. Walker Evans, *Sharecropper's Family, Hale County, Alabama* (Ivy, Ellen, Pearl, Thomas, and Bud Woods, and Miss Molly Gallatin), 1936. Courtesy Library of Congress, Washington, D.C.

22. Walker Evans, *Floyd Burroughs' Workshoes*, Hale County, Alabama, 1936

comes a symbol of "then." In other words, Warhol manipulates the image to visualize the loss of a historical sense that Jameson deplores. This loss can in turn serve to anesthetize those who, like John Kennedy during his 1960 primary campaign in West Virginia, were shocked to discover the extent of rural white poverty. Warhol (or his studio assistant) indicates the dislocating effects of deprivation by cropping the third image from the left to delete Rauschenberg's parents. To the far right, as in a number of the disaster pictures of the early 1960s, he introduces a white blank, the only open space in the painting. The white space comments on the mechanical character of the production of the original photographic images. At the same time, the blank functions as a metaphor of temporal gap or rupture, of mortality.[60]

Beneath this row of images is a repeating image of a photograph of Rauschenberg as a young, successful artist. In other handlings, for example in *Young Rauschenberg #1* (1962), the portrait is placed above the family group, which invites the "before" and "after" reading of a conventional American success story: rural obscurity to begin with, personal achievement and celebrity afterward. The images even invite reading in terms of "cause" and "effect": anonymity and relative deprivation prompt a dramatic upward mobility. Warhol's staging of the images draws attention to their status as a myth. This analytic presentation, however, resonates with history, in part because the "hero" is a bohemian artist, in part because both the subject of the painting and its painter were old enough to have experienced the Great Depression. The space between the two different kinds of image functions as a metaphor of the distance that both men covered in a generation. For Warhol, whose own father emigrated from Slovakia and worked in a coal mine, the myth is also biography and autobiography.

In *Let Us Now Praise Famous Men*, Warhol repeats the portrait-image, overlaps it, and erases it with irregular white spaces or heavy inking. The repetitions highlight the conventionality and reproducibility of celebrity; the manipulations suggest its temporality. The pose and lighting of the original photograph also define the masculine character of this version of the myth. With head lifted and eyes raised above the viewer, the image recalls Hollywood publicity stills, in particular a shot of Montgomery Clift.[61] Richard Dyer, who classes these images as "male pin-ups," argues that the look up and away spiritualizes the male body while validating the ideal of straining, which he regards as the central suggestion of male pin-up imagery: "It is precisely *straining* that is held to be the great good, what makes a man a man."[62] Straining in this painting, however, is straining with a difference since it is expressly loaded with the urgencies of social mobility—and dislocation—of working-class Americans born ei-

23. Andy Warhol, *Young Rauschenberg #1*, 1962. Courtesy Andy Warhol Foundation.

ther shortly before or during the depression. Moreover, the fame referred to in the title is marked as the fame of a male who is homosexual. Rauschenberg, who was better known in 1963 than Warhol was, and Jasper Johns were both prototypical pop artists and gay men; they also were lovers.[63] Warhol's homage to Rauschenberg, then, is a homage to a man who was able to overcome the stigma of homosexuality.

Gay reference in *Let Us Now Praise Famous Men* works with other aspects of the painting to undercut univocal interpretation. These displacements destabilize the subjects of the images represented while enacting Warhol's strategy of return—of gay men to each other and to others, to

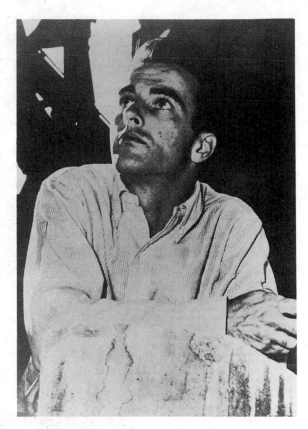

24. Montgomery Clift. Provenance unknown.

workers, to women, to family, and to the patterns of self-improvement in America that Warhol both acknowledges and calls into question. The element of resistance in this affirmation should not be underestimated. Warhol was negating the assertion, urged in the preceding decade, that fags were commies or child molesters or any other sort of monstrous Other.[64] Warhol's counterassertion was: "I am another; I am one of you."

In *Let Us Now Praise Famous Men*, Warhol was able to turn his position as an "unsubject" to good use in fashioning a politics of location. If one were to pursue the question of how his work continued to be marked by gay reflexivity, one could consider an ever-changing range of practices. Warhol did other "unsubject" works in the early 1960s. These works—referring to newspaper reports about anonymous deaths in major accidents; the "car crash" pictures, whose iconography is drawn from sensational photographs in the print media; the electric chair series; the images of falling and fallen suicides; the images of racial violence in

Birmingham, Alabama; the images of the *Thirteen Most Wanted Men*, a twenty-foot-square mural commissioned by Philip Johnson for the exterior of the New York State Pavilion at the 1964 New York World's Fair and covered over by direction of Governor Rockefeller—all these images play with a public exposure that leaves subjectivity a blank.[65] This extreme sense of alienation between the subject and its public appropriation registers Warhol's awareness of his psychically and socially exposed position. During the decade of the 1960s, Warhol also was a frequent collaborator with young gay men, most notably in his adaptation of underground film technique in both experimental and commercial filmmaking, often dealing with homosexual material, between 1963 and 1969.[66]

Engendering the Subject

In the final lines of the opening chapter Jameson invokes the name of Althusser when arguing that critical theorists have yet to address the need to theorize the relationship between "the Lacanian Symbolic" (54) and the issues of agency and representation in postmodern culture. In his essay, "Freud and Lacan," Althusser contends that the formation of the contemporary subject, whose existence is necessary to the functioning of late capitalism, occurs through the processes of education and family life. Althusser especially emphasizes this inculturation as a process of gender formation. Commenting on Lacan's "Symbolic Order," Althusser argues that "Lacan demonstrates the effectiveness of the Order, the Law, that has been lying in wait for each infant born since before his birth, and seizes him before his first cry, assigning to him his place and role, and hence his fixed destination."[67] In his discussion, Jameson transcodes "Lacan's account of schizophrenia" (26) from psychoanalysis to aesthetics. He remarks: "I must omit the familial or more orthodox psychoanalytic background to this situation" (26). In response, Jacqueline Rose has observed that Jameson elides precisely the psychoanalytic etiology that has made schizophrenia especially a female condition.[68] The exclusion of this context guarantees other significant absences. Rose points out "the omission . . . of any women artists from his account of postmodern cultural production, and more specifically of those who might be said to make the representation of sexual difference, or sexual difference *as* representation, their chief object of concern." Rose also observes that "the concept of representation that is at stake" for Jameson "seems to bring with it a kind of nostalgia for direct and unmediated vision," for "a moment or an epoch when vision was direct and possible, when the viewing subject looked out on and greeted the world, and greeted too, without perversion or aggressivity, the other human subjects who peopled it."[69] I would add to these comments that in the context of the opening chapter of *Post-modernism*, the subject of this innocent gaze is a heterosexual male, who occupies the position of Heidegger/van Gogh. Establishing this position, even if equivocally, requires Jameson to negate not only feminine differ-ence but also differences within masculine existence, particularly femi-nized male homosexual difference.

Recent gay critique has associated schizophrenia with the play of visi-bility and invisibility within the regime of closeting. Commenting on the Russian dancer, Nijinsky, for instance, Michael Moon writes: "The strain of being a visible and intensely mystified embodiment of the open secret of male homosexuality in Paris and London in the decade or two after the epochal downfall and death of Oscar Wilde no doubt played a significant part in what was diagnosed as Nijinsky's schizophrenic disintegration in his late twenties, at the end of World War I."[70] In *Postmodernism*, Jame-son belatedly begins to attend to the sexual contexts of schizophrenia. He adds to the discussion of Lacan a footnote that refers the reader to Lacan's discussion of the Schreber case, which Freud analyzes in terms of "a re-gression to a passive homosexuality."[71] In this limited way, Jameson pro-vides a trace of male-male desire in his own account of schizophrenia.

By failing to address the psychoanalytic structure of schizophrenia, Jameson ensures that the play of gender and sexuality in his text will act out rather than act on the implications of Althusser's reflections. The dis-solution of the subject in the hysterical sublime, however, also functions as a symptom of Jameson's resistance to apocalypse in Marxist theory. This resistance shows in two ways: first, in his preoccupation with "the unavoidable representational problem that there is no 'late capitalism in general'" (xx), and second, in his evacuation of the revolutionary subject. As for the problem of representation, one might argue that Jameson's reduction of Mandel's model of capitalist development to a thumbnail sketch is more problematic than Mandel's portrayal of that development within *Late Capitalism*. In Mandel's account of capitalist expansion in the nineteenth and the twentieth centuries, he offers persuasive illustrations of his general thesis that *"the accumulation of capital itself produces de-velopment and underdevelopment as mutually determining moments of the uneven and combined movement of capital."*[72] He also provides a credible account of these effects in the relation between postcolonial economies and multinational corporations since the end of World War II.[73] In light of this analysis, there appears to be no need for a "representation" of "late capitalism in general." Mandel provides a good basis for understanding the effects of further capital accumulation in the metropolitan countries.

Far more problematic is the apocalyptic turn that Mandel takes in the final chapter, in which he argues the imminence of the revolutionary overturn of the capitalist economy by a "working-class" whose "cultural and political horizon" is ever "widening."[74] The subjects of this revolution are unitary, and Mandel uses terms like "workers" and "democracy" in altogether reified fashion. In contrast, Jameson presents a postmodern subject who is not transparent but thick—even if only with sensation. In positing this subject, Jameson indicates how different from Mandel's is his assessment of political possibilities in the waning years of the century.

The movement of the narrative of "The Cultural Logic of Late Capitalism" is not toward the recovery of representation and agency but toward an occluded subject altogether suitable for the *fin de millennium*. This account is symptomatic of blockage at both the social and psychological levels. Yet impasse, as I have attempted to show in analyzing the practices of Andy Warhol, is by no means the only or even a necessary outcome of postmodern theory and practice. Avoiding impasse, however, requires the continued work of engendering theory, including Jameson's; of attending to the specificities of experience of those subject to hegemonic masculinity; and of an inventive use of macro- and micropolitical politics in both metropolitan countries and elsewhere.

7

• • •

APOCALYPTIC
UTTERANCE
IN EDMUND WHITE'S
"AN ORACLE"

Questions about specifically gay male agency in the wake of AIDS are to the fore in Edmund White's short story "An Oracle." White shows the disintegrative impacts of AIDS on personal identity, intimate relations, and group identification in New York City in the mid-1980s. Nonetheless—and however unwished for—the illness and death of Ray's partner, George, and Ray's probable infection put in question the premature consolidation of a white, upper-middle-class style of gay existence during the preceding decade. In White's story, this style can include love and loyalty but not the egalitarian reciprocity that Walt Whitman and other American sexual radicals had long called for. By making visible the inadequacies of Ray and George's existence, White exposes it to judgment; but he also opens the possibility that the devastations of AIDS and the anxieties surrounding HIV-infection will provide Ray an opportunity to change his life. To this end, White emphasizes the semantic structure of oracle in the narrative. In this way, he avoids the coincidence of individual death with narrative closure typical of AIDS fictions. In AIDS writing, the doubling of mortality and fictional ending are freighted ideologically in ways that gay writers find difficult to manage. But oracular structure also portends a reorganization of gay subjectivity at the individual, interpersonal, and social levels that will enable new configurations to arise. White does not guarantee such an outcome. Indeed, he shows how limited the possibilities for Ray and Marco are. But opening the possibility is ethically and politically important. For the major challenge facing white middle-class gay men, whether addressing AIDS or other issues, is whether they will be able to engage with other subjects of male-male desire across the differences that separate, objectify, or render invisible.

As the title suggests, the most important aspect of apocalypse in White's short story is the oracular. Apocalyptic texts such as the Apocalypse of St. John include many oracles; indeed, an apocalyptic narrative is, in a sense, an oracle. In his essay "Of an Apocalyptic Tone Recently Adopted in Philosophy" Derrida distinguishes between "articulated discursive content" and "tone" in apocalyptic texts. Further, he distinguishes two sorts of tone: a unified tone that produces a single meaning for the narrative and another that he refers to as "a generalised derailment, a *Verstimmung* multiplying the voices and making the tones shift [*sauter*], opening each word to the haunting memory of the other in an unmasterable polytonality, with grafts, intrusions, interferences [*parasitages*]. Generalised *Verstimmung* is the possibility of the other tone, or the tone of another to come at no matter what moment to interrupt a familiar music." In other words, tonal interference amplifies the range of oracular signification. Moreover, Derrida regards the second tone as necessary to the very possibility of "emission." Obversely, he contends that "the unity of tone, if there was any, would certainly be the assurance of destination, but also death, another apocalypse."[1] Poised at a moment when the onset of AIDS had put in question gay identity as constituted during the preceding decade, "An Oracle" poses the possibility that "another tone" can come that will enable the rethinking of gay existence on other bases.

White's story ends with the message, "You must look out for yourself." The phrase is one that Ray's deceased lover, George, often addressed to him. It is repeated frequently in the text. At the end, it returns in "the tone of another" as spoken by Marco, the young man with whom Ray falls in love while on vacation in Crete. Derrida's use of the adjective "haunting" is apt, since although the tone is Marco's, Ray also hears George. The question arises whether the meaning of the message changes in this altered context or whether Ray is condemned to hear it with an unvarying "unity of tone" that Derrida correlates with death itself. The question has political significance since it implies other questions that became important following the onset of AIDS. Do those who, like George, have died as a result of AIDS continue to speak to those who are left behind and do they speak differently? How does AIDS affect the possibility of listening to others who are markedly different? The second question is especially pointed in view of the differences of race, class, nationality, and gender that characterize PLWAs.

In addition to questions about apocalyptic utterance, "An Oracle" addresses the phenomenon of blockage in responses to AIDS. White sets the story among upper-middle-class whites in New York City in the early mid-1980s when public agencies had not yet responded to the epidemic.

In this milieu, blockage functions at both macro- and micropolitical levels. The absence of a public discourse of AIDS management and prevention enforces the isolation of gay men like Ray and George within the wider population. Blockage also operates within their quasi-closeted personal lives, a fact indicated by the absence of the word "AIDS" from the story. Absent too is any explicit indication that those who are not white and well to do have also been adversely affected by AIDS. The psychologically and socially destructive aspects of blockage are suggested in contrast to the model of mourning among women in Greek peasant villages that White uses to counter Ray's sense of drift and dislocation. In Loring M. Danforth's book *The Death Rituals of Rural Greece* (1982), the grief of mourning ends with a return to community, but for Ray this is not possible, since his social existence dissolves after the onset of AIDS.

In the most telling image of AIDS that Ray uses, he thinks: "If and when the disease surfaced (for it seemed to him like a kid who's holding his nose underwater for an eerily long time but is bound to come crashing, gasping up for air), when the disease surfaced he wouldn't mind much. In a way dying would be easier than figuring out a new way of living."[2] The image is one of delayed but inevitable return, a return that also refers to a departure. Once the "kid" returns to the surface, his presence will mark something new, namely, the changed terms of existence after AIDS can no longer be denied. What modes will sociality take after awareness of AIDS can no longer be avoided? The image directs the reader's attention beyond the frame of the narrative to find answers to this question.

Altered Fictions

"An Oracle" is a cruising narrative within the subgenre of sexual tourist fiction. The story exploits the exotic aspects of gay sex and depends on the same binary structures "of self/other, origin/return that structure the myths and stereotypes which make visible institutional patterns of stigmatization and discrimination."[3] The genre is one in which White has long been proficient. "The Beautiful Room Is Empty," of the mid-1960s, is a story about two New Yorkers cruising in San Juan, Puerto Rico. In "An Oracle," the life that Ray leads with George before George's illness is a satiric caricature of the lifestyle of middle-class gay couples living in "open" relationships in New York City in the decade before AIDS. Along with other writers of gay fiction, such as Andrew Holleran, White may be said to be a major installer of the myth that this lifestyle constituted the norm of gay existence. By excluding reference to the non-WASP majority of New York City (Ray, George, and company apparently live in a cocoon), White exacerbates the "otherness" of the Cretan locale to which Ray goes after George's death as a result of AIDS "had tossed all the sandbags overboard and Ray had been floating higher and higher towards extinction" (222).

Within the context of the AIDS epidemic, the political significance of White's representations is precisely sited. By the mid-1980s when he wrote "An Oracle," mainstream gay responses to AIDS were taking a pro-monogamy line. Sex, relabeled "promiscuity," was out. This view is in sharp contrast to gay activist responses to AIDS earlier in the decade. In the booklet, *How to Have Sex in an Epidemic* (1983), now and then "the single most comprehensive guide to safe sex," members of the News from the Front collective wrote: "Once you understand how diseases are transmitted, you can begin to explore medically safe sex. Our challenge is to figure out how we can have gay, life-affirming sex, satisfy our emotional needs, and stay alive!"[4] White's story is pro-sex at the same time that it lampoons obsessive concern about bodily fitness. He is very satirical about gay partnerships on the model of heterosexual marriage.

"The Beautiful Room Is Empty" circles around a scene of trauma: a disastrous car crash that has left one of the two protagonists permanently injured.[5] "An Oracle" circles around Ray's fear that he will develop AIDS: "He thought it very likely that he was carrying death inside him, that it was ticking inside him like a time bomb but one he couldn't find because it had been secreted by an unknown terrorist. Even if it was located it couldn't be defused. Nor did he know when it might explode. He didn't want to expose anyone to contagion" (225). The very clichés with which Ray describes his situation suggests how incomprehensible he finds it. If HIV-positive, he is not in a position to know when or where he became infected. Additionally troubled by unexpressed grief over the death of George, he can neither trace his disturbance to a moment of origin nor can he makes sense of his vulnerability in terms of the life that he led before George's death. Sexually, Ray responds with a burst of "lust" shortly after George's death, followed by celibacy. With Marco, he practices safe sex. At no time, however, has he been able to bring himself to be tested for HIV antibodies.

On Crete, Ray is in limbo, cruising in hope of finding answers to questions that he is unable to frame. The image he uses to express his anxiety about AIDS—"The disease . . . seemed to him like a kid who's holding his nose underwater for an eerily long time but is bound to come crashing, gasping up for air" (219)—recalls Ray's memories of his youth in Findlay, Ohio, which he recovers while abroad, and foreshadows Marco, the "kid" with whom Ray becomes sexually involved. All three of these kids (Ray's adolescent self, AIDS, Marco) function as interior voices that Ray addresses in the course of the story.[6] In this way, oracular utterance is described as inward, a possibility that Derrida touches on when he suggests that "the other tone" that interrupts "self-identity" readily occurs "in analysis."[7] Listening means that the subject changes, hopefully to the point where what is blocked can become accessible to conscious comprehension. But in order for this change to occur, the concept of self, which in Ray's case means a particular formation of *gay* identity, has to be transformed.

Ray experiences his crisis, in familiar humanist terms, as the loss of a sense of self: "'You must look out for yourself,' George had always said. But what self?" (211). Within the terms of sexual identification as Ray understands it, regaining selfhood means finding a lover who can confirm the identity of Ray's desire. Cruising, in this scenario, can yield love, which can in turn secure a disabled ego. It is important to emphasize the psychological character of sexual politics in this trajectory (which is also the trajectory of the genre within which the story unfolds) despite the fact that, as the story proceeds, one learns that when Ray first came out, sexual politics to him meant community politics. In his life with George, however, the public dimension of gay politics has been reduced to mainstream gay fund-raising.

At the urging of his friend Betty, Ray decides to accept an invitation to travel to Crete with a prominent painter and gay acquaintance, Ralph Brooks. There Ray becomes involved in sex for pay with a young Greek named Marco. Predictably, Ray falls in love. When he proposes to Marco that the pair open a gay guest house together at Xania, Marco declines but responds in words that may—or may not—hold a clue to how Ray can fashion "a new way of living" (220). In the course of the story, Ray experiences a number of oracles that offer an equivocal prospect for establishing relations between subjects different from those that existed before the AIDS epidemic.

One way to describe the sorts of change that Ray needs to undergo is to observe the distinction that Michel Foucault makes between defining male-male sexuality in terms of a hermeneutic of the self, the definition inscribed by sexologists and criminologists in the 1890s, and defining it in relation to erotics, "pleasure and the aesthetics of its use."[8] In spite of the very different sexual paradigms that each brings to the relationship, Ray and Marco begin to fashion an erotics. Translating Ray to Greece permits White to bring to bear the genealogy of sexual relations between men that Foucault began to trace in the final decade of his life.[9] Indirectly, the shift of locales also permits White to address the interrogation of group identities in poststructuralist theory that began to affect gay identity in the United States at the same time that AIDS became a cause of concern. In the 1983 introduction to *States of Desire*, White comments on the solvent effect of both phenomena on established norms of gay identity in the opening years of the decade.

Foucault traces the development in medieval and later culture of what he refers to as "individualizing power"—that is, the power to fashion individuals—in the Church and subsequently in the modern state.[10] In the first volume of the *History of Sexuality*, Foucault argues that the formation of homosexuals has been one effect of the exercise of this power.[11] In contrast, in ancient Greek tradition he finds a technology of the self in relation to male-male sexual practices that is aesthetic rather than confessional in character.[12] Foucault describes "sexual activity and sexual practices . . . problematized through practices of the self, bringing into play the criteria of an 'aesthetics of existence'" (12). In this context, the term "aesthetic" refers to a specific set of practices, especially apt for gay men, that have the potential to be articulated in resistance to an individualizing power whose forcefulness has been exacerbated in the proliferation of discourses around AIDS. Although Foucault specifically rejects the use of Greek solutions as an alternative to current gay existence, he does find pertinent the problematic relation between ethics and an aesthetics of existence in Greek thought. In an interview with Paul Rabinow and Hubert Dreyfus conducted at Berkeley in April 1983, Foucault comments: "You can't find the solution of a problem in the solution of another problem raised at another moment by other people. You see, what I want to do is not the history of solutions, and that's the reason why I don't accept the word *alternative*. I would like to do the genealogy of problems, of *problématiques*."[13] In the later volumes of *The History of Sexuality*, Foucault implicitly reads a Greek aesthetics of existence across the grain of the erotics, especially sadomasochistic, that he encountered in California and elsewhere in North America during visits in the late 1970s and early 1980s.[14] In White's story, Ray's trip to Greece offers an opportunity to make the contrast between these aesthetics explicit.

Ray's Greek destination implies a narrative of return to origin since reconstructions of ancient Greek culture have played a important part in the formation of models of male-male desire in Western culture. Here again, however, a familiar trajectory is put in doubt. The disparity between Ray's preconceived ideas of Greek sexuality and the practices that he finds on Crete provides much of the material of the story. As a crossroads of Mycenaean, Greek, West Asian, and African cultural influences, Crete also subverts notions of "white" superiority based on nineteenth-century identifications of northern Europeans with Dorian Greeks. Ray's sojourn comments unexpectedly on the structure of familiar versus exotic relations on which narratives of sexual tourism depend. Tacitly, the trip likewise comments on the fiction of ethnic quarantine that characterizes

Ray and members of his set in New York City. This fiction provides a defense against acknowledging the vast differences in individual and group opportunities that are cause and effect of de facto segregation along lines of race and class.

Missives

"An Oracle" begins with the following paragraph:

> After George died, Ray went through a long period of uncertainty. George's disease had lasted fifteen months and during that time Ray had stopped seeing most of his old friends. He'd even quarreled with Betty, his best friend. Although she'd sent him little cards from time to time, including the ones made by a fifty-year-old California hippie whom she represented, he hadn't responded. He'd even felt all the more offended that she'd forgotten or ignored how sickening he'd told her he thought the pastel leaves and sappy sentiments were. (207)

These sentences register a concern about the prescribed character of messages that recurs throughout the story. In this case "the pastel leaves and sappy sentiments" of Betty's friendship cards do not really suit the crisis that George and Ray face. There are also lapses in relaying messages. Ray is unable to communicate his irritation in a way that will prompt Betty to change her behavior. There are contingencies that further limit communication: Betty is using cards that are, apparently, her stock in trade. The use of the word "hippie" and the observation that the hippie referred to is middle-aged suggests another limit, an inability to change with time.

These limits are not simply limits to language, identity, or intersubjective relations. They are immediately inscribed within and begin to describe the micropolitics of a mode of gay existence: a couple, one of whom has died as a result of AIDS and the other of whom has yet to accomplish the work of mourning. Betty, the woman who is Ray's "best friend," provides another key element in that micropolitics since the role of the-woman-who-is-a-gay-man's-best-friend is characteristic of gay existence as represented in the story. Betty functions as a link between gay friends and existence outside gay networks. Her presence implies the need for further analysis, not only of the apparent necessity of the role she plays for gay men but also about reciprocity. What support do Ray and Ralph provide *her* and women like her?

Later in the story, the issue of women's mourning comes to the fore when Ray becomes fascinated with an account he reads in Loring M. Danforth's *Death Rituals of Rural Greece* about a Greek mother's loss of her daughter. Because Ray's attempt to draw analogies between this experience and his own ignores cultural differences, his efforts to do so produce incongruous and at times inadvertently humorous results. Nevertheless, his perception of the losses faced by Greek women prompts reflection about his responsibility and that of other gay men to women who mourn. The question is yet more apt since, like gay men in face of AIDS, women who mourn women often find themselves in the position of needing to invent modes of expression, literary genres, and rituals to express the meaning of relationships between women that traditionally have had limited or no possibility of expression.[15]

"An Oracle" implies the need to consider such questions as well as their difficulty. The semi-closeted life of Ray and George as a gay "couple" constitutes an incipient and, to a large degree, blocked social form, for which rituals of mourning are wanting.[16] However satirical White is about a gay lifestyle, one has to bear in mind how radically new gay existence is as a set of openly expressed social formations and that it continues to exist under duress. The very novelty of gay social forms exacerbates the disruption caused by AIDS while also inviting, indeed almost requiring, the existence of oracular utterance, since if there is one constant in gay experience since Stonewall it has been the need to adapt to quickly changing circumstances. Of these, AIDS is only the most recent and the most daunting. In the oracle with which the story ends, the possibilities of misunderstanding and failure, personal and political, are magnified, in part because the words of the oracle, "Take care of yourself," are ones that George often repeated. The oracle raises the possibility of communication with those who have died with AIDS. But in what way can those who have died with AIDS speak to those who have been left behind? Moreover, the oracle is spoken by Marco, in Ray's parlance a "hooker" (246), a term which in its very mischaracterization of the relations between well-to-do tourists and young Greek islanders indicates Ray's insensitivity to evident asymmetries between members of the two groups. The sender and receiver of this message are marked by differences of class, age, sexual and gender identity, language, and nationality. How will Ray receive these familiar words? Will he see that coming from Marco, they must have a different meaning? Or will he regard Marco as simply the narcissistic pretext for delivering a message that Ray in effect already knows and wishes to hear reflected back to him? And does narcissism here belong not only to Ray but also to White and to a reader specified by the text since this Aegean sojourn produces an exotic love already mapped in the imaginary of a Manhattanite?

White underscores the general validity of a critical assessment of Ray's lifestyle by tracing his life from boyhood on a farm in Ohio, to graduate study of Émile Durkheim's concept of anomie at the University of Chicago, to life in a gay commune in Toronto, to adjustment to corporate life in New York. In his efforts to come to terms with the effects of the epidemic, Ray obscurely envisages a need to reacquaint himself with "his old boyhood goals and values" (248). Precisely because his past is so stereotypically an image of the development of middle-class gay ethnicity out of the social movements of the 1960s, the relevance of his need implies a widespread need among gay men in face of AIDS.[17]

Postmarked Greece

The shift to a Greek context provides a number of different social formations in relation to which Ray's sexuality can be interpreted: urban and rural modern Greek, Homeric, classical Athenian, Minoan, Dorian, and Hellenistic. Ray's ignorance about AIDS (for instance, his belief that the penetrator in anal intercourse is not at risk), though understandable in the early 1980s, leaves him just as ignorant of crucial matters as the Greek villagers described in *The Death Rituals of Rural Greece*. Moreover, Ray and George's experiment in a durable but nonmonogamous relationship entails a cultivated lack of awareness that veils anxieties about gender inversion no less intense than those Foucault detected in classical Greek culture or that Ray finds on arriving in Crete (*Use of Pleasure*, 18–20). As George's "doll" (218), Ray has been a kind of "hooker," reduced in status to the level of a high-priced commodity-object ("George saw him obviously as a sort of superior home entertainment centre," 216). Within the couple, Ray is loving, loyal, and patient but also alienated, seeing himself as "impersonating George's lover" (218). White associates the relationship with Ray's loss of direction and with an ignorance on the part of George that has the advantage of helping him pass for straight in the upper echelons of corporate America but affords no gains in awareness even when George faces illness and death. George's opacity is especially marked in the phrase, "You must look out for yourself," a leitmotif repeated with ever-varying meaning in the story and becoming, at last, the equivocal oracle of the story's title. George keeps using it to tell Ray he needs a job (that is, a "well-paying" job, 211). And before he dies George finds for Ray "a gig" in public relations for Amalgamated Anodynes, an irresponsible corporation that "produced a fabric for children's wear that had turned out to be flammable" (212). George himself specializes in high-priced face-lifts for corporations. White's satire of the illusion and misinformation that George and Ray produce reflects their complicity in a late capitalist "we" contoured along lines of race, gender, nationality, and class.

When Ray, before leaving for Greece, gives the cat Anna into Betty's keeping, he thinks of George's injunction: "'You must look out for yourself,' George had said, and now he was trying" (221). In Marco, Ray seeks first intimacy and, second, a chance to regain a sense of self. But the cash-nexus of the relationship enacts and parodies relations of exchange within the corporate economy and in Ray's earlier life with George. Ray's pleasurable, semiguilty fantasies about sex with Marco show that he is aware that asymmetries in the relationship do not tell in Ray's favor: "He whose conscience years of political struggle had raised now sank into the delicious guilt of Anglo fag servicing Mexican worker, of cowboy face-fucked by Indian brave, of lost tourist waylaid by wily camel boy" (239). Near the end of his stay, Ray reflects:

> When he'd first arrived in Crete he'd had the vague feeling that this holiday was merely a detour and that when he rejoined his path George would be waiting for him. George or thoughts of George or the life George had custom-built for him, he wasn't quite sure which he meant. And yet now there was a real possibility that he might escape, start something new or transpose his old boyhood goals and values into a new key, the Dorian mode, say. Everything here seemed to be conspiring to reorient him, repatriate him, even the way he'd become in Greece the pursuer rather than the pursued. (247–248)

This anticipated repatriation is ironic since the patterns of sexual relation in ancient Greece indicate by contrast how unsatisfactory life with George has been. He will not be permitted to remain. Instead, he is told: "Do not rest here. You must go" (250).

In *The Use of Pleasure*, Foucault observes how the "use of the pleasures" was codified in classical Greece to produce an "individual" who is "an ethical subject of sexual conduct" (32). Foucault identifies "four great axes of experience" as relevant to this process. One of these, *dietetics*, refers to one's relation to one's body. This set of practices constitutes "a form of moderation defined by the measured and timely use of the *aphrodisia*." The second axis, termed *economics*, refers to marriage and is "a form of moderation defined not by the mutual faithfulness of marriage partners, but by a certain privilege, which the husband upholds on behalf of the lawful wife over whom he exercises his authority." The third axis, *erotics*, refers to moderation in sexual relations between men and boys. The fourth axis refers to meditation on properly philosophic issues that arise for Plato in response to "the love of boys" (*The Use of Pleasure*, 251, 252). Ray's "use of the pleasures" appears to parody the classical model. He has translated dietetics into "years of [weight] training" that "had in point of absolute fact turned him into a physical commodity" (216).

"Marriage" to George installed a "hierarchical structure," to use Foucault's phrase (*The Use of Pleasure*, 252) in which Ray was left permanently in the role of "the looker with the brain, exactly like the starlet whom the studio hypes wearing a mortarboard and specs above her adorable snub nose and bikini" (218).

Foucault's remarks about the third axis are in marked contrast to aspects of the Ray-Marco relationship. The ethics of erotics between a male adult and an adolescent in the ancient model excluded the exchange of money (*The Use of Pleasure*, 217–219). The relationship between an older and a younger man respects "a fleeting time that leads ineluctably to an end that is near." As well, it "carries with it the ideal," if not the literal reality, "of a renunciation of all physical relations with boys." The moral efficacy of the connection depends on "the respect that is owing to the virility of the adolescent and to his future status as a free man. It is no longer simply the problem of a man's becoming the master of his pleasure; it is a problem of knowing how one can make allowance for the other's freedom in the mastery that one exercises over oneself and in the true love that one bears for him." This "problem" is precisely Ray's at the end of the story. He has yet to think through the ethical implications of age difference in his relationship with Marco although the "black and shiny" evidence of Marco's moustache, the "first hair sprouting" on his chest, place him at the threshold of male love as understood in ancient Greece (see *The Use of Pleasure*, 252, 243).

In addition to the classic model of pederastic love, other patterns of male-male intimacy are intimated by Ray's trip to Xania. One is the pattern of sexual and emotional ties between men that existed in preclassical Crete. Gay activists have exploited the cult of the Cretan bull-god and the mother goddess in Minoan culture in order to associate love between men with feminism in an alliance against patriarchy.[18] Ray affiliates Marco with this culture when he compares him with "the slim-waisted matador" (249) found in Minoan painting.[19] Yet the murals at Knossos, rediscovered in the twentieth century by the English anthropologist, Sir Arthur Evans, have been "absurdly over-restored" (235). This fact serves as a reminder that processes of colonization and tourism make impossible any exclusive affinity between Marco and his antecedents. Through his love of Marco, Ray is affiliated with the ethos of preclassical civilization in Crete. But countertendencies also abound. For one, when Ray invokes "the Dorian mode," he associates himself with the culture of the Dorians, a group of Greek invaders who overran Crete.[20] First there and later in the Peloponnesus, the Dorians developed a model of pederastic relationship that became central to the formation of the soldier/citizen of Sparta. This form of pederasty helped them maintain their dominance over subject populations. White uses geographical references to associate Ray and Marco with the roles of colonizer and colonized in history. Ray, who lives on one island, Manhattan, travels to another island, Crete. White dots the story with the traces of past conquests: for example, the Turkish minaret, located on an island in Xania.[21] Ray and Ralph rent "a Venetian palace" (221), a monument to four centuries of rule by the island city. Ray is also associated with imperial Rome during the Hellenistic period: "His body had acquired a certain thickness, as though the original Greek statue had been copied by a Roman" (224).

If Ray is, as I have suggested, associated with Minoan as well as Dorian and other imperial cultures, so is Marco, whose Italian name connotes the ascendancy of "the Venetian lion [of San Marco] . . . emblazoned" on the walls of Xania (227). By further associating Marco with figures of lions and cats, White draws on Minoan and Venetian referents of Marco's virility. "Marco in his white Keds and Levi jacket came treading stealthily around the corner, noble and balanced as a lion; he winked his approval and Ray felt his own pleasure spread over his whole body like the heat of the sun" (244). These lion images imply a process of revirilization in the Ray-Marco nexus that carries negative connotations but is also validated. The images, moreover, are associated with affectionate intimacy: Marco's "ass" is "hairy with nice friendly fuzz" (240). Moreover, the lion can be associated not with Western dominance but with crisscrossing exchanges between Crete, Egypt, and black Africa. The lion, "borrowed from the Egyptian word for a lion-statue, *rw*, vocalized as *re-wo*, already attested as a man's name in the Linear B tablets of Knossos in Crete, [is] our first 'European' Leon."[22] No single framing, West/Oriental, North/South, contains the significations of this figure.

White uses reference to a lion to register yet one other form of affiliation between men, this time in Homeric Greece. Sitting on a beach reading the *Odyssey*, Ray is moved to tears by the laments of "lion-hearted Achilles" (226) over the death of Patroclus. David Halperin has argued that the representation of this friendship in Homer celebrates a nonsexualized model of pair-bonding between male heroes.[23] The reference to Achilles, then, is a reminder of yet further diversity in the Greek imagination of male romance. Failing to recognize the cultural distance between his relationship and Achilles', Ray imagines Achilles' loss of Patroclus in terms of his own loss of George. Yet this distorting assimilation of heroic friendship to gay partnership is countered by an experience that issues in what might be characterized as a second or minor oracle in the story. The unexpected appearance on the beach of an old herdsman and his sheep prompts Ray to see his "grief" in a new light, "as a costly gewgaw, beyond the means of the grievously hungry and hard-working world" (226) of the shepherd. Recognizing someone else's condition enables Ray to look at his own experience differently. This double recognition, moreover, raises a further possibility: "Maybe it was precisely his grief that joined him to this peasant" (226). I call this moment oracular because for the first time Ray's identity is altered by recognizing someone else's difference.

Home Truths

This discovery invites further reflection on how "the tone of another" can "interrupt a familiar music" and thereby disrupt "the self-identity" of the listener. White brings this concern reflexively into the text by incorporating a number of passages from Danforth's book, a study of the rites of exhumation that form part of the process of mourning in northern Greece. At the start of his book, Danforth tells the story of Irini, whose twenty-year-old daughter Eleni died in August 1974 in a hit-and-run accident in Thessaloniki. Eleni was a bright, attractive young woman whose parents had sent her from home at the age of twelve so she could attend high school and prepare for work as an elementary-school teacher. She was killed one month before taking up her first post.[24] When Ray decides to accept an offer of a vacation in Greece, he is drawn in part by her story. "It would be all new—new place, new language, no ghosts. He even liked going to the country where people expressed their grief over dying so honestly, so passionately. In that book he liked the way a mother, when she exhumed her daughter's body after three years of burial, said, 'Look what I put in and look what I took out! I put in a partridge, and I took out bones'" (221).[25] Ray's interest in Irini's grief suggests questions about alterity. Do subjects—and discourses—permit the expression of difference in ways that alter those subjects and discourses? Or are such expressions always recuperated in a binary structure of signification in which the meaning of one term is subordinated to the meaning of the other?

White is familiar with such questions not only from his reading in poststructuralist theory but also from the consideration that Danforth gives them in the introduction of the book.[26] Danforth describes the goal of humanist anthropology as one of reducing "the distance between the anthropologist and the Other," of bridging "the gap between 'us' and 'them.'" He contends that "an investigation of the Other involves an exploration of the Self as well. The central problem of anthropology is thus, in Paul Ricoeur's words, 'the comprehension of the self by the detour of the comprehension of the other.' The anthropologist sets out to investigate the Other, only to find the Other in himself and himself in the Other. For the anthropology of death, this means that the study of 'how others die' becomes the study of 'how we die.' We must come to see in the deaths of Others our own deaths as well."[27] In this passage, eloquent though it is, "Others" tends to become a transparent overlay of "we." Danforth misses a key step necessary if ethnographic study is to increase self-knowledge, namely, the analysis of the investments that the ethnographer brings to his object of study. Ethnography progresses not by finding "us" in the "Other" (and vice-versa) but by analyzing the ethnographer's "own social self as it engages in the observation of others."[28]

Ray's attraction to Danforth's book arises in part from the emotional deprivations of his sometimes closeted existence. (He cannot, for instance, let his boss, Helen, know about George's death.) Ray's response to the situation of the Greek women is complicated by the fact that as a gay man living in New York City, he too is in some contexts not one of the "we" but rather an "Other." Since the advent of AIDS, the tendency of gay men to be regarded as sources of contagion has exacerbated their alienation. Although Ray sometimes passes as a straight upper-middle-class WASP, his sexual difference means that in part he approaches Greece as an Other approaching an Other. His subordination within hegemonic masculinity and in relation to George intensifies his identification with the widows in Danforth's book. Danforth describes the women as experiencing a crisis of identity when they lose the male through whom their status in the village has been secured.[29]

Ray shifts with considerable confusion between the positions of "we" and Other. In "An Oracle," the term gay provides a touchstone of individual and ethnic identity; but the continual variation of nominatives for subjects of male-male desire indicates continual oscillation in the significance of being such a subject. This variation amplifies once Ray is in a society where the political structure of desire between men differs from that of his own. Gay men are referred to as muscle queens, "lovers," pooves, boys, "the Stonewall generation," pick-ups, *poosti*, dirty old men, "girls," *putana*, transvestites, and faggots. This proliferation of terms indicates that *gay* refers to a subject whose meaning is continually shifting under the pressure of varying knowledge (and ignorance).

In Xania, Ray relies on a frequent visitor from the United States, a sixty-year-old Classics professor named Homer, to explain to him the construction of sexuality that permits Greek men to engage in sex for pay as long as they take the active role but that licenses a shepherd to murder a son whom he learns "was getting fucked" (244). Homer acts as a gay ethnographer who understands the differences between sexuality at home and in Greek bar culture. Moreover, he understands the compatibility of sexuality at Xania with his own sexual ritual—namely, photographing the "locals" (229) in the nude. As his name wryly suggests, Homer, whose modern Greek is patched together from an expert knowledge of ancient Greek, respects the differences between modern and ancient Greek male-male sexual practices; he is also likely aware that his hobby is imbricated in a specifically gay tradition.[30] Of the characters in the story, he is the one most capable of understanding male-male sexual differences across time and space.

Barbara Godard has pointed out that translation effects are graphic traces of linguistic meaning that remind readers that they are reading a text through the lenses of a language other than that in which the text was written earlier.[31] Translation effects are visible signs of differences in meaning that depend on differences in language. In "An Oracle," White both acknowledges and denies linguistic differences in ways that culminate in the open semantic structure with which the story ends. When Ray first meets Marco, it is Marco who initiates verbal exchange: "'Ya,' he said, that short form of *Yassou*, the all-purpose greeting" (235).[32] It is possible to hear this word as *yeah*, yes, that is, as an utterance with which the Cretan elects the Manhattanite for a possible intimacy. Intimacy may occur, however, only if Marco can prevent Ray from sentimentally misconstruing what is about to happen. "What you want?" Marco asks, "and his faint smile suggested he already knew and that Ray's desire was disgusting and entirely practicable" (235). Ray's answer, "You," [Ya, You] strikes a false note because it is a pretext. What he wants at this moment is not "you" but sex.

In response, Marco "frowned angrily." Ray reads the gesture: "'Sex,' Ray said, and this time the boy nodded. 'But money!' he threatened, rubbing his thumb and forefinger together." The narrator surmises that Marco's reaction occurs because the fact that "the word [you] apparently was not one of the boy's dozen English words." Marco immediately continues: "I fuck you!" (235). He does know the word "you" in the sense of sexual object and insists on specifying the difference between sentimental rhetoric and exchange value. This difference is crucial for Marco since in his sexual culture being the fucker validates his masculinity even when he is fucking another man. Marco's assertion demystifies Ray's position at the same time that it glances at a subtext of appropriation that surfaces at the end of the story. The performative, "I fuck you," also undermines the knowingness of the narrator, who momentarily believes, as does Ray, that Marco does not know what the word "you" means.

By the end of the story, Ray has fallen in love with Marco, a condition not likely to give rise to improved cognition. Paul de Man has remarked that "'Love' is a figure that disfigures, a metaphor that confers the illusion of proper meaning to a suspended, open semantic structure."[33] Ray's delusion takes the shape of the fantasy of buying a house in Xania, turning it into a guest house, and living there with the younger man. He finds a gay Greek journalist who agrees to translate this proposal into a letter for Marco. The expedient seems to overcome the possibility of translation effects: Ray's meaning will be transparent to Marco because the translator is both gay *and* Greek. Along with the letter, however, Ray sends the gift of a "gold necklace . . . , the sort of sleazy bauble all the kids here were wearing" (249). It prompts semantic interference. "Kids" is condescending; and the phrase "sleazy bauble" itself, whether the narrator's or Ray's in indirect discourse, undercuts Ray's stated intentions. Is Ray attempting to buy a sleazy bauble? And is it possible for him to go "Greek" or for Marco to be gay in Xania?

For his part, Marco reads the letter silently, pauses, then returns the gift unopened. After a long silence, he says in English: "I know you love me and I love you. But Xania is no good for you. Too small. Do not rest here. You must go." (250). In the sentence, Marco uses English with a difference of intonation: "I know you love me," he says; and he does know what Ray intends. Ray's letter, written in the same grammar of possession in which George had spoken, proposes a future in which his relation with Marco will mirror the 'marriage' whose ending has left Ray adrift. Although Marco rejects this grammar, he continues by responding, "and I love you." He uses the predicate with another intonation. Love in this register demystifies Marco's earlier defensive positioning of himself within Greek conventions of sexual exchange while simultaneously suspending the chain of substitutions (George-Ray, Ray-Marco) in which Ray is caught. The "kid" enjoins Ray to depart from Greece, to return elsewhere. But the return will also be a departure from the life spent "impersonating George's lover" (218) in which Ray is still enmeshed.

The possibility of speaking love in a different intonation opens the semantic structure for Ray and Marco both. Even in this moment, negation is possible since the best known apothegm about Crete is Epimenides' maxim: "All Cretans are liars." The point of the maxim is not to vilify Cretans but to say something about the limits of linguistic reference. Since Epimenides himself was a Cretan, the sentence creates doubts about the claim of the subject to speak the truth. The statement "disproves its own validity, and thus cannot be relied upon as a model of sincerity, authenticity—or even of deconstructive strategy."[34] Both the meaning and the truth of Marco's statement ("I love you") remain open to question.

Within this context of radical uncertainty, the final oracular utterance of the story occurs. Marco says to Ray: "You must look out for yourself." The imperative echoes the maxim, "Know thyself," which has become a synonym for the Platonic/Christian hermeneutic of the self. But "Know thyself" pertains earlier to the inscription on the temple of Apollo at Delphi, where, according to Hellenistic accounts, the priestess of Apollo/ Dionysus uttered oracles as vapor rose from the floor of the temple. In *Oedipus Rex*, the oracle speaks to the inhabitants of Thebes, which was, as New York is, a "plagued city" (266).

Marco then leaves, and Ray is transported: "Ray felt blown back in a wind-tunnel of grief and joy. He felt his hair streaming, his face pressed back, the fabric of his pants fluttering. In pop-song phrases he thought 'this guy' had walked out on him, done him wrong, broken his heart—a heart he was happy to feel thumping again with sharp, wounded life. He was blown back on to the bed and he smiled and cried as he'd never yet allowed himself to cry over George, who'd just spoken to him through the least likely oracle" (250). Even at the moment of oracle, Ray's thinking does not escape the clichéd lyrics of popular song.[35] He continues to speak in an already given language. Yet, in challenging Ray's narrative, Marco has opened the possibility of other trajectories, including the possibility for Ray to hear George differently. To return to the terms of Danforth's analysis of Greek ritual, the "liminal period" of mourning issues in a "conversation" in which Ray's body speaks with sobs, and George speaks by way of an echo.[36]

In rural Greece, the exhumation of the bones of the dead confirms the mortality of the deceased while marking the return of the bereaved to the community. With this recognition, mourners are received back into the everyday life of the village—to the celebrations of rites of passage, to the bickering, to the struggles over property and sustenance. In Ray's case, the equivocal character of the oracle leaves suspended the possibility of such a return. He invokes songs expressing the position of the wronged woman, neither the same as his nor decisively different. And the return to community remains outside the frame of the story as do the referents of community, which appear no longer to exist back in Manhattan. During George's illness, Ray and George had "chased away their friends" (208). And now that Ray suspects that he is HIV-positive, the customary sexual routes to intimacy are closed. Looking back to his youth and forward to the prospect of untimely illness and death, Ray sees no obvious route into social existence.

The one possibility that White proposes is that Ray may turn to his long neglected interest in writing. In contrast to the abuse of Ray's intelligence in "public relations" (211), the erotics of the Marco-Ray relation is productive: Ray thinks of Marco as a "co-worker," of "the high seriousness of the work they did together every night" (243). The development of relationship at the site of erotics leads to reflection, contemplation (another meaning of apocalypse), and writing.[37] If Ray must leave, as in Foucault's model of Greek love, to permit Marco's coming of age, perhaps he must write to bring about his own.

White's purpose in "An Oracle" is to remind his readers that sexual practices have been at the heart of the struggle for gay identity: "It is our sexuality that is contested, not the color of our hair. To build a political identity around this is therefore no mean feat."[38] His phrasing echoes a line in a poem by A. E. Housman in which Housman refers to a man who is being imprisoned "for the colour of his hair." The poem, "Oh who is that young sinner with the handcuffs on his wrist?" was occasioned by the Wilde trials in 1895.[39] In recalling this occasion, White also recalls that homosexual identity is built directly in relation to homophobic oppression.

Before the advent of AIDS, White was in a position to speak as the representative of a consolidated gay community. In 1980, he could look back on the Stonewall riots, which he witnessed in 1969 and speak in the first person plural.[40] The onset of AIDS has made that harder, and those who do so usually find themselves on the defensive. Moreover, the professionalization of voluntary organizations that had rapidly taken shape among gay men in response to AIDS was already well under way when White wrote "An Oracle" in 1986. The bitter reaction against the neglect of minority and other marginal gay groups in mainstream gay philanthropy was also evident.[41] In interviews and on panels, White still speaks in the "we" as he does not in this story. On a panel at a book fair in Miami in November 1989, White spoke of how it came about that he and a British writer, Adams Mars-Jones, decided to collaborate on a book of AIDS short stories, White remarks: "We thought that fiction was the best medium for communicating what it was like actually to be living through these experiences as an insider. We were seeing so many programs on television where experts were discussing our problem as a medical phenomenon, even as a social phenomenon, but always from the outside. What was being lost sight of was that actual human beings were suffering, watching their lives crumble, and having to confront very deep fears."[42] Probably more than White recognized at the time, this comment indicates how representative gays and the gay first-person-plural pronoun continue to be constructed as objects of the gaze of outside "experts." The pertinent point is not that "we" are "actual human beings" as White says, attempting to reverse the rhetoric that defines "being-human" by excluding homosexuals. Rather, the point is that "we" continue to be "insiders" in the sense that word is used colloquially to refer to prisoners.[43]

The fact that escape is no easier for White and others like him than it is for Ray makes all the more significant the production of stories like "An Oracle," of which White also says: "Fiction becomes a kind of monument that one can raise to what we've actually lived through. It's also, of course, a way of communicating the most subtle, the least easily disciplined or programmatic feelings, all those little thoughts and half-thoughts that flicker through your mind, thoughts that may not be politically correct, that aren't what people want you to say or think but are in fact what you really do think."[44]

In the passage, White slips into middle voice, referring to a "you" that is both himself and possibly his reader. In the 1983 introduction to *States of Desire*, White reaffirms the view he put forward in the first edition of 1980 that "gay men . . . will eventually lead us to a proper sense of sex as a pleasure or a kind of communication, as opposed to the current doctrine of sex as transcendence, of sex as the ultimate meaning of experience."[45] White then cites the publication, nearly simultaneous with the first edition, of Foucault's view that "one should aim instead at a desexualization, at a general economy of pleasure not based on sexual norms."[46] This hope motivates White's emphasis in "An Oracle" and validates his and Foucault's emphasis not on sexual truth but on erotics.

White is interested in the possibility that around erotics gay men may devise new modes of sociality. By the end of the story, the oracle, "Take care of yourself," has been translated from its late capitalist meanings (look out for number one; get a good job) into a number of traditions of desire between men in Greece. In context, the most important of these is the Foucauldian model in which what mattered was "the use of pleasure" in "the care of the self." The subject stood in relation to sexual practices in a moral-aesthetic reflection that became a way of relating to self and others. Foucault observes that reflection and existence were often at odds in Athenian pederasty. But the effort to bring both terms into alignment enabled a sense of self among male lovers. White's double glance, backward as well as forward, in face of bereavement reminds gay men, in particular, of the need to continue this work.

8

•••

TRADITION AND APOCALYPSE IN ALAN HOLLINGHURST'S *THE SWIMMING-POOL LIBRARY*

The "end" that dominates *The Swimming-Pool Library* is the advent of AIDS. The primary narrator of Hollinghurst's novel acknowledges this moment in gay existence when he refers to the novel's temporal setting as "that summer, the last summer of its kind there was ever to be."[1] Although the catastrophic end of this existence is never named, it is everywhere implied, inflecting homosexual and gay signifiers with supplementary meaning. And because the novel is written after that end has already occurred, the book, though written in the midst of an epidemic whose end is not yet in sight, is posteschatological.

The absence of the word "AIDS" signifies the traumatic structure of the history that the novel adumbrates. Cathy Caruth argues that trauma provides a way for individual or collective subjects to reclaim as history "an overwhelming experience of sudden, or catastrophic events."[2] But such a history is necessarily constituted on the basis of loss since it is a defining characteristic of trauma that a crucial portion of memory continues to escape consciousness. The absence of explicit reference to AIDS is part of the history that Hollinghurst represents. For most of its duration, a second set of events is also missing—an account of the prosecution of upper-middle-class and aristocratic homosexuals in London during the early 1950s. In particular, Will Beckwith, the young gay flaneur and rentier who is the novel's principal narrator, is unaware that the privileges that enable his sexual gourmandise have been purchased by the avidity with which his grandfather, Lord Beckwith, persecuted homosexuals in the 1950s. Insofar as one novelistic code is concerned with the disclosure of moral truth,[3] the truth that Beckwith eventually learns is that of his implication in this shameful past, a past of which his family, friends, and associates have carefully kept him ignorant. Lord Nantwich intervenes to make this past accessible to Beckwith, but he does so ambiguously. At the end of the novel, Beckwith is trying to secure photographs that disclose that the undercover policeman who arrested his friend James Brooke is an agent provocateur. But Nantwich may be partially responsible for the disappearance of the incriminating evidence. This loose end suggests that the gaps in historical understanding can never be fully closed and that new gaps will continue to open. Or, in other words, although one mode of gay existence may end and another begin, the structure of collective history continues to be characterized by trauma.

Hollinghurst's novel takes the form of a postmodernist metafiction. Undertaking a literary project more or less by accident, Beckwith begins in a desultory way to prepare to write the biography of Charles Nantwich. Lord Nantwich is an old queen, a former colonial hand who swims at Beckwith's club. Beckwith meets him after administering "the kiss of life" when Nantwich passes out while "cottaging" in a public lavatory at Kensington Gardens. The journals and other materials that Nantwich gives Beckwith provide a fragmentary secondary narrative that Hollinghurst interleaves through the framing story as Beckwith reads them. In this way, Beckwith functions as a hermeneutic figure of the process of "reading" gay history. In the relation between the texts of these two "I"s, the problematics of being gay, white, and privileged in Great Britain in the twentieth century become evident. But, as will also become evident, the hermeneutic process lacks a ground which the process of interpretation can be completed.

The sense of imminent apocalypse floats across other ways of organizing time in the novel. The time that Will narrativizes as "sheer crammed, single-minded repetition" (7–8) may also be construed as the *saeculum* of apocalypse, undifferentiated time whose very profanity signals the proximity of transformed time, the "faint flicker of calamity, like flames around a photograph, something seen out of the corner of the eye" (6). One effect of approaching catastrophe is to convert much of Will's memoir into a retrospective apocalypse of gay bliss. This effect is analogous with the widespread tendency in contemporary gay existence to project back onto the period between Stonewall and AIDS a myth of sexual and social plenitude that depends for its believability on the contrast between gay visibility in the 1970s and the isolation, anger, and grief of the following years.

The ominous golden body that Beckwith at one moment imagines signifies both Ends: "The steady rumble of far-off traffic, the thinning haze, the suited people hurrying past, all seemed invitations to some wearying and majestic happening. I almost seemed to see, above the houses across the street, an immense golden athlete stretching into the sky like the drop-curtain of a ballet or a gigantic banner at a Soviet rally, full of appalling promise. It was a relief to go indoors" (249). The "immense golden athlete" carries reminders of the blond American actors in the porno flicks that Beckwith sees at the Brutus Cinema, images that suggest the further "image of a new society we had made, where every desire could find its gratification" (60). Yet the passage (ironically enough, one of the few that identifies Will as a member of a gay "we") also suggests that the golden body is a phantasm articulated in a number of different scenarios—economic, aesthetic, and political—in which Beckwith is participant and observer.

Some of these narratives are fixed in the form of traditions, including ones that organize relations among men of different races over time so that not only sexual history but other histories, the history of African diaspora, for instance, begin to come visible through repeated instants in the book. The pattern of homoerotic patronage and loyalty between white master and black attendant is observed in the eighteenth-century portrait of a former slave which Will sees in Nantwich's drawing room. Brought to England from Virginia by an English general after the War of Independence, Bill Richmond became a boxer and a valet. There's the story of Makepeace, the young Trinidadian sailor who stayed behind after missing his ship in London during World War II. He is picked up in the National Gallery by a gay painter and drawn into a homosexual network where he is passed from friend to friend. And there are also the stories of Nantwich and his manservant and his manservant's son, Abdul. Lugubriously, Nantwich says to Will: "All my true friends were black" (284).

In contrast to repetitive time and apocalypse, there is also time turned into self-story in what Will refers to as "the 'romance of myself'" (8). The transparency of this fiction is indicated by the single quotation marks in which Will sets the phrase. Nantwich too is a romancer in the dream in which he relives his days in Africa. The romance of the self overlaps the "enigmatic path" (281) that men with power can lay out for themselves and others. Nantwich is "a fixer and favouritiser" (287) both in the aboveground world of Parliament and boys' clubs and in the world of homosexual secrets, coding, and conspiracy that is produced by the criminalization of sex between men. Lord Beckwith is another "fixer and favouritiser." Both manipulate Will, who already at the start of the novel finds himself manipulating and being manipulated by Arthur, who flees to him for help after knifing a drug dealer. At the end, Will seems about to embark on his own course of fixing things as, ominously, he resolves to "get" James's betrayer (336). The negative effects of either romancing or emplotting time reflect back on textual operations. Hollinghurst's novel, with its carefully prepared mysteries and disclosures, is another example of characters, narratives, and meanings fixed in place with authorial skill. Should the reader be any less skeptical of Hollinghurst's plotting than of Bill's, Nantwich's, Will's, or Lord Beckwith's? And yet, by slight displacements in the many references to a homosexual and gay past in London, Hollinghurst unfixes memory from any single casting of time.

Apocalypse, like other constructions of time, can be a consciousness effect produced by institutional factors—as in the "notebooks of visions and apocalypses" (291) that "Barmy" Barnes writes while he is in prison. Nantwich, who stubbornly refuses to write under those circumstances, composes his prison journal only after he is released Ronald Staines makes camp fun of this effect in his exhibition of photographs of young male nudes posing as Christian martyrs or "crossed and half-obscured by the shadows of prison bars" (270). Nonetheless, apocalyptic time, like the drifting banner, evades traditions, conspiracies, and the determinate meanings of narrative and genre. Apocalyptic pattern moves Hollinghurst and his readers beyond the limits of careful construction, beyond the limits too of the exploitation of apocalyptic rhetoric in mass media coverage of the "gay plague."[4]

Another kind of time in the novel is bodily time, the time it takes to shape the body at the gym, the time in which scars occur, both those that Will sees on Abdul's body at Staines's studio and the metaphorical ones inflicted on Nantwich by his time in prison. Or the changes to the body and the mind incurred in face of sexual isolation as by James. There is the time too of human mortality, of the collapse, quick or protracted, of bodily functions, that Hollinghurst represents in Nantwich's old age. This time is a sort of bass line against which other times are played.

Whose Memoirs Are These?

Will/Willy/willie/will/will he? is the unthinking beneficiary of a struggle that goes back at least as far as the late eighteenth century to decriminalize the very sexual pleasures he pursues. In ways that surprise him, he learns a good deal about that struggle before he finishes reading Nantwich's papers. In addition, the materials that Nantwich entrusts to him contain information that traces through a single lifetime the pattern of public service in which "earnest" (207) young men sexually and emotionally attracted to other men traditionally sublimated their desires. Nantwich thinks that the men who chose colonial officers for the Sudan had a shrewd awareness that young homosexuals might prove to be especially useful: "On the gay thing, they were completely untroubled—even to the extent of having a slight preference for it, in my opinion. Quite unlike all this modern nonsense about how we're security risks and what-have-you. They had the wit to see that we were prone to immense idealism and dedication" (282).

Through the use of modified repetition, Hollinghurst attempts to span the periods of persecution by emphasizing sense-making, solidarity-building traditions, traditions that are as persistent as they are socially and psychologically inadequate. When Beckwith reads Nantwich's memoir of his school days at Winchester, written while serving as a district commissioner in the Sudan during the 1920s, he finds that Nantwich did not separate his recognition of himself as a subject of male-male desire from his induction as a schoolboy into sociopsychological patterns of personal mastery and dependence among his fellows, an induction that bonded him into the male homosocial world of Britain's future leaders while setting the paradigm of the relationship of trust that he attempted to recreate with Taha, his personal attendant and closest subordinate in Africa. That Beckwith recognizes similar mores in his own schooling at Winchester and Oxford during the 1970s provides Hollinghurst with a way of suggesting that the patterns of power and desire in public school and at Oxbridge at the beginning of the century continue to this day despite legislative and cultural changes.

The temporal reach of the novel extends even earlier than 1900, since Nantwich thinks that "the 1880s must have been an ideal time, with brothels full of off-duty soldiers, and luscious young dukes chasing after barrow-boys" (289).[5] Yet that decade was also the decade of the Berlin Conference, of the massacre of General Gordon and the Egyptian garrison at Khartoum, and the start of the Scramble for Africa. The dependence of the Sudanese economy on slave labor prior to the British takeover corroborates Nantwich's belief in the ethical project of late Victorian imperialism (239).[6] His career links the Victorians of the 1880s with aspects of contemporary life in England, including the changing demographics that accompanied immigration from Commonwealth countries in the 1950s and later. The immigration of blacks to England provides an additional frame for Hollinghurst's tale of Beckwith's sexual exploits and mishaps. Both he and Nantwich are sexually fixated on black men.

Nantwich's life, however, took a turn that holds a big surprise for Beckwith. The tradition of homosocial clubability in which Nantwich was nurtured is ruptured after his return to England. Entrapped by police in a London "cottage" in 1954, he is tried, found guilty, and sent to prison for six months. This experience forces him into yet another tradition, the Wildean tradition of the homosexual as the criminal, outcast Other of the homosocial/homosexual milieu in which Nantwich has previously lived. In this way, Nantwich's homosexual identification becomes yet further specified, though in terms forced on him from without. After Beckwith saves his life, Nantwich asks him to write his biography. The story that he wants told is the process of induction, exclusion, and resistance that I have just sketched.

If Beckwith were to write the story, a particular truth would be produced: Nantwich would be translated into a typical character in the way in which Georg Lukács used the term to refer to characterization in the realist novel as the "living human embodiment" of "historical-social types." For Lukács, writing in exile in Russia in the winter of 1936–1937, types were defined primarily in terms of class. He contends that in such characterizations "great historical trends" of the development of capitalism "become tangible."[7] More modestly, by representing Nantwich as a sexual type, Beckwith will be able to discover and write the history of how men of Nantwich's station and generation came to be differentiated and to differentiate themselves as homosexual. In the end, though, Will cannot write this book. His text explains why another text—the book of gay history written in terms of the formation of identity—cannot be written. The combination of his journal with Nantwich's records describes a set of textual limits within which such an exploration can be carried on. But because neither of the narrating personas can find a vantage point external to these limits, the project can never be completed. Personal identity remains incomplete because it is always implicated in someone else's identity, and someone else's identity is always implicated in a variety of discursive practices, including the operations of the legal system.

Representation of Nantwich is bound to be ambivalent since he is both privileged and victimized, both generous and hard working and compromised by the erotic implications of his interest in his charges, including Taha, whom he idolizes and whom he takes back to England with him after his period abroad. Nantwich's penchant for interfering in the lives of his subordinates, what Beckwith refers to as "the Nantwich feudal system" (159), results in tragedy when Taha is beaten to death "by a gang of youths" in "an act of racial hatred and ignorance" (302) while Nantwich is in prison. Later, Nantwich arranges for the man's son, Abdul, to be hired as chef at his club; still later, he involves him and the young waiters in pornographic filmmaking. This path of metonymic reduction (of love and dedication to prurience) mimics Nantwich's account of the experience of arriving at Port Said. There he first admires a smiling black boy in a store, "a pure Negro, from far south evidently, like the people we are going to, quite different from the crossbred scamps who haunt the quays" (211). Next, he watches admiringly from a tea terrace as Egyptian stevedores load coal onto a ship. "A handsome young man," noticing the "pleasure & fascination evident perhaps in my gaze" (213), approaches Nantwich with postcards of local sights in a valise, then, immediately before leaving him, flashes "from inside his robe, from somewhere mysterious about his person, a hand of postcards which he quickly fanned & as quickly swept together again and & covered. . . . I was keenly dismayed, humiliated, feeling that he had read me like a book & I, in the glimpse I caught of naked poses—all male, young boys, fantastically proportioned adults, sepia faces smiling, winking—had confusedly admitted as much" (214). The flash exposes Nantwich's specifically sexual interest in subaltern subjects. What is humiliating is to be readable as a subject of low desires.

The narrative whereby Nantwich becomes homosexual comes to Will in "private bits and pieces" (253) together with blanks—Nantwich has a habit of "'blanking' as he called it" (281) in the midst of conversations, sometimes spontaneously, sometimes because he is reserving information. Will has to fill in the blanks as well as put the pieces together. As he does so, he learns that Nantwich's biography and his own intersect. This discovery changes the project from a historicist one to one about the relation between the two narrating personas. The process becomes most dramatic near the end of the novel when Nantwich gives Will a final document. In it, Will learns that his grandfather, Denis Beckwith, was responsible for Nantwich's prosecution. This moment fills in for Will not only a gap in his personal history but also a "blind spot" (326) in his awareness of the history of gay existence in England.

Beckwith is able to enjoy a measure of sexual freedom as a result of the passage of the Sexual Offences Act in 1967. Reprising the events of the 1950s helps Beckwith become aware of how recent and limited the decriminalizination of sex between men in England has been. In point of fact, both his relationship with Arthur Hope, a seventeen-year-old Afro-Caribbean, and his relationship with an eighteen-year-old weight trainer named Phil violate the legal age of consent stipulated in the act. Getting mugged by three skinheads makes Will suddenly aware of the dangers run by "poofs." Shortly afterward, Nantwich's story is repeated when James falls victim in an updated instance of police entrapment. The tactics of the police indicate their continuing intent to criminalize men who enjoy sexual and emotional ties with other men and to render the protections of privacy provided by the act so dubious that the public expression of gay existence is severely inhibited. It is this public expression, not sexual acts per se, that are the prime target of post-1967 law enforcement. Limited decriminalization of sex between men has permitted men publicly to express cultural differences that are articulated in relation to a wide range of sexual practices between and among males. In qualifying the dominance of hegemonic culture in this way, gay erotics have effects that are akin to cultural expression by members of the South Asian, African, and other diasporas in the British cities. Cultural differences are much more likely to be the objects of police surveillance than are literal differences, whether sexual or racial.

The repetition of vindictive juridical interventions underscores the existence of a pattern of homophobic oppression with the history of homosexual and gay networks and subcultures. So too do the repeated references to customary practices within homosexual and gay existence, such as "cottaging," which occur at the margin where male homosocial and homosexual sexual interests intersect. Gay existence has been from the start and continues to be articulated in relation to homophobia among police, in the courts, and elsewhere. The novel demonstrates and assumes these referents in canvassing gay existence. In this way, the novel crosses the categories of class, status, occupation, party, religion, and education that are also significant in characterizing the history of homosexual and gay groups in England. These distinctions contribute to the constitution of homosexual and gay subjectivities, but they do so in relation to framing institutions that are homophobic. Accordingly, assessment of one set of terms requires consideration of others as well. Further, the novel demystifies the split between expressions of gay sexuality in high culture and in the low culture of the pub, disco, or "cottage." Nantwich, Will, and James but also Abdul, Arthur, Bill, Phil, and others cross these lines.

In terms of sexual politics, the novel focuses on how to reimagine and reengage gay existence so that it is not encompassed within binary oppositions that while continually crossed, permit the manipulation and abuse of players on both sides. This question exceeds the understanding that Beckwith is able to garner as a belated interpreter of homosexual and gay history. Hollinghurst emphasizes the double bind within which homosexual and gay representation are caught. For example, Nantwich's memoirs are an attempt to ascertain the truth of his desire. Yet once that desire is identified as homosexual, Nantwich is rendered as readable as a page of print. "He had read me like a book," Nantwich complains about the vendor at Port Said. Nantwich experiences his inscription as "homosexual" to be humiliating even though it becomes his lifelong vocation to read himself as homosexual. This double bind follows inevitably from the formation of homosexuality as a set of representations within the dominant discourse. Hollinghurst responds to this situation, which affects him equally with his characters, by taking a revisionary view of a number of interweaving traditions in elite male culture. In this way, he demonstrates the discursive character of aspects of homosexual consciousness. Second, he exploits scenarios drawn from genres within the mass media such as contemporary pornography and the clichéd images and incidents of the evening news on television. The scene in which Beckwith is mugged by skinheads is an example of the latter sort of representation.[8]

Hollinghurst emphasizes that gay existence must be seen in relation to the low, déclassé, and disreputable aspects of gay experience and in relation to the stereotypes generated in the media and the marketplace. This second set of referents qualifies any theory of representation that is based on a concept of typical characterization since typicality always needs to be gauged in relation to stereotypical representations generated at a number of different sites of cultural production. *The Swimming-Pool Library* begins, for instance, with the description of a maintenance worker on the underground, "a severely handsome black of about thirty-five" (3), who is about to begin his shift. "He was very aloof," says Beckwith, "composed, with an air of massive, scarcely conscious competence" (4). As a type, he appears to be the counter of Arthur, also introduced in the opening pages, a virtually illiterate young member of what English writers refer to as the underclass.[9] Yet the immediate sympathy that the representation of the worker evokes from Beckwith is not much different from the "imagination" (281) with which Nantwich regards Africans. The description emphasizes, in a way that the Nantwich of the 1920s could have shared, the erotic fantasy within which the figure of the ennobled black worker stands: "I looked," Beckwith says, "with a kind of swimming, drunken wonder" (3). Contaminating with racial difference and erotic fascination a traditional image of the manual worker, the description blurs any one truth—of class, race, *or* sexuality—that the image might be said to convey, attract, or disclose. The double narrative of *The Swimming-Pool Library* requires that Will visit sites in Nantwich's experience, but these sites (re)visited have been changed by and can only signify in relation to the details of life and their representation in latter-day London. For gay reflection this fact entails acknowledging and addressing intractable realities of economic and racial disparity. In the shadow of AIDS, it means re-presenting gay experience in the present.

Homosexual Dissidence

What happens when the kind of group formation that went on among feminists, socialists, and homosexuals in the mid-1880s and early 1890s is suddenly interrupted?[10] What happens, when, in the terms of Forster's "Albergo Empedocle," the dream of recapturing a "Greek" existence results in ostracism and virtually complete solipsism? In "Arthur Snatchfold," written in 1928 and published posthumously in 1972, Forster suggests a kind of erotic malaise in which men donned armor, entered the world of business, joined clubs, married, parented, pursued other women—and enjoyed "pleasures" on the side that signified a lack in philistine existence.[11] As Sir Richard Conway says in Forster's story: "He got the feeling that they were all of them looking for something which was not there, that there was an empty chair at the table, a card missing from the bridge-pack, a ball lost in the gorse, a stitch dropped in the shirt; that the chief guest had not come."[12] A significant number of privileged young men in England in the 1920s and 1930s rejected this compromise. For these men, sex with other men became a political choice.

In *Our Age* (1990), Noel Annan, a member of the House of Lords and the former provost of King's College, Cambridge University, has written a memoir of the group that he refers to in the subtitle of his book as *English Intellectuals Between the World Wars*. Intellectuals in this context refers to writers, educators, public servants, and some clergymen who were born into the upper or middle classes and who attended first public schools and afterwards Oxford, Cambridge, or the London School of Economics.[13] Among members of this group, "homosexuality became a way of jolting respectable opinion and mocking the Establishment," particularly those members of it who were responsible for the huge casualties incurred during the Great War.[14] During the economic depression of the thirties and the rise of fascist regimes in Germany, Italy, and Spain, many young men took the additional step of becoming socialists and communists. Annan emphasizes that their rebellion was conceived specifically in relation to gender. They rejected "the insufferable ideal of the English gentleman," an ideal in which masculinity was defined in terms of "civic duty and diligence. Every man's first loyalty should be to the country of his birth and the institution in which he served. Loyalty to institutions came before loyalty to people."[15] Many elite homosexuals in the 1920s and 1930s rejected this sort of corporate loyalty.

Annan's construction of homosexuality as an oppositional practice is pertinent to Beckwith and Nantwich's cross-class, cross-race sexual interests.[16] His presentation also serves as a reminder of the erotic investments that traditional class analyses of "historical-social types" blank out. In the Annan model, rebellion against norms of class, gender, race, and nationality are aligned, though they can coexist with snobbery and with a wide range of political positions. Second, the oppositional stance of male homosexuals helps make sense of the importance of camp as a leading aspect of the sensibility of the Oxford Wits of the 1920s, a group with whom Nantwich is affiliated in Hollinghurst's novel. Ronald Firbank, a literary hero for James, is a former acquaintance of Nantwich (101).[17]

And Will, who likes to think of himself as disidentified from the norms of his class, finds it easiest to see Nantwich as "a Firbankian figure" (283). But Hollinghurst's novel presents a more ambivalent and contradictory view than Annan's model provides. In the 1920s Nantwich combines a love of pleasure that was associated at the time with the Oxford Wits; a critical view of racial prejudice; and a formidable attachment to personal loyalty plus "civic duty and diligence." Both a gentleman and a homosexual, he is unaware how oppositional his sexual preferences are. In Nantwich, Hollinghurst represents simultaneous identification and disidentification with gentlemanly values. As for Will, he is far more a member of the upper class than he is prepared to recognize.

Effective means existed to protect institutions from homosexual dissidence. The Labouchère amendment of 1885, under which Wilde had been tried, could be selectively enforced against casual sexual partners from the wrong side of the class divide, or, seemingly at random, against some privileged persons and not others. In the denouement of "Arthur Snatchfold," the social deference existing in rural areas operates to buttress this juridical model when Arthur, the young milkman with whom Conway has a fling, refuses to betray the older man's identity to the police. Selective enforcement had the advantage of extorting complicity from rebels, thereby increasing class alienation but also alienation from oneself and other subjects of same-sex desire. A generation later, in the 1950s, this approach would come back to haunt British officials when Guy Burgess and Donald Maclean, homosexual double agents, defected to the Soviet Union. The point would be underscored again when it was later discovered that the homosexual Anthony Blunt, surveyor of the Queen's pictures, had also been a spy.

Alan Sinfield's study *Literature, Politics, and Culture in Postwar Britain*, appeared in 1989, after Hollinghurst's novel and before Annan's memoir. Sinfield presents British social history since World War II as a narrative in which wartime promises made to members of the working classes and other subordinate groups were translated into the social policies of welfare capitalism after the war. When structural economic problems brought welfare into crisis in the 1970s, political consensus failed. Under the leadership of Margaret Thatcher, during the 1980s the British government reneged on its commitment to ensure the civil status of all sectors of the British public. Sinfield uses the language of social contract to describe this promise proffered, translated, and finally withdrawn. But what Sinfield refers to as the "rare opportunity to recast British society" after Word War II is also apocalyptic.[18] Success would have meant the transformation of British culture and society. Writing in the late 1980s after widespread loss of faith that such change is conceivable, much less achievable, Sinfield faces the challenge of describing an emerging set of cultural practices that can help recuperate the project.

Sinfield focuses on literary and popular culture as sites of contestation in the social and political struggles of the postwar decades. He is the first specifically to consider how the contaminating association of literary writing with male effeminacy and homosexuality affected cultural politics, especially between 1945 and 1955. And he is the first to analyze gay writing as an attempt to intervene in these conflicts. During World War II, elite intellectuals were drawn into the war effort. Sinfield argues that, among these, writers with sexual and emotional ties to other men came to identify with working-class soldiers and civilians, some of whom were their lovers. Gay writers with cross-class affiliations identified against the culture of their upbringing and, in particular, against middle-class homosexuals, whom they stereotyped as effete, art-loving pansies, unwilling and incapable of contributing to the struggle against Hitler. After the war, when members of the working classes appeared at last to be achieving full civil status within the British state, Sinfield reports that homosexual writers tended to fall into two groups. One group was nostalgically identified with the values of a refined, leisure-class elite that was rapidly disappearing from public view. The other with the newly admitted and upwardly mobile cadres.

Sinfield provides a literary model of cultural difference in the fifties in the following diagram:

dominant	the state	the working class	'masculinity'
literary	the personal	the leisure class	'femininity'

In the model, terms aligned horizontally support or are in affinity with one another; terms aligned vertically or diagonally oppose one another. The term *femininity* need not necessarily refer to gender difference but can also, perhaps even more significantly, refer by a chain of associative terms (feminine → effeminate → homosexual) to sexual difference within a gender. The model describes literature as a set of male homosocial discourses and institutions. But the model is rendered unstable insofar as "feminized," that is, homosexual, middle-class, and upper-class men were often attracted across differences of class, education, and sexual style to working-class men. This possibility relieved the contraries—as well as the injuries, stresses, incomprehensions, and resentments—among homosexual and gay men themselves and implied the possibility of change in their relations.[19] In this way, Sinfield sees sexual and emotional ties between men across binary divides as contributing to democratic change within British society.

During the 1950s the old gentlemen's agreement that had regulated homosexual dissidence was discarded in favor of "Red Scare" witch hunts of homosexuals in the public eye. This shift is a major referent of Hollinghurst's novel, which recasts the prosecution of Lord Montagu by Theobald Mathew and Sir David Maxwell-Fyfe in 1954 into the fictional standoff between Lord Nantwich and Lord Beckwith. The change came about in part as a result of Britain's new status as a client of the United States; cold war enthusiasts in Washington wanted a cleanup in England. The change also indicated the waning power of traditional elites in Britain itself. Furthermore, there was, in Annan's view, an intramural aspect as undergraduate "hearties" of the prewar years finally gave their comeuppance to the "aesthetes." Prosecutions increased sharply. After the appointment of Mathew, a Roman Catholic, as Director of Public Prosecutions in 1944, "the number of convictions for the commonest homosexual offence, gross indecency, rose from eight hundred cases before the war to 2,300 in 1953."[20] In the same year, a new Metropolitan Police Commissioner, Sir John Nott-Bower, came to Mathew's assistance. Mathew also had the support of Maxwell-Fyfe, later Earl of Kilmour, Home Secretary during the last Churchill government. The popular press pitched in, especially in the wake of the Burgess scandal.

The campaign climaxed in October 1953. During that month, an appeal filed by the Labour MP William Field, who had been convicted in January on the basis of evidence presented by two police officers, was dismissed; he was forced to resign his seat in Parliament. "In the same month, the well known author Rupert Croft-Cooke was found guilty of offences concerning two young sailors and sent to prison for nine months." Two weeks later, John Gielgud was fined on a minor charge. On October 16, "Lord Montagu of Beaulieu, and his friend, film director Kenneth Hume, were . . . charged with 'serious offences' involving two boy scouts."[21] In December, Montagu was acquitted on the principal charge after it was shown that police had tampered with the evidence.[22] On January 9, while awaiting retrial on the lesser charge, he was arrested on new counts involving RAF servicemen.[23] "Telephones were tapped, searches made without warrant, the Crown committed forgery and . . . Mathew assured the RAF men that however many offences they had committed they would not be prosecuted. Mathew later sat gloating in court when the accused were sentenced."[24] Despite this renewed zeal, however, government excess had already set in motion a reaction. Early in December 1953, two members of Parliament proposed establishment of a Royal Commission to consider reform of antihomosexual legislation.[25] By summer, Maxwell-Fyfe was forced to establish what came to be known as the Wolfenden Committee on Homosexual Offenses and Prostitution.

For elite homosexuals, who had thought themselves protected from attack, the campaign had major effects. Some—such as Nantwich in Hollinghurst's novel—walked out of the closet and stayed out. Liberal and social democratic intellectuals were offended by the pliancy of Whitehall in face of the U.S. State Department. The irregularities of the prosecution of Montagu provoked a reaction—in public opinion, Parliament, and the press.[26] The excesses of prosecutorial zeal set the stage for a gradual change in establishment opinion. In 1953, Forster wrote an article in the *New Statesman* in which he proposed decriminalizing homosexual activities between consenting adults.[27] A committee was set up "under Jack Wolfenden, then vice-chancellor of the University of Reading, to consider homosexuality and prostitution."[28] When the committee issued its report in 1957, it contained a recommendation in line with Forster's, though it was to not to be enacted for another decade.

The targeting of middle-class homosexuals took by surprise men like Croft-Cooke and Peter Wildeblood, who had assumed that their respectability and discretion shielded them from the law.[29] Ironically, the breakdown of the model impelled them toward homosexual identification. Media publicity propagated negative stereotypes of homosexuals but had the unintended consequence of increasing the awareness of many men sexually involved with other men. Bringing the topic into public discussion fostered the formation of a politically self-conscious gay subculture. At the same time, cross-class relations were riskier than hitherto for upper-middle-class men. In face of conflicting pressures, "closeting" became a yet more intensified and damaging reality for elite homosexuals, threatened on the one hand with prosecution but, on the other, finding it more and more difficult to conceal or disavow sexual difference at a time when bishops, parliamentarians, medical doctors, and journalists conducted public roundtables about homosexuality. As the decade continued, the "open secret" became more and more open.[30] The breaking of the gentlemen's agreement that had once offered protection of a sort to some elite queers led to decisive changes in the existence of homosexual and gay men in Britain. There are many reasons why Will Beckwith should be aware of these changes, from which he has benefited. But he is not. On this score, for him, the early 1950s are a blank. Unconsciously, he still lives within the illusory security of privilege. But in modeling Nantwich's prosecution in part on that of Montagu and by conflating aspects of Mathew and Maxwell-Fyfe in the characterization of Lord Beckwith, Hollinghurst provides Will with a quick course of study.

The lesson is not a pleasant one, since becoming aware of Nantwich's arrest and imprisonment means becoming aware of complicity in the injustice done to Nantwich. Will is free to pursue sex and to contemplate writing Nantwich's biography because of the financial support that he receives from the same man who made his political reputation and won his title by the vigor with which he pursued Nantwich and his ilk. When Will discovers the connection, he realizes that he cannot possibly write Nantwich's biography. He tells him: "All I could write now . . . would be a book about why I couldn't write the book" (329). The fact of complicity resonates beyond the accidents of individual kinship, since the connection between Will's grandfather and Lord Nantwich describes a relationship in which success in the predominantly male purlieus of the Establishment could be purchased by scapegoating other members of the Establishment who happened to be homosexual. This very success, in turn, permits self-appointed moral commissars like Will's grandfather to protect and indulge attractive young homosexuals with the right credentials. Yet this favor, as Will learns through James's predicament, can be revoked at any moment.

The ambiguity and ambivalence of this symbiotic relationship is evoked in a scene of the novel in which Will and James attend Lord Beckwith in his box at the opera during a performance of Benjamin Britten's *Billy Budd* (1951), an opera whose exploitation of homosexual *Sehnsucht* depends on the refusal to acknowledge that the sacrificial body of a beautiful young man is its object of desire. This silence, which is a closeting, made possible a coded expression of desire that permitted Britten to carry on collaborative work with his lover and other homosexual men, including Forster, who helped write the libretto; but the work and the expression remain subordinate to heterosexual presumption.[31]

Apocalyptic Overtures

While still at school, Will resolves on a career of sexual picaresque after his housemaster shames him for his lack of "vocation" (101). Nantwich wants to find a vocation for Will by persuading him to write the biography. The question of how errant desires can be translated into writing returns the characters to the moment in which the first wave of homosexual polemicists in the 1890s were faced with the question of what (social) utilities would be left if their project of dissociating male-male desire from institutional service was achieved.[32] Nantwich asks Will to undertake the biography while showing him the remnants of a Roman bath in the basement of his London house. "This little bit of the baths is all that's left to show how all those lusty young Romans went leaping about. Imagine all those naked legionaries in here" (94), says Nantwich. What remains is a

25. Masaccio, *Expulsion of Adam and Eve from Paradise* (pre-restoration), 1427–1428. Santa Maria del Carmine, Brancacci Chapel, Florence. Courtesy Alinari/Art Resource, New York.

portion of a mosaic in which "the upper parts of two figures could be seen, the one in front turning to the one behind with open, choric mouth as they dissolved into the nothingness beyond the broken edge of the pavement" (93). As Will looks at them, he thinks:

> Perhaps they were already standing in water, lapping round their long-eroded legs. They were intensely poignant. Seen close to, their curves were revealed as pinked, stepped edges, their moving forms made up of tiny, featureless squares. The boy in full-face had his mouth open in pleasure, or as an indication that he was speaking, but it also gave a strong impression of pain. It was at once too crude and too complex to be analysed properly. It reminded me of the face of Eve expelled from Paradise in Masaccio's fresco. But at the same time it was not like it at all; it could have been a mask of pagan joy. The second young man, following closely behind, leaning forward as if he might indeed be wad-

ing through water, was in profile, and expressed nothing but attention to
his fellow. What did he see there, I wondered—a mundane greeting or
the ecstasy which I read into it? (94)

Set in a scene in which this image appears, Nantwich's appeal to Will to
turn a career of sexual pursuit into a vocation as biographer suggests hope
that such a conversion can throw light on the "enigma" (94) of male play,
comradeship, and pleasure-pain. Will's response to the image is colored
by sublime affects. Seen close up, the forms of the mosaic turn into "tiny,
featureless squares" describing nothing yet together signifying the "moving forms" of the boys. These forms suggest in turn a likeness that speaks
chorically the voices of an ancient knowledge, but the visual/aural representation escapes Will's ken. Further, the fragmentary state of the mosaic conveys an impression of the representation of something of infinite
magnitude characteristic of the mathematical sublime as well as the perception of threatened existence proper to the experience of the dynamic
sublime. Within this complex affect, Will is not in a position to know, but
he can "wonder" at the prospects of "ecstasy," of paradisal expulsions, of
meanings that escape definition.

The boys who dissolve "into nothingness" portend the dissolution of
many lives. But their existence can also be imaged in terms of other temporal narratives. One could argue that the fresco indicates a continuity of
male sexual "swimming" from the beginnings of Britain's existence as a
colony to the present day. Yet, rather than continuity, the baths might be
taken to represent what historians refer to as invented tradition, "a set of
practices, normally governed by overtly or tacitly accepted rules and of a
ritual or symbolic nature, which seek to inculcate certain values and
norms of behaviour by repetition, which automatically implies continuity
with the past."[33] In this view the mosaicists have produced cultural capital calculated "to define and to justify" the roles of the colonizers.[34] If one
adopts the view of Roman invaders that Conrad takes in *The Heart of
Darkness*, then they, like many Victorian colonists in central Africa, were
surplus members of "an extended governing class," redundant at home
but needed abroad.[35] Like cricket grounds laid out in Kenya or South
Africa, the baths in a Roman context signify the superior civilization that
justified the invaders' inroads while simultaneously sustaining a "neo-
traditional title to gentility" for expatriates involved in boring, menial,
and distasteful tasks.[36] In this reading, the images signify not ecstasy but
cultural dominance.

Late-nineteenth-century colonization in Africa depended heavily
on invented traditions—for both Europeans and Africans. In addition to
the functions described above, these practices also "provided models of

subservience into which it was sometimes possible to draw Africans." While serving as modes of governance, these traditions paradoxically were main avenues of modernization since they provided means whereby Africans could adjust to the immense political, cultural, and economic changes taking place around them. In *The Swimming-Pool Library*, Taha al-Azhari travels remarkable cultural distances from the time when he enters Nantwich's service as a houseboy in the Sudan at the age of sixteen in 1926 to his life as a husband and father living in North Kensington in the 1950s. In the postcolonial period, "the invented traditions of European . . . gentlemen and professional men" have had negative consequences among comprador bourgeoisie who defined their own modernity in terms of those traditions. Another European tendency, that of viewing customary African societies as traditional in the sense of being static and unchanging, falsified the past while "transforming flexible custom into hard prescription."[37] "The glowing trance, aerial & romantic" (240), in which Nantwich sees the Sudan is correlative with this mode of reconstructing individual and group relations in Africa.

Nantwich has organized his life through personal relations—of loyalty, trust, and friendship. At the end of the novel, his "feudal system" retains enough integrity to check Will's effort to absorb Phil. Traditions in the novel are enacted through such relationships, without which they cannot exist. Yet the negative consequences of tradition are produced through the same operations. The implication is that the waters of male-male sexual interaction cannot be successfully navigated on the basis of personal relations alone. This *sotto voce* moral again echoes with the political effects of AIDS. Gays usually contract HIV-infection in moments of intimacy. That being so, individuals can scarcely rely on what one AIDS activist, Cindy Patton, has referred to as "an unefficacious 'trust,'" to protect them.[38] Too many have died of trust.

If personal relations, emplotting, traditions, and apocalyptic pattern are all equivocal ways of organizing gay existence, what is left? Lives, texts, and practices. Patton suggests that "we" might better understand "community" not as "an essential, stable, social institution" but as "a historically specific site of contestation that is in the process of reinvention."[39] When Nantwich makes his offer to Will while Will wonders at the unheard speech of a figure in a Roman mosaic, Hollinghurst positions the reader to perceive a number of different sites of contestation. It is as an ensemble of these that Hollinghurst provides his text to readers touched by apocalyptic anxieties.

At the end of his prison narrative, Nantwich uses the language of St. Paul as he speaks of the need to "take on a new man." After leaving prison, he does fulfill his intention of doing "something for others like myself, and for those more defenseless still" (304); yet the change in Nantwich is scarcely apocalyptic. A more useful option might exist in Will's awareness, after he learns about Nantwich's arrest and imprisonment, that "I needed . . . to know more" (309). Hollinghurst's novel grows out of the conviction that, after the check put by AIDS to a decade of American-style gay existence in London, there is need for gay men to learn more about the motivated absences that mark the history of gay existence in Great Britain.

As is so often the case, the inability to "fill in the blanks" in a narrative about one mode of gay existence impels a turn to the past. And the pasts tend to be multiple: the past of the 1920s, the 1880s, the early 1950s. In no case does the story that is generated end by dovetailing neatly with the narrative whose incompleteness provoked it in the first place. Something always escapes. Accordingly, there is no total story, no total comprehension. Kant's dream of sublime intelligibility remains a dream—as I believe he knew it to be. As there is no master story, there is no single gay subject or collectivity. Instead of achieving closure, the apocalyptic narratives that arise out of the continuing existence of gay men keep generating new music, new apocalyptic overtures.

AFTERWORD

On 10 March 1993, the final manuscript of this book was dispatched to Rutgers University Press. Later that day, I traveled by N.J. Transit to New York to see David Drake's performance piece, *The Night Larry Kramer Kissed Me*. Drake charts the progress of a young queer from childhood in suburban Baltimore to the scenes of gay life in the Big City—the bar, the gym, and so on. Drake energizes stereotypes he assumes his audience shares. Sometimes the vignettes work; sometimes they don't. Near the end, there is a long section during which he memorializes friends lost to AIDS.

The final section, *"The Way We Were,"* takes a new direction. The text jumps to the future—to New Year's Eve 1999—then turns in retrospect to the years between then and now. The speaker reminds his listeners of the uprising of gay men that occurred in the year 1996. Like the battle of Armageddon in Apocalypse (Rev. 19), this is a final great battle against the forces of Satan (Pat Buchanan, we are told with satisfaction, has been assassinated). Following victory, a thousand-year reich begins, the period known in the Bible as "the first resurrection" (Rev. 20.5) of the saints. When I saw the play, the final section galvanized the audience, for a moment, into a community. It was a curious sensation: to hear unfolded before one a fiction of the future that expressed unformulated wishes as though they were accomplished facts, at once private, secure, and shared.

As a rhetorical structure, the advantage of invoking apocalypse, especially after an AIDS memorial, is evident. Mortal closure gives way to (a proleptic recollection of) possibility. The structure also does political work, reminding listeners, queer, straight, or otherwise, that "the first resurrection" is still around the corner. For a moment, we "focus," to invoke a much-used word of 1993.

Even more revealing than Drake's play is the place where it is staged. The Perry Street Theatre is located on a block in the West Village that presents something like a material dream of gay existence. Constructed originally as a stable for the New York City Police Department, the building was converted to use as a theater in 1975. In 1988, Tammis Day purchased and renovated it in order to create a venue permanently dedicated to the presentation of lesbian and gay theater in New York City. *The Night Larry Kramer Kissed Me* is the first production mounted under the new management. The advent of this space along with the development of other cultural institutions such as the Sager Symposium at Swarthmore

College are signs of the determination of lesbians and gays to define spaces for themselves in a world where outcomes are unpredictable and, too often, negatively apocalyptic. As a sign of this continuing work, the Perry Street Theatre is an oracular sign in its own right.

Apocalyptic narrative characterizes a number of the first gay literary responses to AIDS in the mid- to late-1980s. As the *fin de millennium* approaches, this tendency has intensified in ever more flamboyant terms. Last summer, it occurred in the figure of Jonathan, the Canadian actor with AIDS, who is the protagonist of Geoff Ryman's novel, *Was*. Setting out on a search for Judy Garland/Dorothy, Jonathan is finally relieved of physical and emotional torment by the expedient of turning shaman and—simply—disappearing. A few weeks after I saw Drake's performance, the angel of the millennium crashed through the ceiling of Prior Walter's bedroom in Tony Kushner's play *Angels in America: A Gay Fantasia on National Themes*, at the Walter Kerr Theatre.

Apocalypse in minority discourse responds to the apocalyptic terms in which political discourse was framed during the twelve years of the Reagan and Bush administrations. This phenomenon has a point of origin in the divide-and-conquer strategy devised by Republicans after 1968 in order to win the support of Wallace Democrats. Kevin Phillips and others argued that resentment among working- and middle-class whites against legislative efforts on behalf of equality for blacks could be mobilized in order to fashion a Republican majority in presidential politics. The apogee of this effort was the Willie Horton ad campaign that Bush strategists used with great success against Michael Dukakis in the 1988 presidential campaign.[1]

By the fall of 1992, voters were out of sympathy with crude attempts to target the black underclass. The politics of *ressentiment* was no longer attractive at a time when protracted recession faced the families of white blue- and white-collar workers with many of the same economic problems that distressed African-Americans. Accordingly, 1992 was the year in which apocalyptic rhetoric would find a new target in the menace of homo-sex-YOU-al-ity. Pat Buchanan, the politician of *ressentiment* par excellence, managed to wangle a prime-time slot as a speaker on the opening night of the Republican convention. On that memorable occasion, when Phyllis Schlafly crowed: "None of the big tent garbage," Buchanan declared that, with the end of the cold war, Republicans must prepare for a new battle:

> There is a religious war going on in this country for the soul of America. It is a cultural war, as critical to the kind of nation we shall be as the Cold War itself, for this war is for the soul of America. And in that

struggle for the soul of America, Clinton & Clinton are on the other side, and George Bush is on our side.

Buchanan "ended with an extended analogy: as the brave young men of the 18th Cavalry retook streets after the Los Angeles riots, block by block, so 'we must take back *our* cities, and take back *our* culture and take back *our* country.'" Take back, yes, but from whom? In another speech, a commencement address given at Jerry Falwell's Liberty College in May, Buchanan fingered "the adversary culture, with its implacable hostility to Judeo-Christian teaching."

Enter gays and lesbians. What better targets to pose against (Republican) family values? As the party platform, embracing the Boy Scouts, asserted:

> We also stand united with those private organizations, such as the Boy Scouts of America, who are defending decency in fulfillment of their own moral responsibilities. We regret the irresponsible position of those corporations that have cut off contributions to such organizations because of their courageous stand for family values. Moreover, we oppose efforts by the Democratic Party to include sexual preference as a protected minority receiving preferential status under civil rights statutes at the federal, state, and local level.[2]

I was one of those who watched Buchanan, on the assumption that it is always better to know what one's antagonists are up to. Suddenly, however, I asked myself why I exposed myself to abuse? I switched off the set. In retrospect, I am glad that I saw as much as I did because, apparently, Buchanan's venom turned off lots of other people, who may have very little direct contact with gay men and lesbians. The politics of scapegoating backfired in a year when, finally, citizens were concerned that action be taken to bring medical expenses under control and to extend medical insurance to all. (More people in the United States are without *any* medical insurance coverage than the total number of people served by the Canadian national health service.)

As the unsatisfactory compromise over military service by gay men and lesbians reached in July 1993 indicates, it would be a mistake to believe that the apocalypse of the moral and religious Right disappeared, like the Wicked Witch of the West, on election night in 1992. For those on the Right, Washington will continue to be a favored stage for apocalyptic performances. Apocalypse has become a permanent feature of American politics. The fates of members of a wide range of minority groups depends on further successes against the Pat Buchanans of this world.

The signs of the times register apocalypse as an important aspect of gay existence and cultural practice. Lesbian and gay existence, as much and more than ever, are enmeshed as subject and object in national tropes and obsessions. As the 1990s unfold, the time of apocalypse, as before, is now.

NOTES

Introduction

1. Marie Françoise Plissart and Jacques Derrida, "Right of Inspection," 34.
2. Ernest Tuveson, "The Millenarian Structure of *The Communist Manifesto*," 324.
3. Ibid., 325.
4. Frank Kermode, *The Sense of an Ending: Studies in the Theory of Fiction*, 98, 101.
5. Ibid., 25.
6. I consider a number of these in Chapter 5.
7. Jacques Derrida, "The Ends of Man," 113.
8. Lee Edelman, "Seeing Things: Representation, the Scene of Surveillance, and the Spectacle of Gay Male Sex," 104.
9. Ed Cohen, *Talk on the Wilde Side: Towards a Genealogy of a Discourse on Male Sexualities*, 4.
10. Mary Poovey gives the phrase, "the ideological work of gender," two meanings: "In one sense, it means 'the work of ideology': representations of gender . . . [are] part of the system of interdependent images in which various ideologies . . . [become] accessible to individual men and women. In another sense, however, the phrase means 'the work of making ideology': representations of gender constitute one of the sites on which ideological systems . . . [are] simultaneously constructed and contested" (*Uneven Developments: The Ideological Work of Gender in Mid-Victorian England*, 2).
11. I discuss the enigmatic circumstances surrounding introduction and passage of this amendment in *Masculine Desire: The Sexual Politics of Victorian Aestheticism*, 199–202.
12. Chushichi Tsuzuki, *Edward Carpenter: 1844–1929*, chap. 6.
13. Jan Zita Grover, "AIDS: Keywords," 18.
14. Simon Watney, *Policing Desire: Pornography, AIDS, and the Media*, chaps. 1, 4, 5, 6.
15. Geoff Bennington, "Cogito Incognito: Foucault's 'My Body, This Paper, This Fire,'" 5.
16. Michel Foucault, *The History of Sexuality. Volume I: An Introduction*, 43.
17. Michel Foucault, *The Use of Pleasure*, 3.
18. Ibid., 4, 5–6.
19. Ibid., 12, 18.
20. Regenia Gagnier, *Subjectivities: A History of Self-Representation in Britain, 1832–1920*, 9.
21. Michel Foucault, "On the Genealogy of Ethics: An Overview of Work in Progress," 343, 346.
22. Ed Cohen, "Foucauldian Necrologies: 'Gay' 'Politics'? Politically Gay?" 88.
23. Foucault says: "What I mean in fact is the development of power techniques

oriented toward individuals and intended to rule them in a continuous and permanent way. If the state is the political form of a centralized and centralizing power, let us call pastorship the individualizing power" (*Politics, Philosophy, Culture: Interviews and Other Writings 1977–1984*, 59).

24. Quoted in Cohen, "Foucauldian Necrologies," 91.

25. Quoted in Cohen, "Foucauldian Necrologies," 93. This paragraph is indebted to Cohen's essay.

26. Consider, for example, Edward W. Said, "The Problem of Textuality: Two Exemplary Positions," 673–714; but see also Ann Wordsworth, "Derrida and Foucault: Writing the History of Historicity," 124.

27. Michel Foucault, "My Body, This Paper, This Fire," 27. For a translation of Derrida's review, see chapter 2 of Jacques Derrida, *Writing and Difference*, 31–63.

28. Jacques Derrida, *Margins of Philosophy*, 114, 113.

29. Jacques Derrida, "Of an Apocalyptic Tone Recently Adopted in Philosophy," 23.

30. Jacques Derrida, *The Truth in Painting*, 19; and "The Principle of Reason: The University in the Eyes of Its Pupils," 3–20.

31. Foucault, *The History of Sexuality*, 102.

32. Foucault, *Politics, Philosophy, Culture*, 95.

33. Immanuel Kant, *Political Writings*, 262.

34. Foucault, *Politics, Philosophy, Culture*, 93. Jean-François Lyotard comments on the same passage in "The Sign of History," 168–177.

35. Christopher Norris, *What's Wrong with Postmodernism: Critical Theory and the Ends of Philosophy*, 195–199.

36. Dietmar Kamper and Christoph Wulf, eds., *Looking Back on the End of the World*, 1, 2, 3.

37. Dominick LaCapra, "The Temporality of Rhetoric," 119–120.

38. These structures can be called "chronotypes." See the definition in John Bender and David E. Wellbery, eds., *Chronotypes: The Construction of Time*, 2–3.

39. Jean-François Lyotard, "On the Strength of the Weak," 205.

40. Jean-François Lyotard, *The Postmodern Condition: A Report on Knowledge*, 81.

41. Lyotard, "On the Strength of the Weak," 207.

42. Lyotard, *The Postmodern Condition*, 81, 82.

43. Immanuel Kant, *The Critique of Judgement*, 98. Christopher Norris argues that Lyotard treats "the Kantian sublime as a topos whose significance extends far beyond the realm of aesthetic judgement. For it is precisely the mark of the sublime, as theorized by Kant, that it sharpens this sense of the distance separating cognitive from ethical truth-claims, or sensuous intuitions that can be brought under adequate concepts (in the mode of theoretical understanding) from judgements belonging to the realm of 'suprasensible' ideas, values or principles. Thus it is that the sublime comes to figure, for Lyotard, as an index of the radical heterogeneity that inhabits our discourses of truth and value, or the kinds of injustice that inevitably result when one such 'phrase-regime'—most often the cognitive—seeks to mo-

nopolize the whole conversation" (Christopher Norris, "Deconstruction *Versus* Postmodernism: Critical Theory and the 'Nuclear Sublime,'" 98).

44. Derrida, *Truth in Painting*, 103. I delete Derrida's added parentheses. For a standard translation, see Kant, *The Critique of Judgement*, 91.

45. Thomas Weiskel discusses the tripartite structure in *The Romantic Sublime: Studies in the Structure and Psychology of Transcendence*, 23–24. Concerning the description of this kind of structure as a narrative, see J. Hillis Miller, "Narrative," 75–78.

46. Lyotard, "The Sign of History," 179.

47. Thomas Yingling, "AIDS in America: Postmodern Governance, Identity, and Experience," 298–299.

48. Kant, *The Critique of Judgement*, 98, 110–111.

49. Quoted by Neil Hertz in *The End of the Line: Essays on Psychoanalysis and the Sublime*, 51. See J. M. Bernstein's comments on this way of reading Kant's definition in *The Fate of Art: Aesthetic Alienation from Kant to Derrida and Adorno*, 38–44.

50. Hertz, *The End of the Line*, 57, 60.

51. Lyotard, *The Postmodern Condition*, 79.

52. "Too Much Laughter Gone," *Detroit Free Press*, 26 January 1992, G1.

53. Allan Stratton, "Of Largesse and Neglect," *Xtra!*, 10 January 1992, XS3.

54. Jacques Derrida, *Spurs: Nietzsche's Styles; Éperons: Les Styles de Nietzsche*, 147 n. 2. Unless otherwise noted, subsequent page citations to this work will be given in the text.

55. See, for example, 147 n. 2.

56. Jacques Derrida and Christie V. McDonald, "Choreographies," 76.

57. Ibid., 76.

58. These texts are by no means Derrida's final word on woman, feminism, femininity, or lesbian difference. I consider these issues in some detail in "Responsibilities: Deconstruction, Feminism, and Lesbian Erotics," forthcoming in a special issue of *The Canadian Review of Comparative Literature*.

59. Jacques Derrida, *The Post Card: From Socrates to Freud and Beyond*, 9, 12. In the illustration, "Plato" is not capitalized. For another reading of *The Post Card* by a gay critic, see Edelman, "Seeing Things," 95, 110–113. Wayne Koestenbaum plays on Derrida's interest in postal effects in his article, "Wilde's Hard Labor and the Birth of Gay Reading," 180–183.

60. Derrida, *The Post Card*, 18.

61. Ibid., 19, 15.

62. Ibid., 22.

63. George Chauncey, "From Sexual Inversion to Homosexuality: The Changing Medical Conceptualization of Female 'Deviance,'" 89–90.

64. Derrida, "Of an Apocalyptic Tone," 26.

65. Derrida, *The Post Card*, 179. Consider, for instance, the grammatically required masculine form in the phrase, "mon immense," in the following sentence: "Que peut signifier cette lettre chiffrée, ma trés douce destinée, mon immense, ma toute-proche inconnue." Derrida exploits parataxis in the sentence to render ambiguous the syntactic function of the train of phrases after "lettre." The play on gender and sexuality is accentuated in the immediately

succeeding sentences: "Peut-être ceci: même si c'est plus mystérieux en-core, je te dois d'avoir découvert l'homosexualité, et la nôtre est indestruc-tible. Je te dois tout et je ne te dois rien du tout. Nous sommes du même sex, c'est aussi vrai que deux et deux font quatre ou que S est P. CQFD" (Jacques Derrida, *La Carte postale*, 60). In these sentences, Derrida plays on the ambiguity of the term "l'homosexualité," which can refer either to (male or female) homosexuality or, exploiting the Greek root, homo- (same, equal, like), can refer to "same-sexuality" as in Luce Irigaray's concept of (male) *hom(m)o-sexualité*: "Reigning everywhere, although prohibited in prac-tice, hom(m)o-sexuality is played out through the bodies of women, matter, or sign, and heterosexuality has been up to now just an alibi for the smooth workings of man's relations with himself, of relations among men" (Luce Irigaray, *This Sex Which Is Not One*, 172). What better figure of hom(m)o-sexuality than "Derrida's" relay of "cette lettre chiffré" between an infatu-ated man and his "trés douce destinée?"

66. Derrida, *The Post Card*, 18.

67. Derrida, *La Carte postale*, 165; Derrida, *The Post Card*, 53.

68. Derrida, *La Carte postale*, 63–64. "She touches me, she takes me in her voice, while accusing me she cradles me again, she makes me swim, she engulfs me, you becloud me like a fish, I let myself be loved in the water" (Derrida, *The Post Card*, 56). If one were to pursue the possibility that the recipient of "Derrida's" correspondence is a woman or women, the analysis of signification would need to be tracked differently. See the preface by Gayatri Chakravorty Spivak to Derrida, *Of Grammatology*, xxxvi. See also, by the same author, "Displacement and the Discourse of Woman," 169–195. Spivak discusses *The Post Card* in "Love Me, Love My Ombre, Elle," 19–36. For a more recent discussion, see Spivak, "Feminism and Deconstruction, Again: Negotiating with Unacknowledged Masculinism," 206–223. See also Linda S. Kauffman, *Special Delivery: Epistolary Modes in Modern Fiction*, 81–130.

69. Kauffman, *Special Delivery*, 103–105. In middle voice, the speaker ("I") uses the second-person "you" to refer to him- or herself: for example, "you'd think that . . . ," used to mean, "I think that. . . ."

70. Osbert Sitwell, "Introduction," in Ronald Firbank, *Five Novels*, xiii, xxiii.

71. David Halperin, *One Hundred Years of Homosexuality and Other Essays on Greek Love*, 114.

72. Samuel Weber provides the translation and the comment in "The Debts of Deconstruction and Other, Related Assumptions," 37.

73. Edelman discusses "an overdetermined multiplicity of identifications" that accompanies the Wolf Man's fantasy of the primal scene ("Seeing Things," 112).

74. Derrida, *The Post Card*, 8, 138.

75. Ibid., 53, 56. See also 57 and Alan Bass's comments in the glossary (xxiv).

76. "Derrida" exclaims: "Lacan in truth meant to say what I said, what I will have said, under the heading of dissemination. What next!" (Derrida, *The Post Card*, 151). The irony exists in its being a woman who draws Derrida's work into the conventional model of logocentric inversion. Derrida's point is

that one's sex does not necessarily determine one's position in the sex-gender system. A female academic can also be a good "son."

77. Claude Summers, *Gay Fictions: Wilde to Stonewall, Studies in a Male Homosexual Literary Tradition*, 51.

78. Luce Irigaray, *Speculum of the Other Woman*, 136.

79. Jacques Derrida, "The Rhetoric of Drugs," 5–6, 20, 21. Michael Israel translates "l'experience" as "our experience"; I prefer "the experience."

80. Cathy Caruth, "Introduction," 419.

81. See Lee Edelman, "The Mirror and the Tank: 'AIDS,' Subjectivity, and the Rhetoric of Activism," 9–38.

82. Consider Edelman, "Seeing Things," 113.

83. Alexander García-Düttmann, "What Will Have Been Said about AIDS," 111–112.

84. Quoted in ibid., 99.

85. Derrida, "Of an Apocalyptic Tone," 4.

86. Ibid., 23.

87. Ibid., 22, 12.

88. Ibid., 23–24.

89. Spivak, "Love Me," 24–25.

90. Derrida, "Of an Apocalyptic Tone," 9, 17, 6, 16–17.

91. Dellamora, *Masculine Desire*, 10–12.

92. Sheila Rowbotham and Jeffrey Weeks, *Socialism and the New Life: The Personal and Sexual Politics of Edward Carpenter and Havelock Ellis*, 159.

93. Jacques Derrida, *Cinders*, 27, 61.

94. Jacques Derrida, "No Apocalypse, Not Now (Full Speed Ahead, Seven Missiles, Seven Missives)," 20–31; *Cinders*, 43, 53, 55.

95. See, for example, William J. Scheick, "Nuclear Criticism: An Introduction," 5. For a contrasting practice of nuclear criticism that attempts to critique apocalyptic thinking, see Peter Schwenger, "Circling Ground Zero," 255, 260.

96. Norris, "Deconstruction," 94–95.

97. Derrida, "No Apocalypse, Not Now," 22.

98. Ibid., 28.

99. Robert Glück, *Jack The Modernist*, 100.

1. Neil Bartlett's Gift for Oscar Wilde

1. Joseph Dewey, *In a Dark Time: The Apocalyptic Temper in the American Novel of the Nuclear Age*, 12, 41, 10.

2. Jan Zita Grover, "AIDS: Keywords," 27.

3. Wayne Koestenbaum, "Wilde's Hard Labor and the Birth of Gay Reading," 187.

4. Some of these authors are Charles Bernheimer, Ed Cohen, Christopher Craft, Jonathan Dollimore, Wayne Koestenbaum, Kevin Kopelson, Eve Kosofsky Sedgwick, and Elaine Showalter.

5. Neil Bartlett, *Who Was That Man? A Present for Mr Oscar Wilde*, 219. Henceforth cited in the text.

6. Stephen Jeffery-Poulter, *Peers, Queers, and Commons: The Struggle for Gay Law Reform from 1950 to the Present*, 176.
7. Cf., for instance, Sander L. Gilman, "AIDS and Syphilis: The Iconography of Disease."
8. In Balzac's *Illusions perdues* and *Splendeurs et misères des courtisanes*, de Rubempré is seduced by the master criminal, Vautrin.
9. Virginia Woolf, *Between the Acts*, 156.
10. Quoted in Ed Cohen, *Talk on the Wilde Side: Towards a Genealogy of a Discourse on Male Sexualities*, 171; slightly modified.
11. Ibid., chap. 5.
12. Harford Montgomery-Hyde, *The Trials of Oscar Wilde*, 224, 234.
13. Quoted by Jeffery-Poulter, *Peers, Queers, and Commons*, 23–24.
14. Jeffery Schmalz, "Gay Politics Goes Mainstream." For the situation in Britain following passage of Section 28 of the Local Government Act of 1988, see Jeffery-Poulter, *Peers, Queers, and Commons*, 242–267.
15. See, for instance, Dennis Altman, *Coming Out in the Seventies*.
16. I have in mind the political struggle surrounding Section 28 (Jeffery-Poulter, *Peers, Queers, and Commons*, 199–241). See also Anna Marie Smith, "A Symptomology of an Authoritarian Discourse: The Parliamentary Debates on the Prohibition of the Promotion of Homosexuality."

2. Dorianism

1. Quoted in Jacques Derrida, *The Truth in Painting*, 68n.
2. Elaine Scarry, *The Body in Pain: The Making and Unmaking of the World*, 63. For studies of the ideological structure of nation-building, see Benedict Anderson, *Imagined Communities: Reflections on the Origins and Spread of Nationalism*, and Ernest Gellner, *Nations and Nationalism*.
3. Michel Foucault, *The History of Sexuality. Volume I: An Introduction*, 139.
4. David Halperin, *One Hundred Years of Homosexuality and Other Essays on Greek Love*, ix.
5. In contrast to the Spartan model, Halperin points out that in a number of early texts "pair-bonding" within a military or political context is not sexualized (*One Hundred Years of Homosexuality*, 75). He instances the relationships of Achilles and Patroclus in the *Iliad*, of David and Jonathan in the Books of Samuel in the Old Testament, and of Gilgamesh and Enkidu in the Gilgamesh epic.
6. See Paul Cartledge, "The Politics of Spartan Pederasty."
7. George Mosse, *Nationalism and Sexuality: Middle-Class Morality and Sexual Norms in Modern Europe*, 88, chap. 2; Barry D. Adam, *The Rise of a Gay and Lesbian Movement*, 21–22.
8. Ernst Curtius, *The History of Greece*, 1: 190–197.
9. Hector Hugh Munro ("Saki"), a British writer who died in military action in World War I, was one such subject (Mosse, *Nationalism and Sexuality*, 43).
10. Paul de Man, *The Rhetoric of Romanticism*, 264.
11. Immanuel Kant, *On History*, xii.
12. Immanuel Kant, *The Critique of Judgement*, 112–113.

13. In his *Anthropology* (1798), Kant refers to Jews as "a nation of cheats, . . . a nation of traders" (Paul Lawrence Rose, *Revolutionary Antisemitism in Germany: From Kant to Wagner*, 94. See Rose's general discussion of Kant and Judaism, 91–97).

14. Robert Rosenblum, "Reconstructing David," 196.

15. In this sentence and in the remainder of the chapter, I observe the distinction that Kaja Silverman draws in *Male Subjectivity at the Margins* between the "look" or "eye" and the "gaze." She writes: "The relationship between eye and gaze is . . . analogous . . . to that which links penis and phallus; the former can stand in for the latter, but can never approximate it. Lacan makes this point with particular force when he situates the gaze outside the voyeuristic transaction, a transaction within which the eye would seem most to aspire to a transcendental status, and which has consequently provided the basis, within feminist film theory, for an equation of the male voyeur with the gaze" (130).

16. C. O. Müller, *The History and Antiquities of the Doric Race*, 2:303.

17. Luc de Nanteuil, *Jacques-Louis David*, 118.

18. Cf. the discussion in de Man, *The Rhetoric of Romanticism*, chap. 4, esp. 77–78.

19. De Nanteuil, *Jacques-Louis David*, 118.

20. Stephanie Carroll, "Reciprocal Representations: David and Theater."

21. Jack Lindsay, *Death of the Hero: French Painting from David to Delacroix*, 131.

22. Sander Gilman, "Opera, Homosexuality, and Models of Disease: Richard Strauss's *Salome* in the Context of Images of Disease in the Fin de Siècle," in *Disease and Representation: Images of Illness from Madness to AIDS*, 155–181.

23. Joan DeJean, *Fictions of Sappho: 1546–1937*, 206.

24. Martin Bernal, *Black Athena: The Afroasiatic Roots of Classical Civilization*, 1:27, 33.

25. Emily Vermeule, "The World Turned Upside Down," 40, 41. Although Vermeule is highly critical of the arguments that Bernal puts forward in the second volume of his study to justify his belief "that [black] Egypt and the Levant inspired the culture of the Greeks," she acknowledges Bernal's "justifiable condemnation" in the first volume "of the narrow-minded teaching of the classics that assumed the cultural superiority of the Greeks without reference to Egypt and the East" (40).

26. DeJean, *Fictions of Sappho*, 204.

27. On *Deutschheit* and related terms in advanced thinking of the period, see Jacques Derrida, "*Geschlecht* II: Heidegger's Hand."

28. DeJean, *Fictions of Sappho*, 209, 214.

29. Müller, *History and Antiquities of the Doric Race*, 2:300. Linda Dowling discusses this claim in "Ruskin's Pied Beauty and the Constitution of a 'Homosexual' Code," 2, as does DeJean in *Fictions of Sappho*, 214–215.

30. Müller, *History and Antiquities of the Doric Race*, 2:304.

31. This demand for a hermeneutic reading persists today. See the discussion in the afterword of my *Masculine Desire: The Sexual Politics of Victorian Aes-*

theticism, as well as in Halperin, *One Hundred Years of Homosexuality*, 10–11 and chap. 3.

32. Halperin, *One Hundred Years of Homosexuality*, 154 n. 12; DeJean, *Fictions of Sappho*, 346 n. 16.

33. John Addington Symonds, *Male Love: A Problem in Greek Ethics and Other Writings*, 17.

34. Ibid., xxi.

35. Müller, *History and Antiquities of the Doric Race*, 2:306.

36. Symonds, *Male Love*, 14.

37. Müller, *History and Antiquities of the Doric Race*, 2:302.

38. Johann Jakob Bachofen, *Myth, Religion, and Mother Right*, 201, 204, 71, 205, 207. See DeJean's discussion in *Fictions of Sappho*, 220–222. For connections between Bachofen and anglophone writers, see Bachofen, li–lvi.

39. Friedrich Engels, *The Origin of the Family, Private Property and the State*, 95.

40. Benjamin Jowett, trans., *The Dialogues of Plato*, 2d rev. ed., 3:26.

41. Walter Pater, *Miscellaneous Studies: A Series of Essays*, 181–182. Subsequent page citations to this work will be given in the text.

42. Matthew Arnold, *Complete Prose Works*, 5:134, 136, 283.

43. Ibid., 5:282.

44. Ibid., 5:292, 294.

45. Walter Pater, *Plato and Platonism*, 202, 198.

46. Ibid., 220.

47. William Shuter, "Walter Pater and the Academy's 'Dubious Name,'" 140.

48. Used in conversation with the author, September 1990. Lesley Higgins has made clear to me the polemical relation between Pater's later writing about *Phaedrus* and Jowett's translation. In the introduction to his translation of *Phaedrus*, Jowett attempts to evade the emphasis on desire between males in Plato's text by substituting for male love a nearly asexual ideal of Victorian marriage (Benjamin Jowett, trans., *The Dialogues of Plato*, 3d rev. ed., 1:406–409).

49. Pater refers to these discourses at the beginning of "Emerald Uthwart" when the narrator meditates on the epitaphs of "German students" who studied at Siena early in the eighteenth century. Pater links these men with the paintings of "Sodoma" (*Miscellaneous Studies*, 170; Rudolf Wittkower and Margot Wittkower, *Born under Saturn: The Character and Conduct of Artists—A Documented History from Antiquity to the French Revolution*, 173–175) in the same church and, allusively, with later German students—such as those who studied with Winckelmann in Rome or like the Nazarenes, Friedrich Overbeck, Peter Cornelius, and Franz Pforr, who made "friendship pictures" for each other early in the nineteenth century (*German Masters of the Nineteenth Century: Paintings and Drawings from the Federal Republic of Germany*, 176; Keith Andrews, *The Nazarenes: A Brotherhood of German Painters in Rome*, frontispiece; for an account of apologies for desire between men in late eighteenth-century German philosophy, see Gert Hekma,

"Sodomites, Platonic Lovers, Contrary Lovers: The Backgrounds of the Modern Homosexual," 435–440).

50. Gerald Monsman, *Pater's Portraits: Mythic Pattern in the Fiction of Walter Pater*, 178n. On 171–183 Monsman traces the connections between the portrait and *Plato and Platonism*.

51. For the post-1870 history of British aristocracy, see Noel Annan, "The Death of 'Society.'"

52. William Shuter discusses Pater's use of the Greek *stele* in a number of texts. See his "Arrested Narrative of 'Emerald Uthwart,'" 15–18.

53. Pater, *Plato and Platonism*, 222, 231.

54. Oscar Wilde, *The Picture of Dorian Gray*, 180. Henceforth cited in the text.

55. See Dellamora, *Masculine Desire*, 114.

56. See Royston Lambert, *Beloved and God: The Story of Hadrian and Antinous*.

57. Richard Kaye is studying the fin de siècle interest, heterosexual and homosexual, in Saint Sebastian.

58. Dellamora, *Masculine Desire*, 202.

59. Halperin argues that the Platonic lover falls in love with the love of beauty pouring forth from the eye of the beloved. The latter responds to the reflection of this love in the look of the lover (David Halperin, "Plato and Erotic Reciprocity," 62–63, 75 n. 49).

60. Pater, *Plato and Platonism*, 232.

61. In Wilde's novel, Dorian appears to be attracted to both men and women. For Wilde's relationship with John Gray, see Richard Ellmann, *Oscar Wilde*, 291.

62. Brocard Sewell, *In the Dorian Mode: A Life of John Gray, 1866–1934*, 18.

63. Ibid., 138.

64. Havelock Ellis, cited in Christopher Craft, "'Kiss Me with Those Red Lips': Gender and Inversion in Bram Stoker's *Dracula*," 113. For Raffalovich, see Timothy d'Arch Smith, *Love in Earnest: Some Notes on the Lives and Writings of English 'Uranian' Poets from 1889 to 1930*, 29–30, 34.

65. Mosse, *Nationalism and Sexuality*, 41, 42.

66. Sewell, *In the Dorian Mode*, 79.

67. Edward Carpenter, *Selected Writings. Volume One: Sex*, 217. Carpenter's *Intermediate Types Among Primitive Folk: A Study in Social Evolution* (1914) includes a chapter, "Military Comradeship Among the Dorian Greeks."

68. Dellamora, *Masculine Desire*, 160–161.

3. J. Hillis Miller and Walter Pater

1. For a recent study of Pater's engagement, see James Eli Adams, "Gentleman, Dandy, Priest: Manliness and Social Authority in Pater's Aestheticism."

2. I discuss this aspect of Abrams's confrontation with deconstruction in Chapter 5.

3. J. Hillis Miller, "Tradition and Difference," 6, 8.

4. Ibid., 8.

5. Miller's "Tradition and Difference" and Paul de Man's "Rhetoric of Temporality," which I discuss in Chapter 5, are essays that mark the advent of deconstruction in the work of both men.

6. Miller, "Tradition and Difference," 8. The phrase, "apocalyptic mood" is Gary Indiana's.

7. Ibid., 12.

8. Donald Pease, "J. Hillis Miller: The Other Victorian at Yale," 85, 88–89. Pease's essay specifies the cultural moment of Miller's critique of Abrams.

9. The tendency continues in other critics. See, for example, W. David Shaw, *The Lucid Veil: Poetic Truth in the Victorian Age*, 168.

10. Walter Pater, *Letters*, 13.

11. Linda Dowling, *Language and Decadence in the Victorian Fin de Siècle*; Robert Crawford, "Pater's *Renaissance*, Andrew Lang, and Anthropological Romanticism"; Morse Peckham, *Victorian Revolutionaries: Speculations on Some Heroes of a Culture Crisis*, chap. 5.

12. Walter Pater, *Appreciations with an Essay on Style*, 68–69, 66. John Goode argues the centrality of this essay to the Decadence in "The Decadent Writer as Producer," 113–115.

13. Pater, *Appreciations* 104. Translation: [Love is the] father of delicacy, of splendor, of luxury, of the Graces, of desire, and of longing.

14. Ibid., 103–104.

15. Walter Pater, *Studies in the History of the Renaissance*, viii.

16. Quoted in Jeffrey Wallen, "On Pater's Use and Abuse of Quotation," 1.

17. See, for instance, a letter that Richards wrote to Eliot at the time that he was completing his book on Coleridge, in I. A. Richards, *Selected Letters*, 77.

18. J. Hillis Miller, "Walter Pater: A Partial Portrait," 98, 106, 108.

19. See the discussion of the passage in my *Masculine Desire: The Sexual Politics of Victorian Aestheticism*, 139–140.

20. Miller, "Walter Pater," 99.

21. Quoted in ibid., 102.

22. Ibid., 106.

23. Ibid., 112.

24. Monique Wittig, *The Straight Mind and Other Essays*, 21–32.

25. Walter Pater, *Miscellaneous Studies: A Series of Essays*, 122, 123, 122. In Miller's/Freud's terms, the murder of Hyacinth might be seen as the psychological destruction of desire, fixed at an "adolescent homosexual stage," in the Prior.

26. Crawford, "Pater's *Renaissance*," 867.

27. See Richard M. Dorson, "The Eclipse of Solar Mythology."

28. Quoted in Crawford, "Pater's *Renaissance*," 865.

29. Ibid., 859.

30. See Robert Peters, "The Cult of the Returned Apollo: Walter Pater's *Renaissance* and *Imaginary Portraits*."

31. Pater, *Miscellaneous Studies*, 127.

32. Miller, "Walter Pater," 108, 109.

33. Walter Pater, *The Renaissance: Studies in Art and Poetry. The 1893 Text*, 165.

34. Wallen, "On Pater's Use and Abuse," 15.
35. Ibid., 17.
36. Walter Pater, *Marius the Epicurean: His Sensations and Ideas* (1885), 2 : 132.
37. Ibid., 2 : 114, 98.
38. Peter Clarke, *Liberals and Social Democrats.*
39. Patrick Brantlinger, *Rule of Darkness: British Literature and Imperialism, 1830–1914,* 202.
40. Matthew Arnold, *Complete Prose Works,* 3 : 145–146.
41. John Lee, Tim Garrigan, and Bob Connell, "Toward a New Sociology of Masculinity," 587.
42. I adapt the phrase "homosexual existence" from Adrienne Rich, "Compulsory Heterosexuality and Lesbian Existence."
43. Sharon Bassett, "*Marius* and the Varieties of Stoic Will: 'Can the Will Itself Be an Organ of Knowledge, of Vision?'" 57.
44. Arnold, *Complete Prose Works,* 3 : 149. For examples of British brutality after the Sepoy Mutiny, see Jenny Sharpe, "The Unspeakable Limits of Rape: Colonial Violence and Counter-Insurgency," 37–40.
45. Daniel T. O'Hara, *The Romance of Interpretation: Visionary Criticism from Pater to de Man,* 16.
46. Pater, *Marius the Epicurean,* 2 : 66.
47. Ibid., 2 : 68, 72, 70.
48. Bernard McGinn, "Early Apocalypticism: The Ongoing Debate," 23.
49. Cathy Caruth, "Introduction," 419
50. Walter Pater, *Marius the Epicurean: His Sensations and Ideas* (1910), 2 : 209. Unless otherwise noted, subsequent references are to this edition.
51. Ibid., 2 : 223.
52. Thanks to Christopher Keep for drawing my attention to the possibility of this reading.
53. Jonathan Loesberg, *Aestheticism and Deconstruction: Pater, Derrida, and De Man,* 169.
54. Pater, *Marius the Epicurean,* 2 : 217.
55. Ibid., 2 : 118.
56. Richard Gilman, *Decadence: The Strange Life of an Epithet,* 51.
57. Dellamora, *Masculine Desire,* 148–149.
58. See David Hilliard, "Unenglish and Unmanly: Anglo-Catholicism and Homosexuality."
59. O'Hara, *The Romance of Interpretation,* 41; italics added.
60. Pater, *Marius the Epicurean,* 2 : 115.
61. The final phrase is from the second edition of *Marius the Epicurean,* 2 : 110. Loesberg also criticizes O'Hara; see *Aestheticism and Deconstruction,* 216 n. 11.
62. Pater, *Studies in the History of the Renaissance,* 92; Walter Pater, *Imaginary Portraits,* 52–53.
63. Pater, *The Renaissance,* 106.
64. Ibid., 105.
65. Miller, "Walter Pater," 101. Cf. Loesberg's discussion of "sensation" in Pater's epistemology (Loesberg, *Aestheticism and Deconstruction,* chap. 1).

66. Oscar Wilde et al., *Teleny*, 10.
67. Edward Carpenter, *Selected Writings, Volume One: Sex*, 235. "Urning" is Carpenter's term for subjects of male-male desire.
68. Miller, "Walter Pater," 112.
69. Nancy K. Miller, *Subject to Change: Reading Feminist Writing*, 91, 100 n. 21.
70. J. Hillis Miller, "Ariadne's Thread: Repetition and the Narrative Line," 159.
71. Ibid., 164.
72. J. Hillis Miller, *Illustration*, 51.

4. E. M. Forster at the End

1. The scandal attending publication of *Jude the Obscure* later in 1895 indicates the negative impact for male heterosexual writers of the Wilde trials. See Richard Dellamora, *Masculine Desire: The Sexual Politics of Victorian Aestheticism*, 212–217.
2. Quoted in Oliver Stallybrass, "Introduction," in E. M. Forster, *The Life to Come and Other Stories*. In-text citations to "Albergo Empedocle" refer to this edition. Unless otherwise cited, biographical information is from Claude Summers, *E. M. Forster*, chap. 1.
3. I adapt the phrase from Teresa de Lauretis, "The Female Body and Heterosexual Presumption," esp. 260, 277 n. 1, and from Monique Wittig, *The Straight Mind and Other Essays*, 24–25. See also Teresa De Lauretis, "Eccentric Subjects: Feminist Theory and Historical Consciousness," 128–129. I supplement her work by suggesting that the contract is implemented with special aggressiveness in the years immediately following Wilde's imprisonment.
4. My suggested dates for the installation of this shift in the construction of conventional sexuality parallel the development, in Continental psychoanalysis, of Freud's model of female sexual difference, a model that Mary Jacobus argues establishes "the phallus" as "an arbitrary and divisive mark around which sexuality is constructed" (Mary Jacobus, *Reading Woman: Essays in Feminist Criticism*, 122). For a discussion of the problematic of "woman" in male modernity, see Alice Jardine, *Gynesis: Configurations of Woman and Modernity*, chap. 4.
5. See Ross Chambers, *Room for Maneuver: Reading (the) Oppositional (in) Narrative*, 24, 32.
6. Ibid., 237–241.
7. Ibid., 217.
8. I follow Alan Sinfield's argument in *Literature, Politics, and Culture in Postwar Britain*, esp. chap. 5.
9. I mean showing us how in the sense described by David Halperin in a discussion of heroic male friendship in the *Iliad* and other early texts. Halperin argues that interpretations of "homosexuality" in these works tell us more about the understanding of sexuality in the culture of the interpreter than in the cultures in which the works themselves were first performed or written (*One Hundred Years of Homosexuality and Other Essays on Greek Love*, 87).

10. See Eve Kosofsky Sedgwick, *Between Men: English Literature and Male Homosocial Desire*, esp. chap. 9.
11. Ibid., 177.
12. Eve Kosofsky Sedgwick, *Epistemology of the Closet*, 210.
13. For the wives of Oscar Wilde and Edmund Gosse, see Anne Clark Amor, *Mrs. Oscar Wilde: A Woman of Some Importance*, and Ann Thwaite, *Edmund Gosse: A Literary Landscape, 1849–1928*. See also Francis King, *E. M. Forster*, 22–23.
14. Quoted in Lesley Higgins, "Essaying 'W. H. Pater Esq.': New Perspectives on the Tutor/Student Relationship Between Pater and Hopkins," 90.
15. Linda Dowling, "Roman Decadence and Victorian Historiography." Similarly, in "Ansell," another early story, the narrator's upper-class father is distressed when his son loses interest in the history of Rome after he makes friends with a garden boy: "My father did not like my entire separation from rational companions and pursuits. I had suddenly stopped reading and no longer cared to discuss with him the fortunes of the Punic War or the course of Aeneas from Troy" (Forster, *The Life to Come*, 28).
16. Acragas is the Greek name of Girgenti, known to the Romans as Agrigentum and, since 1927, as Agrigento, a change of name consonant with the Fascist program of invoking an earlier empire. Forster visited the town in April 1902.
17. See John Frow, "Tourism and the Semiotics of Nostalgia."
18. Tom Waugh, "Photography, Passion and Power," 30; also personal communication, 11 August 1992.
19. For a discussion of "Apollo in Picardy," see Dellamora, *Masculine Desire*, chap. 9. For the connections between Pater and Forster, see Robert Martin, "The Paterian Mode in Forster's Fiction: *The Longest Journey* to *Pharos and Pharillon*," 99–112.
20. Walter Pater, *Miscellaneous Studies: A Series of Essays*, 170.
21. Quoted in King, *E. M. Forster*, 17. One of the features of the last fifteen years of the century, as discussed in George Gissing's *New Grub Street* (1891) and in such recent studies as Jonathan Freedman's *Professions of Taste: Henry James, British Aestheticism, and Commodity Culture*, is the emergence of what is now referred to as "middlebrow" taste. Middlebrow taste, which might be described as the revenge of Philistinism on Matthew Arnold, was—and is—averse to *thinking Greek*.
22. Quoted in King, *E. M. Forster*, 19.
23. For a discussion of the sexual politics of the Apostles in the 1830s, see Dellamora, *Masculine Desire*, chap. 1.
24. P. N. Furbank, *E. M. Forster: A Life*, 1:78, 98.
25. King, *E. M. Forster*, 34.
26. Furbank, *Forster*, 1:140.
27. Ibid., 1:141.
28. Ibid., 1:111.
29. See Noel Gilroy Annan, *Our Age: English Intellectuals Between the World Wars—A Group Portrait*, chaps. 7, 8.
30. Richard Dellamora, "Textual Politics/Sexual Politics," 162–163.

5. Framing William Burroughs

1. Alan Hollinghurst, *The Swimming-Pool Library*, 289.
2. Andreas Huyssen, "Mapping the Postmodern," 236, 234.
3. Ibid., 237.
4. Susan Sontag, "Notes on 'Camp,'" in *Against Interpretation and Other Essays*, 290. This opposition is true despite the Jewish backgrounds and the elite, usually East Coast, university educations of many of the young men engaged in the emerging field of gay literary and cultural studies in the late 1980s. Larry Kramer and other Jewish men have also played a prominent role in AIDS activism since the early 1980s.
5. Leslie Fiedler, "The New Mutants," in *A Fiedler Reader*, 192.
6. Ibid., 194.
7. Teresa de Lauretis, "The Female Body and Heterosexual Presumption," esp. 260, 277 n. 1; Monique Wittig, *The Straight Mind and Other Essays*, 24–25. See also de Lauretis, "Eccentric Subjects: Feminist Theory and Historical Consciousness," 128–129
8. Robert Alter, "The Apocalyptic Temper," 62. I would like to thank David Robson for providing me a copy of this essay. I am likewise in the debt of his expert knowledge of the relation between Fryean apocalypse and straight(-identified) male postmodernist fiction in the United States during the 1960s.
9. Frank Kermode, *The Sense of an Ending: Studies in the Theory of Fiction*, 116, 117.
10. Ibid., 123.
11. James Joyce, *Ulysses*, vii–xiv.
12. Kermode appeared as a witness for the defense in the successful prosecution on obscenity charges of the English publishers of Hugh Selby's novel, *Last Exit to Brooklyn*. See Frank Kermode, "Obscenity and the Public Interest."
13. Paul Cellupica, "The Political Dawn Arrives for Gays," L21.
14. M. H. Abrams, *The Mirror and the Lamp: Romantic Theory and the Critical Tradition*, 225. See also Donald Pease, "J. Hillis Miller: The Other Victorian at Yale," 70.
15. Kermode, *The Sense of an Ending*, 103.
16. M. H. Abrams, "Rationality and Imagination in Cultural History: A Reply to Wayne Booth," 462.
17. Jacques Derrida, "Of an Apocalyptic Tone Recently Adopted in Philosophy," 23.
18. Dominick LaCapra, "The Temporality of Rhetoric," 120, 122.
19. M. H. Abrams, *Natural Supernaturalism: Tradition and Revolution in Romantic Literature*, 445–446; quoted in LaCapra, "The Temporality of Rhetoric," 125.
20. Abrams, *The Mirror and the Lamp*, 102.
21. De Man singles out Abrams for a view of romantic symbol that "resembles a radical idealism" (Paul de Man, "The Rhetoric of Temporality," 180).
22. Ibid., 198, 199.
23. Abrams, *Natural Supernaturalism*, 447.

24. Alan Sinfield, *Literature, Politics, and Culture in Postwar Britain*, 55–56.

25. John Sutherland, "The Politics of English Studies in the British University, 1960–1984," 127.

26. Ibid., 128.

27. Ibid., 131.

28. Ihab Hassan, "The Question of Postmodernism," 118.

29. Kermode, *The Sense of an Ending*, 45, 5, 12, 10, 110.

30. Ibid., 5, 103, 113.

31. Jan Gorak, *Critic of Crisis: A Study of Frank Kermode*, 32, 32–33, 33.

32. Frank Kermode, *Continuities*, 119.

33. Michael Payne compares and contrasts Kermode and Frye in his introduction to Frank Kermode, *Poetry, Narrative, History*, 1–4.

34. Northrop Frye, *Anatomy of Criticism: Four Essays* , 116.

35. Ibid., 119.

36. Ibid., 74.

37. Kermode, *The Sense of an Ending*, 95, 103.

38. Sinfield, *Literature, Politics, and Culture*, 187.

39. Kermode, *The Sense of an Ending*, 117.

40. Ihab Hassan, "The Subtracting Machine: The Work of William Burroughs," 6. Burroughs's friend, the Swiss-Canadian painter, Brion Gysin, describes the method as follows:

> Method is simple: Take a page or more or less of your own writing or from any writer living or dead. Any written or spoken words. Cut into sections with scissors or switch blade as preferred and rearrange the sections. Looking away. Now write out result. . . .
>
> Applications of cut up method are literally unlimited cut out from time limits. Old world lines keep you in old world slots. Cut your way out. (Quoted in Hassan, "The Subtracting Machine," 9)

41. Kermode, *The Sense of An Ending*, 117, 122.

42. Quoted in Hassan, "The Subtracting Machine," 5, 16, 10. More literally, elsewhere in the novel, Burroughs "predicts the coming of a viral venereal disease that originates in Africa, as AIDS is believed to have done. . . . 'Males who resign themselves up for passive intercourse to infected partners . . . may also nourish a little stranger'" (Ted Morgan, *Literary Outlaw: The Life and Times of William S. Burroughs*, 355).

43. Quoted in Hassan, "The Subtracting Machine," 16.

44. See Tony Tanner's discussion in *City of Words: American Fiction, 1950– 1970*, 109–140. Tanner finds a context for Burroughs's validation of silence in the work of the composer, John Cage (122, 128–129). Cage, who was gay, influenced the work of many gay artists, including Andy Warhol.

45. For the "crisis" in American criticism in the mid- to late-1960s, see "Criticism and Crisis," in Paul de Man, *Blindness and Insight: Essays in the Rhetoric of Contemporary Criticism*, 3–19.

46. Kermode, *The Sense of an Ending*, 118.

47. Michael R. Solomon and Basil G. Englis, "Reality Engineering: Blurring the

212 NOTES TO PAGES 113–120

Boundaries Between Commercial Signification and Popular Culture" (Paper presented at a Roundtable, Rutgers Center for Historical Analysis, Rutgers University, 3 November 1992), 6.

48. Burroughs, "Interview," 47.

49. Burroughs, *Queer*, 50, 49–50. Henceforth cited in the text.

50. See Oscar Urteaga-Ballón, *Interpretacion de la sexualidad en la ceramica del antiguo Peru.*

51. Morgan, *Literary Outlaw*, 350. In the film, Lee performs the "queer" routine and the "talking asshole" routine.

52. John D'Emilio, *Sexual Politics, Sexual Communities: The Making of a Homosexual Minority in the United States, 1940–1970*, 181.

53. For the work of Jack Smith, see Michael Moon, "Flaming Closets," 19–54. Andrew Ross articulates "hip" in relation to music, class, and race while leaving gay sexuality out of account (*No Respect: Intellectuals and Popular Culture*, chap. 3). For underground filmmaking in the postwar period, see Richard Dyer, *Now You See It: Studies on Lesbian and Gay Film*, 111–173.

54. For a discussion of the term "queer" within theory, see the special issue of *differences* titled *Queer Theory*, especially Teresa de Lauretis, "Queer Theory: Lesbian and Gay Sexualities, An Introduction," iii–xviii.

55. Chris Rodley, ed., *Cronenberg on Cronenberg*, xvii.

56. Ibid., 134; Nik Sheehan, "Naked Lunch: Coming Out with Talking Assholes," *Xtra!* 10 January 1992, XS15.

57. Rodley, ed., *Cronenberg on Cronenberg*, 128, 127.

58. Ross traces this struggle in part in *No Respect*, chap. 5.

59. Carole S. Vance, "The War on Culture." In the final week of February 1992, President Bush fired John Frohnmayer, chairman of the National Endowment for the Arts. Bush took action after Patrick Buchanan, his opponent in the Republican presidential primary in the state of Georgia, began to show a television advertisement linking the Bush administration with financial support for the activities of leaping, muscle-bound, leather queens. In a parting statement, Frohnmayer said: "I leave with the belief that this eclipse of the soul will soon pass and with it the lunacy that sees artists as enemies and ideas as demons" (Brian Wallis, "Pandering to Conservatives, Bush Dumps Frohnmayer," *Art in America* 80 (April 1992): 36; see also in the same issue of *Art in America*, "Gay Images Haunt Campaign," 35).

60. David Cronenberg, interviewed by Michael Ondaatje, Premier Dance Theatre, Toronto, 11 March 1992. Early in 1992, the Supreme Court of Canada ruled, in the Butler decision, that material can be declared obscene if it "raises a reasonable apprehension of harm." This test is liable to result in arbitrary and variable obscenity standards across the country. On the topic of women and obscenity, Cronenberg recommended an article by Sallie Tisdale, "Talk Dirty To Me."

61. Morgan, *Literary Outlaw*, 346.

62. Homosexuality surfaced as a security issue in national party politics during the presidential campaign of 1964. Less than three weeks before the election, Walter Jenkins, President Johnson's chief of staff, was arrested "with another man . . . and charged with performing 'indecent gestures' in a base-

ment restroom of the YMCA two blocks from Jenkins's office in the White House" (Lee Edelman, "Tearooms and Sympathy, or The Epistemology of the Water Closet," 263). For a discussion of current controversies over obscenity legislation, see Judith Butler, "The Force of Fantasy: Feminism, Mapplethorpe, and Discursive Excess."

63. The picture book published simultaneously with the release of the film includes seven pages of photographs of this effect (Ira Silverberg, ed., *Everything Is Permitted: The Making of Naked Lunch*).

64. George L. Mosse, *Nationalism and Sexuality: Middle-Class Morality and Sexual Norms in Modern Europe*, 36; Sander L. Gilman, "Opera, Homosexuality, and Models of Disease: Richard Strauss's *Salome* in the Context of Images of Disease in the Fin de Siècle," in *Disease and Representation: Images of Illness from Madness to AIDS*, 155–181; and "Karl Kraus's Oscar Wilde: Race, Sex, and Difference," in *Inscribing the Other*, 173–190.

65. Mahler was Bohemian and Freud an Austrian.

66. Cronenberg remarks on the subject of being an anglophone Canadian: "I'm very balanced. I'm cursed with balance, which is to say I immediately see all sides to the story. And they are all equal. That can be a curse, maybe it's very Canadian too. This has been noted by some critics like Carrie Rickey, who humorously said that my political stance, since it seems to come down on all sides at once or none at all, seems to be very Canadian" (Rodley, ed., *Cronenberg on Cronenberg*, 118).

67. Ibid., 159.

68. On the Lacanian Symbolic, see Jean Laplanche and J.-B. Pontalis, *The Language of Psycho-Analysis*, 439–440.

69. Rodley, ed., *Cronenberg on Cronenberg*, 162.

70. Sigmund Freud, "Thoughts for the Times on War and Death," in *The Standard Edition of the Complete Psychological Works*, 14:298.

71. I use *imaginary* here as "from the intersubjective point of view, a so-called *dual* relationship based on—and captured by—the image of a counterpart (erotic attraction, aggressive tension)" (Laplanche and Pontalis, *Language of Psycho-Analysis*, 210). For transference and counter-transference, see 455–461 and 92–93.

72. Ibid., 460.

73. Ted Morgan, Burroughs's biographer, does not suggest that the pair were sexually intimate. Feminist analyses of Cronenberg's preceding film, *Dead Ringers* (1988), focus on separation anxiety in male psychology. See Barbara Creed, "Phallic Panic: Male Hysteria and *Dead Ringers*"; Marcie Frank, "The Camera and the Speculum: David Cronenberg's *Dead Ringers*."

74. Rodley, ed., *Cronenberg on Cronenberg*, 162.

75. In contrast, Jackie Burroughs, in her performance piece, the *Jane Bowles Project*, acknowledges Bowles's ethnicity. Bowles was highly ambivalent about her Jewish heritage (Jackie Burroughs, *Jane Bowles Project*, Factory Theatre Studio Cafe, Toronto, 13 March 1992).

76. I am indebted to Sherwood William for these observations on Freud's practice of analysis. Sherwood William, "The Gay Science: Paradox and Pathology in Wilde and Melville" (Paper presented at the conference, Plea-

sure/Politics, Harvard University, Cambridge, Massachusetts, 27 October 1990), 14–16.

77. Rodley, *Cronenberg on Cronenberg*, 169, 158.

78. Cited in Judith Roof, *A Lure of Knowledge: Lesbian Sexuality and Theory*, 178.

79. Ibid., 181–183.

80. Sheehan, "Naked Lunch," XS15.

81. Ibid.

82. Morgan, *Literary Outlaw*, 177.

83. "Dominatrix" is Danny O'Quinn's word; see his "War on. . . ." (Paper delivered at the Colloquium of the English Graduate Students Association, York University, North York, Ontario, 5 March 1992.

84. Ibid.

85. Ibid.

86. Brian D. Johnson, "Sex, Drugs and Bugs," *Maclean's*, 20 January 1992, 50.

87. I discuss fin de siècle, male homosexual versions of the myth in *Masculine Desire: The Sexual Politics of Victorian Aestheticism*, chap. 9.

88. Brett Stewart, "Sissies and Superman," *Xtra!*, 7 February 1992, 11.

89. Silverberg, *Everything Is Permitted*, 122.

90. Ibid., 15.

6. Absent Bodies/Absent Subjects

1. For some of these discussions, see Chapters 2 and 3. In the preface to *The Prison-House of Language: A Critical Account of Structuralism and Russian Formalism* (1972), Jameson writes: "To 'refuse' Structuralism on ideological grounds amounts to declining the task of integrating present-day linguistic discoveries into our philosophical systems; my own feeling is that a genuine critique of Structuralism commits us to working our way completely through it so as to emerge, on the other side, into some wholly different and theoretically more satisfying philosophic perspective" (vii). For an analysis of Jameson's Marxism that critiques his continuing reliance on aspects of Northrop Frye's "North American liberal version of structuralism," see Cornell West, "Ethics and Action in Fredric Jameson's Marxist Hermeneutics," 133.

2. Hilton Kramer, *The Age of the Avant-Garde: An Art-Chronicle of 1956–1972*, 541. For more recent comments by Kramer, see Christopher Reed, "Bloomsbury Bashing: Homophobia and the Politics of Criticism in the Eighties." 67–69.

3. I discuss Lyotard's account of the sublime in the Introduction.

4. Jean-François Lyotard, *The Postmodern Condition: A Report on Knowledge*, 79.

5. In Lyotard's terms, the conflation is not surprising: "The nuance which distinguishes these two modes may be infinitesimal; they often coexist in the same piece, are almost indistinguishable; and yet they testify to a difference (un *différend*) on which the fate of thought depends and will depend for a long time, between regret and assay" (ibid., 80).

6. For an analysis of apocalyptic in Marx and Lenin, see Ernest L. Tuveson, "The Millenarian Structure of *The Communist Manifesto.*"

7. Andrew Ross, *No Respect: Intellectuals and Popular Culture*, 169; see also 147.

8. See Fredric Jameson, *Postmodernism, or The Cultural Logic of Late Capitalism*, which is henceforth cited in the text.

9. Jacques Derrida discusses the two aspects of sublimation in *Margins of Philosophy*, 117–119. See Alan Bass's analysis in the note to page 19.

10. Hal Foster, *Recodings: Art, Spectacle, Cultural Politics*, 140.

11. See also Fredric Jameson, "Postmodernism, or The Cultural Logic of Late Capitalism," 76.

12. See the discussion in Ross, *No Respect*, 165–170.

13. In this connection, a 1962 interview of Rudolf Arnheim is discussed by Jonathan Katz, in "Sexuality in the Art of Johns and Rauschenberg" (Paper delivered at the Fourth Annual Lesbian, Bisexual and Gay Studies Conference, Harvard University, Cambridge, Mass., 28 October 1990).

14. Fredric Jameson, "Reification and Utopia in Mass Culture," 144.

15. On this topic, see Kathleen Martindale, "Fredric Jameson's Critique of Ethical Criticism: A Deconstructed Marxist Feminist Response," 33–43.

16. West, "Ethics and Action," 140.

17. In "The Signification of the Phallus," Jacques Lacan writes: "The phallus is the privileged signifier of that mark in which the role of the logos is joined with the advent of desire" (in *Écrits: A Selection*, 287). See Jane Gallop's discussion of the essay, including her discussion of Jameson's comments on feminists, Lacan, and the phallus, in her *Reading Lacan*, chap. 6, esp. 134–136.

18. Craig Owens, "The Discourse of Others: Feminists and Postmodernism," 64–67.

19. Charles W. Haxthausen discusses the Peircian meaning of the word "icon" in his "Translation and Transformation in *Target with Four Faces: The Painting, the Drawing, and the Etching*," 67.

20. Jameson, "Reification and Utopia," 141.

21. I think, for instance, of Teresa de Lauretis, *Alice Doesn't: Feminism, Semiotics, Cinema*, chap. 6; "Feminist Studies/Critical Studies: Issues, Terms, and Contexts," 1–19; and *Technologies of Gender: Essays on Theory, Film, and Fiction*, chap. 1.

22. Foster, *Recodings*, 139–155; Ross, *No Respect*, 228–232.

23. Martin Heidegger, "The Origin of the Work of Art," 662–663.

24. Ibid., 664–665.

25. A voice refers parodically to "the obvious bisexuality" of the shoes. Derrida provides a basis in Freudian dream theory for making such a reference: "Bisexual symbolization remains an irrepressible, archaic tendency, going back to childhood which is ignorant of the difference of the sexes." To this observation, another voice responds: "So it is always necessary to hold in reserve a sort of excess of interpretation, a supplement of reading—which is decisive, to tell the truth—for the idiom of a syntactic variation" (Jacques Derrida, *The Truth in Painting*, 278, 268). By stating that "Derrida" refers

to the shoes as "a heterosexual pair," Jameson (hetero)sexualizes Derrida's text, excluding exactly that "excess of interpretation" to which the preceding citation draws attention. Jameson's misreading of Derrida has also been noted by John Frow in "Tourism and the Semiotics of Nostalgia," 141.

26. Contrary to Jameson's reading, the passage from Heidegger could be read in another way. The "world" of the peasant woman may be her cultural product rather than that of the male artist and male critics and theorists.

27. Cited in Jameson, *Postmodernism*, 35.

28. Meyer Schapiro, "The Still Life as a Personal Object—A Note on Heidegger and Van Gogh," 206.

29. Ibid., 205.

30. Derrida, *Truth in Painting*, 259, 272.

31. For three different images in this series, see Kynaston McShine, ed., *Andy Warhol: A Retrospective*, plates 390, 391, 392. The indexical j emphasizes the phantasmatic aspect of Jameson's reading, which refers, strictly speaking, neither to the specific painting that appears on the dust jacket nor to the series generally.

32. For a discussion of the serigraphs, see Marco Livingstone, "Do It Yourself: Notes on Warhol's Techniques," 74.

33. Illustrated in McShine, ed., *Andy Warhol*, 42, 64.

34. Rainer Crone, *Andy Warhol: A Picture Show by the Artist*, 63.

35. Crone has pointed out that at the beginning of his career as a pop artist Warhol was aware of these aspects of the star system, including its relation to middle-class fantasies and aspirations (ibid., 68–69).

36. Crone argues that Warhol was an admirer of Bertolt Brecht, in Rainer Crone, "Form and Ideology: Warhol's Technique from Blotted Line to Film," 70–72.

37. Charles E. Stuckey, "Warhol in Context," 24.

38. Nan Rosenthal, "Let Us Now Praise Famous Men: Warhol as Art Director," 37, 40, 41.

39. See Crone, *Andy Warhol*, 63.

40. Sigmund Freud, *The Standard Edition of the Complete Psychological Works*, 11:96. At the end of his life, Warhol was producing images drawn from Leonardo's *Last Supper*, a key image of love between men in both Roman Catholic and nineteenth-century aesthetic culture. One hopes that Warhol, who did a series of cow images in the mid-1960s, knew as well the following passage from Freud's study: "When . . . the child becomes familiar with the cow's udder whose function is that of a nipple, but whose shape and position under the belly make it resemble a penis, the preliminary stage has been reached which will later enable him to form the repellent sexual fantasy" of cocksucking (*Standard Edition*, 11:87).

41. Fig. 219 in Crone, *Andy Warhol*.

42. See Rosenthal, "Let Us Now Praise Famous Men," 41–42.

43. Kynaston McShine, "Introduction," in Kynaston, ed., *Andy Warhol*, 19.

44. Bradford R. Collins, "The Metaphysical Nosejob: The Remaking of Warhola, 1960–1968," 48; also Crone, "Form and Ideology," 74.

45. Mandy Merck, "Figuring Out Andy Warhol."

46. Michael Moon, "Flaming Closets," 37.
47. Freud, *Standard Edition*, 11:116. See the discussion of conversion in Jean Laplanche and J.-B. Pontalis, *The Language of Psycho-Analysis*, 90–91.
48. Italics mine. Rilke writes:

> . . . If there weren't light, the
> curve
> of the breast wouldn't blind you, and in the swerve
> of the thighs a smile wouldn't keep on going
> toward the place where the seeds are.
> (Rainer Maria Rilke, *Selected Poems*, 147)

49. Foster, *Recodings*, 151.
50. Between the terms of comparison in the text fall "Rimbaud's magical flowers 'that look back at you'" (10). The reference to Rimbaud is another coded allusion to homosexual transgression.
51. The phrase is Paul de Man's; see his *Allegories of Reading: Figural Language in Rousseau, Nietzsche, Rilke, and Proust*, 142.
52. For the tradition, see Richard Dellamora, *Masculine Desire: The Sexual Politics of Victorian Aestheticism*, 242 n.18. See also Barry D. Adam, *The Rise of a Gay and Lesbian Movement*, chap. 5.
53. The strong period-sense of New York gays when faced with the onset of AIDS is registered in Andrew Holleran's short story "Friends at Evening" (1986).
54. Jameson, "Postmodernism," 83. I cite the earlier version in order to retain the second-person references, which I place in brackets. These were removed from the 1991 text.
55. Susan Sontag, "Notes on 'Camp,'" in *Against Interpretation and Other Essays*, 290.
56. Jameson, "Reification and Utopia," 141.
57. See also Dan Latimer, "Jameson and Post-Modernism," 118–119.
58. Barbara Rose, *Rauschenberg: An Interview with Robert Rauschenberg*, 13.
59. Rosenthal, "Let Us Now Praise Famous Men," 47, 48, 49.
60. The white space is analogous to the strobe cut used by Warhol in his films (Crone, "Form and Ideology," 89–90).
61. Reproduced in Richard Dyer, "Don't Look Now," 62. It has proven impossible to obtain permission to reproduce this image.
62. Ibid., 72.
63. Personal information is from Jonathan Katz. See also Collins, "Metaphysical Nosejob," 48.
64. John D'Emilio, "The Homosexual Menace: The Politics of Sexuality in Cold War America," 226–240.
65. *Andy Warhol: Death and Disasters*, 106; Stuckey, "Warhol in Context," 16.
66. See, for example, his collaboration with Gerard Malanga, who attached poems to thermofax images from the Death and Disasters works (*Andy Warhol: Death and Disasters*, 24–27). See also David Ehrenstein, "The Filmmaker as Homosexual Hipster."
67. Louis Althusser, "Freud and Lacan," 162, 163. A feminist might respond,

as a number of feminists have, that in this instance, as usual, critical theory limits its attention to the male subject. In this particular essay, however, Althusser at least recognizes the fact that the gender formation of women is also central to the constitution of the economic order (162).

68. Jacqueline Rose, "Sexuality and Vision: Some Questions," 116.
69. Ibid., 117.
70. Moon, "Flaming Closets," 29.
71. Richard Wollheim, *Sigmund Freud*, 157.
72. Ernest Mandel, *Late Capitalism*, 85; see also 48–55, 84–88.
73. Ibid., 556–561.
74. Ibid., 585.

7. Edmund White's "Oracle"

I have conducted workshops on White's story along with material from Foucault and Derrida on two occasions: in a session on theory and literary fictions of AIDS during the International Summer Institute for Semiotic and Structural Studies at the University of Toronto in June 1990 and at the University of Alberta at Edmonton in March 1991. I would like to thank Paul Brophy, Dave Pringle, Bill Whitla, and others who took part in the Toronto session and Glenn Burger, Jonathan Hart, Daphne Read, Stephen Slemon, Janice Williamson, and others who participated at Alberta.

1. Jacques Derrida, "Of an Apocalyptic Tone Recently Adopted in Philosophy," 25, 24, 25.
2. Edmund White, "An Oracle," in *The Darker Proof: Stories from a Crisis*, by Edmund White and Adam Mars-Jones, 219. Henceforth cited in the text.
3. Cindy Patton, *Inventing AIDS*, 5.
4. Ibid., 42, 45.
5. Car crashes were significant within the gay imaginary of the 1960s: in Warhol's car crash paintings, for instance, and in the smashups involving Montgomery Clift and James Dean. The image also occurs in AIDS writing. See, for example, Paul Monette, *Love Alone: Eighteen Elegies for Rog*, 33.
6. See Linda S. Kauffman, *Special Delivery: Epistolary Modes in Modern Fiction*, 105.
7. Derrida, "Of an Apocalyptic Tone," 83, 84.
8. Michel Foucault, *The Use of Pleasure*, 254. Henceforth cited in the text.
9. White met Foucault when he visited New York in 1981. After White moved to Paris in 1983, the two men became friends (letter from Edmund White to the author, 5 August 1991).
10. Foucault says: "What I mean in fact is the development of power techniques oriented toward individuals and intended to rule them in a continuous and permanent way. If the state is the political form of a centralized and centralizing power, let us call pastorship the individualizing power" (Foucault, *Politics, Philosophy, Culture: Interviews and Other Writings 1977–1984*, 59).
11. Michel Foucault, *The History of Sexuality: Volume I: An Introduction*, 42–43.

12. For Foucault's view of the importance of confession in the production of personal identity, see *The History of Sexuality*, 57 – 73.

13. Michel Foucault, "On the Genealogy of Ethics: An Overview of Work in Progress," in *The Foucault Reader*, 343.

14. Foucault uses the term *Californian* to refer to a set of lifestyles of which some gay lifestyles form a subset. He observes: "In the Californian cult of the self, one is supposed to discover one's true self, to separate it from that which might obscure or alienate it, to decipher its truth thanks to psychological or psychoanalytic science" (Foucault, "Genealogy of Ethics," 362). Derrida and Foucault agree on the tendentious character of psychoanalytic claims to locate the truth of personal development, but as I indicate above, Derrida still believes in the heuristic value of an analytic tropology when critiquing the concept of identity.

    The views of Arthur Evans, a gay activist in the Bay area whose writing I comment on later in the book, fall within the sense of "Californian" that Foucault questions. Edward Said exploits the gay connotations of the term in criticism directed toward Foucault at the time of his death: "It was noticeable that he was more committed to exploring, if not indulging his appetite for travel, for different kinds of pleasure (symbolized by his frequent sojourns in California), for less and less frequent political positions" (quoted in Ed Cohen, "Foucauldian Necrologies: 'Gay' 'Politics'? Politically Gay?" 88). For a positive assessment of the importance to Foucault of the visible existence of gay subcultures in California, see Didier Eribon, *Michel Foucault*, chap. 21, esp. 315. Jim Miller's forthcoming biography of Foucault is also significant in this context (see David M. Halperin, "Saint Foucault," 34).

15. In a special issue of *Open Letter*, dedicated to the memory of the Canadian poet Bronwen Wallace, Barbara Godard argues that the specifically male character of poetic elegy has compelled female writers of elegy to devise new forms of writing that transgress the traditional limits of genre. Godard argues that this and analogous operations are a necessary part of the effort by women to invent connections between personal affiliations and meaning within "an affiliative secular order" (Barbara Godard and Mary di Michele, "'Patterns of Their Own Particular Ceremonies': A Conversation in an Elegiac Mode," 43).

16. The phrase "closeted gay," which became familiar during the recent debate over "outing" male homosexuals, is contradictory since gay identity is usually predicated on the process of "coming out." The contradiction between living as a gay man and simultaneously being in the closet at work or in other contexts is, however, one that continues to occur.

17. In the 1970s, middle-class gay culture developed along the lines of other ethnic groups in the United States. See Steven Epstein, "Gay Politics, Ethnic Identity: The Limits of Social Constructionism," 6 – 54.

18. Arthur Evans, *The God of Ecstasy: Sex-Roles and the Madness of Dionysos*, 66 – 68.

19. Willets, *Cretan Cults*, 112; Rodney Castleden, *The Knossos Labyrinth: A New View of the 'Palace of Minos' at Knossos*, chap. 10.

20. Ernst Curtius, *The History of Greece*, 1:192–197.
21. Information provided by Bill Whitla.
22. Emily Vermeule, "The World Turned Upside Down," 42.
23. David M. Halperin, *One Hundred Years of Homosexuality and Other Essays on Greek Love*, chap. 4.
24. Loring M. Danforth. *The Death Rituals of Rural Greece*, 13.
25. Ibid., 65. Ray is an inexact reader. The exhumation occurs five years after burial, not three.
26. Edmund White, *States of Desire: Travels in Gay America*, xiv, xvii–xix.
27. Danforth, *Death Rituals*, 6.
28. Paul de Man, *Blindness and Insight*, 9.
29. Danforth, *Death Rituals*, 138.
30. At the turn of the century, Baron von Gloeden took similar photographs of teenagers in Sicily. See Tom Waugh, "Photography, Passion and Power," 30.
31. See Barbara Godard, "Theorizing Feminist Discourse/Translation."
32. *Yassou* creates a translation effect within the passage, the rest of which is in an ethnographic mode.
33. Paul de Man, *Allegories of Reading: Figural Language in Rousseau, Nietzsche, Rilke, and Proust*, 198.
34. Kauffman, *Special Delivery*, 88, 121.
35. Using the lyrics of popular songs to think through questions about gay existence is a familiar practice within gay culture. Vito Russo, for example, in a late interview, quotes a Phil Ochs song when he says: "I want to be here when it's over to say who's to praise or who's to blame. I want to say I lived through it, to have witnessed it." Quoted in Eric Marcus, *Making History: The Struggle for Gay and Lesbian Equal Rights, 1945–1990, An Oral History*, 418.
36. Danforth, *Death Rituals*, 36, 117, 127.
37. Derrida, "Of an Apocalyptic Tone," 64.
38. Edmund White, *States of Desire*, xviii–xix.
39. Laurence Perrine, "Housman's 'Others, I am not the first,'" 137.
40. Edmund White, "The Political Vocabulary of Homosexuality," 235.
41. Patton, *Inventing AIDS*, chap. 1.
42. Edmund White, "An Essay," 12.
43. Michelle Reynolds, "Self-Subjectification through Confession in Edmund White's 'An Oracle'" (unpublished manuscript), 4.
44. White, "An Essay," 13.
45. White, *States of Desire*, xvii.
46. Quoted in ibid., xviii.

8. *Hollinghurst's* Swimming-Pool Library

I would like to thank Joseph Bristow, Ross Chambers, and Barry Weller for their discussions of this novel, which motivated my reflections.

1. Alan Hollinghurst, *The Swimming-Pool Library*, 5–6. Henceforth cited in the text.

2. Cathy Caruth, "Unclaimed Experience: Trauma and the Possibility of History," 181.

3. I have in mind what Roland Barthes refers to as the hermeneutic or moral code in the novel.

4. See Simon Watney, *Policing Desire: Pornography, AIDS, and the Media.*

5. The text here refers allusively to John Addington Symonds's initiation into homosexual acts in 1877 by "a brawny young soldier" at a house of assignation in London (Symonds, *The Memoirs*, 253). *The Memoirs* were published while Hollinghurst was writing *The Swimming-Pool Library.*

6. Patrick Brantlinger, *Rule of Darkness: British Literature and Imperialism, 1830–1914*, 179.

7. Georg Lukács, *The Historical Novel*, 34, 35.

8. Joseph Bristow, "Being Gay: Politics, Identity, Pleasure," 76–78.

9. Alan Sinfield, *Literature, Politics, and Culture in Postwar Britain*, 294, in which the term is used primarily with economic reference. For suggestions on how the term can be used also to describe blacks and homosexuals, see 307.

10. Homosexual networks in contact with Wilde and Edward Carpenter are only some of these groups. For others, see the survey in Noel Gilroy Annan, *Our Age: English Intellectuals Between the World Wars—A Group Portrait*, chap. 7.

11. E. M. Forster, *The Life to Come and Other Stories*, 134.

12. Ibid., 131.

13. That this group included a few women hardly disproves the general rule of gender exclusivity (Annan, *Our Age*, 3).

14. Ibid., 113.

15. Ibid., 19.

16. Ross Chambers discusses Will Beckwith as an oppositional figure in an unpublished paper, "Messing Around: Gayness and Loiterature in Alan Hollinghurst's *The Swimming-Pool Library*," 2–3.

17. Annan, *Our Age*, 4, 92–97.

18. Sinfield, *Literature, Politics, and Culture*, 1.

19. The preceding two paragraphs summarize information in Sinfield, *Literature, Politics, and Culture*, chap. 5.

20. Annan, *Our Age*, 125.

21. Stephen Jeffery-Poulter, *Peers, Queers, and Commons: The Struggle for Gay Law Reform from 1950 to the Present*, 14.

22. Ibid., 15; Annan, *Our Age*, 126.

23. Jeffery-Poulter, *Peers, Queers, and Commons*, 16.

24. Annan, *Our Age*, 126.

25. Jeffery-Poulter, *Peers, Queers, and Commons*, 15–16.

26. Sinfield, *Literature, Politics, and Culture*, 78.

27. Francis King, *E. M. Forster*, 89.

28. Annan, *Our Age*, 127.

29. The name of Will's nephew in Hollinghurst's novel is Rupert Croft-Parker (66).

30. Information in the paragraph is drawn from Alan Sinfield, "Closet Dramas: Homosexual Representation and Class in Postwar British Theater."
31. Philip Furbank, *E. M. Forster: A Life*, 2:283–286.
32. I describe this moment in Chapter 4. See also Barry Weller, "Uncles and Empire: British Homosexual Culture and the Nurture of Culture" (Paper presented at the conference, Pleasure/Politics, Harvard University, Cambridge, Mass., 27 October 1990).
33. Eric Hobsbawm, "Introduction: Inventing Traditions," in *The Invention of Tradition*, ed. Eric Hobsbawm and Terence Ranger, 1.
34. Terence Ranger, "The Invention of Tradition in Colonial Africa," in *The Invention of Tradition*, ed. Hobsbawm and Ranger, 211.
35. Ibid., 215; Joseph Conrad, *Heart of Darkness*, 20.
36. Ranger, "Colonial Africa," 215.
37. Ibid., 211, 220, 212, 214, 212.
38. Cindy Patton, "Safe Sex and the Pornographic Vernacular," 38.
39. Ibid., 32.

Afterword

1. Andrew Hacker, "Paradise Lost," *New York Review of Books*, 13 May 1993, 33.
2. Gary Wills, "The Born-Again Republicans," *New York Review of Books*, 24 September 1992, 9.

BIBLIOGRAPHY

Abrams, M. H. *The Mirror and the Lamp: Romantic Theory and the Critical Tradition*. New York: Norton, 1958.

———. *Natural Supernaturalism: Tradition and Revolution in Romantic Literature*. New York: Norton, 1971.

———. "Rationality and Imagination in Cultural History: A Reply to Wayne Booth." *Critical Inquiry* 2 (1976): 447–464.

Adam, Barry D. *The Rise of a Gay and Lesbian Movement*. Boston: Twayne, 1987.

Adams, James Eli. "Gentleman, Dandy, Priest: Manliness and Social Authority in Pater's Aestheticism." *ELH* 59 (1992): 441–466.

Alter, Robert. "The Apocalyptic Temper." *Commentary* 41 (June 1966): 61–66.

Althusser, Louis. "Freud and Lacan." In *Essays on Ideology*. London: Verso, 1984.

Altman, Dennis. *Coming Out in the Seventies*. Boston: Alyson Publications, 1981.

Amor, Anne Clark. *Mrs. Oscar Wilde: A Woman of Some Importance*. London: Sidgwick & Jackson, 1983.

Anderson, Benedict. *Imagined Communities: Reflections on the Origin and Spread of Nationalism*. London: Verso, 1986.

Andrews, Keith. *The Nazarenes: A Brotherhood of German Painters in Rome*. Oxford: Clarendon Press, 1964.

Andy Warhol: Death and Disasters. Houston: The Menil Collection, 1988.

Annan, Noel Gilroy. "The Death of 'Society.'" *The New York Review of Books*, 6 December 1990, 29–33.

———. *Our Age: English Intellectuals Between the World Wars—A Group Portrait*. New York: Random House, 1990.

Arnold, Matthew. *Complete Prose Works*. Edited by R. H. Super. 11 vols. Ann Arbor: University of Michigan Press, 1960–1978.

Bachofen, Johann Jakob. *Myth, Religion, and Mother Right*. Translated by Ralph Manheim, with a preface by George Boas and an introduction by Joseph Campbell. Princeton: Princeton University Press, 1967.

Bartlett, Neil. *Who Was That Man? A Present for Mr Oscar Wilde*. London: Serpent's Tail, 1988.

Bassett, Sharon. "*Marius* and the Varieties of Stoic Will: 'Can the Will Itself Be an Organ of Knowledge, of Vision?'" *ELT* 7 (1984): 52–62.

Baudrillard, Jean. "The Anorexic Ruins." In *Looking Back on the End of the World*, ed. Dietmar Kamper and Christoph Wulf. New York: Semiotext(e), 1989.

Bender, John, and David E. Wellbery, eds. *Chronotypes: The Construction of Time*. Stanford: Stanford University Press, 1991.

Bennington, Geoff. "Cogito Incognito: Foucault's 'My Body, This Paper, This Fire.'" *Oxford Literary Review* 4 (1979): 5–8.

Bernal, Martin. *Black Athena: The Afroasiatic Roots of Classical Civilization.* Vol. 1, *The Fabrication of Ancient Greece 1785–1985.* New Brunswick: Rutgers University Press, 1990.

Bernstein, J. M. *The Fate of Art: Aesthetic Alienation from Kant to Derrida and Adorno.* University Park: Pennsylvania State University Press, 1992.

Boffin, Tessa, and Sunil Gupta, eds. *Ecstatic Antibodies: Resisting the AIDS Mythology.* London: Rivers Oram Press, 1990.

Brantlinger, Patrick. *Rule of Darkness: British Literature and Imperialism, 1830–1914.* Ithaca: Cornell University Press, 1988.

Bristow, Joseph. "Being Gay: Politics, Identity, Pleasure." *New Formations* 9 (Winter 1989): 61–81.

Bryson, Norman. *Tradition and Desire: From David to Delacroix.* Cambridge: Cambridge University Press, 1988.

Burroughs, Jackie. *The Jane Bowles Project.* Factory Theatre Studio Cafe. Toronto, 13 March 1992.

Burroughs, William S. "Interview." *Paris Review* 35 (1965): 13–49.

———. *Naked Lunch.* New York: Grove Weidenfeld, 1990.

———. *Queer.* Harmondsworth: Penguin, 1987.

Butler, Judith. "The Force of Fantasy: Feminism, Mapplethorpe, and Discursive Excess." *differences* 2 (Summer 1990): 105–125.

Carpenter, Edward. *Intermediate Types Among Primitive Folk: A Study in Social Evolution.* 2d ed. London: George Allen & Unwin, 1919.

———. *Selected Writings. Volume One: Sex.* With an introduction by Noël Greig. London: GMP Publishers, 1984.

Carroll, Stephanie. "Reciprocal Representations: David and Theater." *Art in America* 78 (May 1990): 198–207.

Cartledge, Paul. "The Politics of Spartan Pederasty." *Proceedings of the Cambridge Philological Society* 207 (1981): 17–36.

Caruth, Cathy. "Introduction." *American Imago* 48 (Winter 1991): 417–423.

———. "Unclaimed Experience: Trauma and the Possibility of History." *Yale French Studies* 79 (1991): 181–192.

Caruth, Cathy, and Thomas Keenan. "'The AIDS Crisis Is Not Over': A Conversation with Gregg Bordowitz, Douglas Crimp, and Laura Pinsky." *American Imago* 48 (Winter 1991): 539–556.

Castleden, Rodney. *The Knossos Labyrinth: A New View of the 'Palace of Minos' at Knossos.* New York: Routledge, 1990.

Cellupica, Paul. "The Political Dawn Arrives for Gays." *New York Times,* 7 November 1992, L21.

Chambers, Ross. *Room for Maneuver: Reading (the) Oppositional (in) Narrative.* Chicago: University of Chicago Press, 1991.

Chauncey, George. "From Sexual Inversion to Homosexuality: The Changing Medical Conceptualization of Female 'Deviance.'" In *Passion and Power: Sexuality in History,* ed. Kathy Peiss, Christina Simmons, and Robert A. Padgug. Philadelphia: Temple University Press, 1989.

Clarke, Peter. *Liberals and Social Democrats.* Cambridge: Cambridge University Press, 1978.

Cohen, Ed. "Foucauldian Necrologies: 'Gay' 'Politics'? Politically Gay?" *Textual Practice* 2 (1988): 87–101.

———. *Talk on the Wilde Side: Towards a Genealogy of a Discourse on Male Sexualities.* New York: Routledge, 1993.

Collins, Bradford R. "The Metaphysical Nosejob: The Remaking of Warhola, 1960–1968." *Arts Magazine* 62 (February 1988): 47–55.

Conrad, Joseph. *Heart of Darkness: A Case Study in Contemporary Criticism.* Edited by Ross C. Murfin. New York: St. Martin's Press, 1989.

Craft, Christopher. "'Kiss Me with Those Red Lips': Gender and Inversion in Bram Stoker's *Dracula.*" *Representations* 8 (Fall 1984): 107–133.

Crawford, Robert. "Pater's *Renaissance,* Andrew Lang, and Anthropological Romanticism." *ELH* 53 (1986): 849–879.

Creed, Barbara. "Phallic Panic: Male Hysteria and *Dead Ringers.*" *Screen* 31 (Summer 1990): 125–146.

Crone, Rainer. *Andy Warhol: A Picture Show by the Artist.* New York: Rizzoli, 1987.

———. "Form and Ideology: Warhol's Technique from Blotted Line to Film." In *The Work of Andy Warhol,* ed. Gary Garrels. Seattle: Bay Press, 1989.

Curtius, Ernst. *The History of Greece.* Translated by Adolphus William Ward. 4 vols. New York: Scribners, 1867.

Danforth, Loring M. *The Death Rituals of Rural Greece.* Photography by Alexander Tsiaras. Princeton: Princeton University Press, 1982.

DeJean, Joan. *Fictions of Sappho: 1546–1937.* Chicago: University of Chicago Press, 1989.

DeLaura, David. *Hebrew and Hellene in Victorian England: Newman, Arnold, and Pater.* Austin: University of Texas Press, 1969.

De Lauretis, Teresa. *Alice Doesn't: Feminism, Semiotics, Cinema.* Bloomington: Indiana University Press, 1984.

———. "Eccentric Subjects: Feminist Theory and Historical Consciousness." *Feminist Studies* 16 (Spring 1990): 115–150.

———. "The Female Body and Heterosexual Presumption." *Semiotica* 67, no. 3/4 (1987): 259–279.

———. "Feminist Studies/Critical Studies: Issues, Terms, and Contexts." In *Feminist Studies: Critical Studies,* ed. Teresa de Lauretis. Bloomington: Indiana University Press, 1986.

———. "Queer Theory: Lesbian and Gay Sexualities, An Introduction." *differences* 3 (Summer 1991): iii–xviii.

———. *Technologies of Gender: Essays on Theory, Film, and Fiction.* Bloomington: Indiana University Press, 1987.

Dellamora, Richard. *Masculine Desire: The Sexual Politics of Victorian Aestheticism.* Chapel Hill: University of North Carolina Press, 1990.

———. "Textual Politics/Sexual Politics." *MLQ* 54 (March 1993): 155–164.

De Man, Paul. *Allegories of Reading: Figural Language in Rousseau, Nietzsche, Rilke, and Proust.* New Haven: Yale University Press, 1979.

———. *Blindness and Insight: Essays in the Rhetoric of Contemporary Criticism.* New York: Oxford University Press, 1971.

———. *The Rhetoric of Romanticism*. New York: Columbia University Press, 1984.

———. "The Rhetoric of Temporality." In *Interpretation: Theory and Practice*, ed. Charles S. Singleton. Baltimore: Johns Hopkins University Press, 1969.

D'Emilio, John. "The Homosexual Menace: The Politics of Sexuality in Cold War America." In *Passion and Power: Sexuality in History*, ed. Kathy Peiss, Christina Simmons, and Robert A. Padgug. Philadelphia: Temple University Press, 1989.

———. *Sexual Politics, Sexual Communities: The Making of a Homosexual Minority in the United States, 1940–1970*. Chicago: University of Chicago Press, 1983.

De Nanteuil, Luc. *Jacques-Louis David*. New York: Harry N. Abrams, 1990.

Derrida, Jacques. *La Carte postale: De Socrate à Freud et au-denà*. Paris: Flammario, 1980. Translated by Alan Bass, under the title *The Post Card: From Socrates to Freud and Beyond*. Chicago: University of Chicago Press, 1987.

———. *Cinders*. Translated by Ned Lukacher. Lincoln: University of Nebraska Press, 1991.

———. *The Ear of the Other: Otobiography, Transference, Translation*. Texts and discussions with Jacques Derrida. Translated by Peggy Kamuf and edited by Christie McDonald. Lincoln: University of Nebraska Press, 1988.

———. "The Ends of Man." In *Margins of Philosophy*. Translated by Alan Bass. Chicago: University of Chicago Press, 1982.

———. "*Geschlecht* II: Heidegger's Hand." In *Deconstruction and Philosophy: The Texts of Jacques Derrida*, ed. John Sallis. Chicago: University of Chicago Press, 1987.

———. *Margins of Philosophy*. Translated by Alan Bass. Chicago: University of Chicago Press, 1982.

———. "No Apocalypse, Not Now (Full Speed Ahead, Seven Missiles, Seven Missives)." *diacritics* 14 (Summer 1984): 20–31.

———. "Of an Apocalyptic Tone Recently Adopted in Philosophy." Translated by John P. Leavey, Jr. *Oxford Literary Review* 6, no. 2 (1984): 3–37.

———. *Of Grammatology*. Translated by Gayatri Chakravorty Spivak. Baltimore: John Hopkins University Press, 1977.

———. "The Principle of Reason: The University in the Eyes of Its Pupils." *diacritics* 13 (Fall 1983): 3–20.

———. *Spurs: Nietzsche's Styles; Éperons: Les Styles de Nietzsche*. Introduction by Stefano Agosti and translated by Barbara Harlow. Chicago: University of Chicago Press, 1979.

———. "The Rhetoric of Drugs: An Interview." *differences* 5 (Spring 1993): 1–25.

———. "Rhétorique de la drogue." *Autrement* 106 (April 1989): 197–214.

———. *The Truth in Painting*. Translated by Geoff Bennington and Ian McLeod. Chicago: University of Chicago Press, 1987.

———. *Writing and Difference*. Translated by Alan Bass. Chicago: University of Chicago Press, 1978.

Derrida, Jacques, and Christie V. McDonald. "Choreographies." *diacritics* 12 (Summer 1982): 66–76.

Dewey, Joseph. *In a Dark Time: The Apocalyptic Temper in the American Novel of the Nuclear Age.* West Lafayette: Purdue University Press, 1990.

Dollimore, Jonathan. "Different Desires: Subjectivity and Transgression in Wilde and Gide." *Genders* 2 (Summer 1988): 24–41.

Dorson, Richard M. "The Eclipse of Solar Mythology." In *Myth: A Symposium*, ed. Thomas A. Sebeok. Philadelphia: American Folklore Society, 1955.

Dover, K. J. *Greek Homosexuality.* New York: Vintage, 1980.

Dowling, Linda. *Language and Decadence in the Victorian Fin de Siècle.* Princeton: Princeton University Press, 1986.

———. "Roman Decadence and Victorian Historiography." *VSt* 28 (1985): 579–607.

———. "Ruskin's Pied Beauty and the Constitution of a 'Homosexual' Code." *VN* 75 (Spring 1989): 1–8.

Dyer, Richard. "Don't Look Now." *Screen* 23 (September-October 1982): 61–73.

———. *Now You See It: Studies on Lesbian and Gay Film.* New York: Routledge, 1990.

Edelman, Lee. "The Mirror and the Tank: 'AIDS,' Subjectivity, and the Rhetoric of Activism." In *Writing AIDS: Gay Literature, Language, and Analysis*, ed. Timothy Murphy and Suzanne Poirier. New York: Columbia University Press, 1993.

———. "Seeing Things: Representation, the Scene of Surveillance, and the Spectacle of Gay Male Sex." In *Inside/Out: Lesbian Theories, Gay Theories*, ed. Diana Fuss. New York: Routledge, 1991.

———. "Tearooms and Sympathy, or The Epistemology of the Water Closet." In *Nationalisms and Sexualities*, ed. Andrew Parker, Mary Russo, Doris Sommer, and Patricia Yeager. New York: Routledge, 1992.

Ehrenstein, David. "The Filmmaker as Homosexual Hipster." *Arts Magazine* 63 (Summer 1989): 61–64.

Ellmann, Richard. *Oscar Wilde.* Markham, Ont.: Penguin, 1987.

Engels, Friedrich. *The Origin of the Family, Private Property and the State.* With an introduction by Michèle Barrett. Harmondsworth: Penguin, 1985.

Epstein, Steven. "Gay Politics, Ethnic Identity: The Limits of Social Constructionism." *Socialist Review* 93/94 (1987): 6–54.

Eribon, Didier. *Michel Foucault.* Translated by Betsy Wing. Cambridge: Harvard University Press, 1991.

Evans, Arthur. *The God of Ecstasy: Sex-Roles and the Madness of Dionysos.* New York: St. Martin's Press, 1988.

Fellows, Jay. *Tombs, Despoiled and Haunted: "Under-Textures" and "After-Thoughts" in Walter Pater.* Stanford: Stanford University Press, 1991.

Fiedler, Leslie. *A Fiedler Reader.* New York: Stein & Day, 1977.

Firbank, Ronald. *Five Novels.* New York: New Directions Books, 1961.

Forster, E. M. *The Life to Come and Other Stories.* Edited and with an introduction by Oliver Stallybrass. Harmondsworth: Penguin, 1975.

Foster, Hal. *Recodings: Art, Spectacle, Cultural Politics.* Seattle: Bay Press, 1985.

Foucault, Michel. *The History of Sexuality. Volume I: An Introduction.* Translated by Robert Hurley. New York: Vintage, 1980.

———. "My Body, This Paper, This Fire." Translated by Geoff Bennington. *Oxford Literary Review* 4 (1979): 9–28.

————. "On the Genealogy of Ethics: An Overview of Work in Progress." In *The Foucault Reader*, ed. Paul Rabinow. New York: Pantheon, 1984.

————. *Politics, Philosophy, Culture: Interviews and Other Writings 1977–1984*. Translated by Alan Sheridan et al., and edited by Lawrence D. Kritzman. New York: Routledge, 1988.

————. *The Use of Pleasure*. Volume 2 of *The History of Sexuality*. Translated by Robert Hurley. New York: Vintage, 1986.

Frank, Marcie. "The Camera and the Speculum: David Cronenberg's *Dead Ringers*." *PMLA* 106 (May 1991): 459–470.

Freedberg, S. J. *Painting in Italy: 1500 to 1600*. Harmondsworth: Penguin, 1971.

Freedman, Jonathan. *Professions of Taste: Henry James, British Aestheticism, and Commodity Culture*. Stanford: Stanford University Press, 1990.

Freud, Sigmund. *The Standard Edition of the Complete Psychological Works*. Translated and edited by James Strachey in collaboration with Anna Freud. 24 vols. London: Hogarth Press, 1971–1974.

Frow, John. "Tourism and the Semiotics of Nostalgia." *October* 57 (Summer 1991): 123–151.

Frye, Northrop. *Anatomy of Criticism: Four Essays*. Princeton: Princeton University Press, 1957.

Furbank, Philip. *E. M. Forster: A Life*. 2 vols. London: Secker & Warburg, 1977, 1978.

Gagnier, Regenia. *Subjectivities: A History of Self-Representation in Britain, 1832–1920*. New York: Oxford University Press, 1991.

Gallop, Jane. *Reading Lacan*. Ithaca: Cornell University Press, 1988.

García-Düttmann, Alexander. "What Will Have Been Said about AIDS: Some Remarks in Disorder." *Public* 7 (1993): 95–114.

Gellner, Ernest. *Nations and Nationalism*. Oxford: Basil Blackwell, 1983.

German Masters of the Nineteenth Century: Paintings and Drawings from the Federal Republic of Germany. New York: Metropolitan Museum of Art, 1981.

Gilman, Richard. *Decadence: The Strange Life of an Epithet*. New York: Farrar, Straus, & Giroux, 1979.

Gilman, Sander L. "AIDS and Syphilis: The Iconography of Disease." In *AIDS: Cultural Analysis, Cultural Activism*, ed. Douglas Crimp. Cambridge: MIT Press, 1989.

————. *Disease and Representation: Images of Illness from Madness to AIDS*. Ithaca: Cornell University Press, 1988.

————. *Inscribing the Other*. Lincoln: University of Nebraska Press, 1991.

Glück, Robert. *Jack the Modernist*. New York: Gay Presses, 1985.

Godard, Barbara. "Theorizing Feminist Discourse/Translation." *Tessera* 6 (Spring 1989): 42–53.

Godard, Barbara and Mary di Michele. "'Patterns of Their Own Particular Ceremonies': A Conversation in an Elegiac Mode." *Open Letter* 9 (Winter 1991): 36–59.

Goode, John, "The Decadent Writer as Producer." In *Decadence and the 1890s*, ed. Ian Fletcher. London: Edward Arnold, 1979.

Gorak, Jan. *Critic of Crisis: A Study of Frank Kermode*. Columbia: University of Missouri Press, 1987.

Grover, Jan Zita. "AIDS: Keywords." In *AIDS: Cultural Analysis, Cultural Activism*, ed. Douglas Crimp. Cambridge: MIT Press, 1989.

Halperin, David M. *One Hundred Years of Homosexuality and Other Essays on Greek Love*. New York: Routledge, 1990.

———. "Plato and Erotic Reciprocity." *Classical Antiquity* 5 (1986): 60–80.

———. "Saint Foucault." *Lesbian and Gay Studies Newsletter* 19 (July 1992): 32–34.

Hassan, Ihab. "The Question of Postmodernism." In *Romanticism, Modernism, Postmodernism*, ed. Harry R. Garvin. Lewisburg: Bucknell University Press, 1980.

———. "The Subtracting Machine: The Work of William Burroughs." *Critique* 6 (Spring 1963): 4–23.

Haxthausen, Charles W. "Translation and Transformation in *Target with Four Faces*: The Painting, the Drawing, and the Etching." In *Jasper Johns: Printed Symbols*, with an introduction by Elizabeth Armstrong. Minneapolis: Walker Art Center, 1990.

Heidegger, Martin. "The Origin of the Work of Art." In *Philosophies of Art and Beauty*, ed. Albert Hofstadter and Richard Kuhns. New York: Modern Library, 1964.

Hekma, Gert. "Sodomites, Platonic Lovers, Contrary Lovers: The Backgrounds of the Modern Homosexual." In *Male Homosexuality in Renaissance and Enlightenment Europe*, ed. Kent Gerard and Gert Hekma. New York: Harrington Park Press, 1989.

Hertz, Neil. *The End of the Line: Essays on Psychoanalysis and the Sublime*. New York: Columbia University Press, 1985.

Higgins, Lesley. "Essaying 'W. H. Pater Esq.': New Perspectives on the Tutor/Student Relationship Between Pater and Hopkins." In *Pater in the 1990s*, ed. Laurel Brake and Ian Small. Greensboro, N.C.: ELT Press, 1991.

Hilliard, David. "Unenglish and Unmanly: Anglo-Catholicism and Homosexuality." *VSt* 25 (1982): 181–210.

Hobsbawm, Eric, and Terence Ranger, eds. *The Invention of Tradition*. Cambridge: Cambridge University Press, 1983.

Holleran, Andrew. "Friends at Evening." In *Men on Men: Best New Gay Fiction*, ed. George Stambolian. New York: New American Library, 1986.

Hollinghurst, Alan. *The Swimming-Pool Library*. New York: Vintage, 1989.

Huyssen, Andreas. "Mapping the Postmodern." In *Feminism/Postmodernism*, ed. Linda J. Nicholson. New York: Routledge, 1990.

Irigiray, Luce. *Speculum of the Other Woman*. Translated by Gillian C. Gill. Ithaca: Cornell University Press, 1985.

———. *This Sex Which Is Not One*. Translated by Catherine Porter with Carolyn Burke. Ithaca: Cornell University Press, 1985.

Jacobus, Mary. *Reading Woman: Essays in Feminist Criticism*. New York: Columbia University Press, 1986.

Jameson, Fredric. "Postmodernism, or The Cultural Logic of Late Capitalism." *New Left Review* 146 (July–August 1984): 53–92.

———. *Postmodernism, or The Cultural Logic of Late Capitalism*. Durham: Duke University Press, 1991.

————. *The Prison-House of Language: A Critical Account of Structuralism and Russian Formalism.* Princeton: Princeton University Press, 1974.

————. "Reification and Utopia in Mass Culture." *Social Text* 1 (Winter 1979): 130–148.

Jardine, Alice. *Gynesis: Configurations of Woman and Modernity.* Cornell: Cornell University Press, 1985.

Jeffery-Poulter, Stephen. *Peers, Queers, and Commons: The Struggle for Gay Law Reform from 1950 to the Present.* London: Routledge, 1991.

Jenkyns, Richard. *The Victorians and Ancient Greece.* Cambridge: Harvard University Press, 1980.

Jowett, Benjamin, trans. *The Dialogues of Plato.* 2d rev. ed. 5 vols. Oxford: Clarendon Press, 1875.

————, trans. *The Dialogues of Plato.* 3d rev. ed. 5 vols. London: Macmillan, 1892.

Joyce, James. *Ulysses.* New York: Random House, 1934.

Kamper, Dietmar, and Christoph Wulf, eds. *Looking Back on the End of the World.* New York: Semiotext(e), 1989.

Kant, Immanuel. *The Critique of Judgement.* Translated by James Creed Meredith. Oxford: Oxford University Press, 1961.

————. *On History.* Edited and translated by Lewis White Beck, Robert E. Anchor, and Emil L. Fackenheim. Indianapolis: Bobbs-Merrill, 1963.

————. *Political Writings.* Edited by Hans Reiss and translated by H. B. Nisbet. 2d ed. Cambridge: Cambridge University Press, 1991.

Kauffman, Linda S. *Special Delivery: Epistolary Modes in Modern Fiction.* Chicago: University of Chicago Press, 1992.

Kermode, Frank. *Continuities.* London: Routledge, 1968.

————. "Endings, Continued." In *Languages of the Unsayable: The Play of Negativity in Literature and Literary Theory,* ed. Sanford Budick and Wolfgang Iser. New York: Columbia University Press, 1989.

————. "Obscenity and the Public Interest." In *Modern Essays.* London: Fontana, 1971.

————. *Poetry, Narrative, History.* With an introduction by Michael Payne. London: Basil Blackwell, 1990.

————. *The Sense of an Ending: Studies in the Theory of Fiction.* New York: Oxford University Press, 1968.

King, Francis. *E. M. Forster.* London: Thames & Hudson, 1988.

Koestenbaum, Wayne. *Double Talk: The Erotics of Male Literary Collaboration.* New York: Routledge, 1989.

————. "Wilde's Hard Labor and the Birth of Gay Reading." In *Engendering Men: The Question of Male Feminist Criticism,* ed. Joseph A. Boone and Michael Cadden. New York: Routledge, 1990.

Kopelson, Kevin R. "Wilde's Love-Deaths." *Yale Journal of Criticism* 5 (Fall 1992): 31–60.

Kramer, Hilton. *The Age of the Avant-Garde: An Art Chronicle of 1956–1972.* New York: Farrar, Straus & Giroux, 1973.

Lacan, Jacques. *Écrits: A Selection.* Translated by Alan Sheridan. New York: Norton, 1977.

LaCapra, Dominick. "The Temporality of Rhetoric." In *Chronotypes: The Construction of Time*, ed. John Bender and David E. Wellbery. Stanford: Stanford University Press, 1991.

Lambert, Royston. *Beloved and God: The Story of Hadrian and Antinous*. London: Weidenfeld & Nicolson, 1984.

Laplanche, Jean, and J.-B. Pontalis. *The Language of Psycho-Analysis*. Translated by Donald Nicholson-Smith with an introduction by Daniel Lagache. New York: Norton, 1973.

Latimer, Dan. "Jameson and Post-Modernism." *New Left Review*, no. 148 (November–December 1984): 116–128.

Lee, John, Tim Garrigan, and Bob Connell. "Toward a New Sociology of Masculinity." *Theory and Society* 14 (1985): 551–604.

Lindsay, Jack. *Death of the Hero: French Painting from David to Delacroix*. London: Studio, 1960.

Livingstone, Marco. "Do It Yourself: Notes on Warhol's Techniques." In *Andy Warhol: A Retrospective*, ed. Kynaston McShine. New York: Museum of Modern Art, 1989.

Loesberg, Jonathan. *Aestheticism and Deconstruction: Pater, Derrida, and De Man*. Princeton: Princeton University Press, 1991.

Luckmann, Thomas. "The Constitution of Human Life in Time." In *Chronotypes: The Construction of Time*, ed. John Bender and David E. Wellbery. Stanford: Stanford University Press, 1991.

Lukács, Georg. *The Historical Novel*. Translated by Hannah Mitchell and Stanley Mitchell. Harmondsworth: Penguin, 1962.

Lyotard, Jean-François. "On the Strength of the Weak." *Semiotexte* 3 (1978): 204–213.

———. *The Postmodern Condition: A Report on Knowledge*. Translated by Geoff Bennington and Brian Massumi. Minneapolis: University of Minnesota Press, 1984.

———. "The Sign of History." In *Poststructuralism and the Question of History*, ed. Derek Attridge, Geoff Bennington, and Robert Young. Cambridge: Cambridge University Press, 1987.

McGinn, Bernard. "Early Apocalypticism: The Ongoing Debate." In *The Apocalypse in English Renaissance Thought and Literature: Patterns, Antecedents and Repercussions*. Manchester: Manchester University Press, 1984.

McShine, Kynaston, ed. *Andy Warhol: A Retrospective*. New York: Museum of Modern Art, 1989.

Malek, James S. "Forster's 'Albergo Empedocle': A Precursor of *Maurice*." *SSF* 11 (1974): 427–430.

Mandel, Ernest. *Late Capitalism*. Translated by Joris De Bres. London: New Left Books, 1976.

Marcus, Eric. *Making History: The Struggle for Gay and Lesbian Equal Rights, 1945–1990, An Oral History*. New York: HarperCollins, 1992.

Martin, Robert K. "Forster's Greek: From Optative to Present Indicative." *KanQ* 9 (1977): 69–73.

———. "The Paterian Mode in Forster's Fiction: *The Longest Journey* to

Pharos and Pharillon." In *E. M. Forster: Centenary Revaluations*, ed. Judith Scherer Herz and Robert K. Martin. Toronto: University of Toronto Press, 1982.

Martindale, Kathleen. "Fredric Jameson's Critique of Ethical Criticism: A Deconstructed Marxist Feminist Response." In *Feminist Critical Negotiations*, ed. Alice A. Parker and Elizabeth A. Meese. Philadelphia: John Benjamins, 1992.

Merck, Mandy. "Figuring Out Andy Warhol." Paper presented at the conference, "Re-Reading Warhol: The Politics of Pop." Duke University, Durham, N.C., 22 January 1993.

Miller, J. Hillis. "Ariadne's Thread: Repetition and the Narrative Line." In *Interpretation of Narrative*, ed. Mario J. Valdes and Owen J. Miller. Toronto: University of Toronto Press, 1978.

———. *Illustration.* Cambridge: Harvard University Press, 1992.

———. "Narrative." In *Critical Terms for Literary Study*, ed. Frank Lentricchia and Thomas McLaughlin. Chicago: University of Chicago Press, 1990.

———. "Tradition and Difference." *diacritics* 2 (Winter 1972): 6–13.

———. "Walter Pater: A Partial Portrait." *Daedalus* 105 (1976): 97–113.

Miller, Nancy K. *Subject to Change: Reading Feminist Writing.* New York: Columbia University Press, 1988.

Monette, Paul. *Love Alone: Eighteen Elegies for Rog.* New York: St. Martin's Press, 1988.

Monsman, Gerald. *Pater's Portraits: Mythic Pattern in the Fiction of Walter Pater.* Baltimore: Johns Hopkins University Press, 1967.

Montgomery-Hyde, Harford. *The Trials of Oscar Wilde.* New York: Dover Publications, 1973.

Moon, Michael. "Flaming Closets." *October* 51 (Winter 1989): 19–54.

Morgan, Ted. *Literary Outlaw: The Life and Times of William S. Burroughs.* New York: Avon Books, 1990.

Mosse, George. *Nationalism and Sexuality: Middle-Class Morality and Sexual Norms in Modern Europe.* Madison: University of Wisconsin Press, 1985.

Müller, C. O. *The History and Antiquities of the Doric Race.* Translated by Henry Tufnell and George Cornewall Lewis. 2d rev. ed. 2 vols. London: John Murray, 1839.

Nadel, Ira. "Moments in the Greenwood: *Maurice* in Context." In *E. M. Forster: Centenary Revaluations*, ed. Judith Scherer Herz and Robert K. Martin. London: Macmillan, 1982.

Norris, Christopher. "Deconstruction *Versus* Postmodernism: Critical Theory and the 'Nuclear Sublime.'" *New Formations* 15 (Winter 1991): 83–100.

———. *What's Wrong with Postmodernism: Critical Theory and the Ends of Philosophy.* New York: Harvester, 1991.

O'Hara, Daniel T. *The Romance of Interpretation: Visionary Criticism from Pater to De Man.* New York: Columbia University Press, 1985.

Owens, Craig. "The Discourse of Others: Feminists and Postmodernism." In *The Anti-Aesthetic: Essays on Postmodern Culture*, ed. Hal Foster. Port Townsend, Wash.: Bay Press, 1987.

Pater, Walter. *Appreciations with an Essay on Style*. London, 1910. Reprint. New York: Johnson Reprint, 1967.

———. *Imaginary Portraits*. London, 1910. Reprint. New York: Johnson Reprint, 1967.

———. *Letters*. Edited by Lawrence Evans. Oxford: Clarendon Press, 1970.

———. *Marius the Epicurean: His Sensations and Ideas*. 2 vols. 2d ed. London: Macmillan, 1885.

———. *Marius the Epicurean: His Sensations and Ideas*. 2 vols. London, 1910. Reprint. New York: Johnson Reprint, 1967.

———. *Miscellaneous Studies: A Series of Essays*. London, 1895. Reprint. New York: Johnson Reprint, 1967.

———. *Plato and Platonism*. London: Macmillan, 1910.

———. *The Renaissance: Studies in Art and Poetry. The 1893 Text*. Edited by Donald L. Hill. Berkeley and Los Angeles: University of California Press, 1980.

———. *Studies in the History of the Renaissance*. London: Macmillan, 1873.

Patton, Cindy. *Inventing AIDS*. New York: Routledge, 1990.

———. "Safe Sex and the Pornographic Vernacular." In *How Do I Look? Queer Film and Video*, ed. Bad Object-Choices. Seattle: Bay Press, 1991.

Pease, Donald. "J. Hillis Miller: The Other Victorian at Yale." In *The Yale Critics: Deconstruction in America*, ed. Jonathan Arac, Wlad Godzich, and Wallace Martin. Minneapolis: University of Minnesota Press, 1983.

Perrine, Laurence. "Housman's 'Others, I am not the first.'" *VP* 28 (Autumn/Winter 1990). 135–138.

Peters, Robert. "The Cult of the Returned Apollo: Walter Pater's *Renaissance* and *Imaginary Portraits*." *PRR* 2 (1981): 53–69.

Plissart, Marie Françoise, and Jacques Derrida. "Right of Inspection." *Art and Text* 32 (Autumn 1989): 20–97.

Poovey, Mary. *Uneven Developments: The Ideological Work of Gender in Mid-Victorian England*. Chicago: University of Chicago Press, 1988.

Reed, Christopher. "Bloomsbury Bashing: Homophobia and the Politics of Criticism in the Eighties." *Genders* 11 (Fall 1991): 58–80.

Rich, Adrienne. "Compulsory Heterosexuality and Lesbian Existence." *Signs* 5 (1980): 631–660.

Richards, I. A. *Selected Letters*. Oxford: Clarendon Press, 1990.

Rilke, Rainer Maria. *Selected Poems*. Translated and with a commentary by Robert Bly. New York: Harper & Row, 1981.

Rodley, Chris, ed. *Cronenberg on Cronenberg*. Toronto: Knopf Canada, 1992.

Roof, Judith. *A Lure of Knowledge: Lesbian Sexuality and Theory*. New York: Columbia University Press, 1991.

Rose, Barbara. *Rauschenberg: An Interview with Robert Rauschenberg*. New York: Vintage Books, 1987.

Rose, Jacqueline. "Sexuality and Vision: Some Questions." In *Vision and Visuality*, ed. Hal Foster. Seattle, Wash.: Bay Press, 1988.

Rose, Paul Lawrence. *Revolutionary Antisemitism in Germany: From Kant to Wagner*. Princeton: Princeton University Press, 1990.

Rosenblum, Robert. "Reconstructing David." *Art in America* 78 (May 1990): 188–197.

Rosenthal, Nan. "Let Us Now Praise Famous Men: Warhol as Art Director." In *The Work of Andy Warhol*, ed. Gary Garrels. Seattle: Bay Press, 1989.

Ross, Andrew. *No Respect: Intellectuals and Popular Culture*. New York: Routledge, 1989.

Rowbotham, Sheila, and Jeffrey Weeks. *Socialism and the New Life: The Personal and Sexual Politics of Edward Carpenter and Havelock Ellis*. London: Pluto Press, 1977.

Said, Edward W. "The Problem of Textuality: Two Exemplary Positions." *Critical Inquiry* 4 (Summer 1978): 673–714.

Scarry, Elaine. *The Body in Pain: The Making and Unmaking of the World*. Oxford: Oxford University Press, 1987.

———. ed. *Literature and the Body: Essays on Populations and Persons*. Baltimore: Johns Hopkins University Press, 1988.

Schapiro, Meyer. "The Still Life as a Personal Object—A Note on Heidegger and van Gogh." In *The Reach of Mind: Essays in Memory of Kurt Goldstein*, ed. Marianne L. Simmer. New York: Springer Publishing, 1968.

Scheick, William J. "Nuclear Criticism: An Introduction." *PLL* 26 (Winter 1990): 3–12.

Schmalz, Jeffery. "Gay Politics Goes Mainstream." *The New York Times Magazine*, 11 October 1992, 18–21ff.

Schmitt, Eric. "Compromise on Military Gay Ban Gaining Support Among Senators." *New York Times*, 12 May 1993, A1.

Schwenger, Peter. "Circling Ground Zero." *PMLA* 106 (March 1991): 251–261.

Sedgwick, Eve Kosofsky. *Between Men: English Literature and Male Homosocial Desire*. New York: Columbia University Press, 1985.

———. *Epistemology of the Closet*. Berkeley and Los Angeles: University of California Press, 1990.

Sewell, Brocard. *In the Dorian Mode: A Life of John Gray, 1866–1934*. Padstow, Cornwall: Tabb House, 1983.

Sharpe, Jenny. "The Unspeakable Limits of Rape: Colonial Violence and Counter-Insurgency." *Genders* 10 (Spring 1991): 25–46.

Shaw, W. David. *The Lucid Veil: Poetic Truth in the Victorian Age*. Madison: University of Wisconsin Press, 1987.

Showalter, Elaine. *Sexual Anarchy: Gender and Culture at the Fin de Siècle*. New York: Viking, 1990.

Shuter, William F. "The Arrested Narrative of 'Emerald Uthwart.'" *NCF* 45 (June 1990): 1–25.

———. Walter Pater and the Academy's 'Dubious Name.'" *VIJ* 16 (1988): 129–148.

Silverberg, Ira, ed. *Everything Is Permitted: The Making of Naked Lunch*. New York: Grove Weidenfeld, 1992.

Silverman, Kaja. *Male Subjectivity at the Margins*. New York: Routledge, 1992.

Sinfield, Alan. "Closet Dramas: Homosexual Representation and Class in Postwar British Theater." *Genders* 9 (Fall 1990): 112–131.

———. *Literature, Politics, and Culture in Postwar Britain*. Berkeley and Los Angeles: University of California Press, 1989.

Smith, Anna Marie. "A Symptomology of an Authoritarian Discourse: The Parliamentary Debates on the Prohibition of the Promotion of Homosexuality." *New Formations* 10 (Spring 1990): 41–65.

Smith, Timothy d'Arch. *Love in Earnest: Some Notes on the Lives and Writings of English 'Uranian' Poets from 1889 to 1930*. London: Routledge & Kegan Paul, 1970.

Sontag, Susan. *Against Interpretation and Other Essays*. New York: Farrar, Straus & Giroux, 1966.

Spivak, Gayatri Chakravorty. "Displacement and the Discourse of Woman." In *Displacement: Derrida and After*, ed. Mark Krupnick. Bloomington: Indiana University Press, 1983.

———. "Feminism and Deconstruction, Again: Negotiating with Unacknowledged Masculinism." In *Between Feminism and Psychoanalysis*, ed. Teresa Brennan. London: Routledge, 1989.

———. "Love Me, Love My Ombre, Elle." *diacritics* 14 (Winter 1984): 19–36.

Stallybrass, Peter, and Allon White. *The Politics and Poetics of Transgression*. Ithaca: Cornell University Press, 1989.

Stuckey, Charles E. "Warhol in Context." In *The Work of Andy Warhol*, ed. Gary Garrels. Seattle: Bay Press, 1989.

Summers, Claude. *E. M. Forster*. New York: Frederick Ungar, 1983.

———. *Gay Fictions: Wilde To Stonewall, Studies in a Male Homosexual Literary Tradition*. New York: Continuum, 1990.

Sutherland, John. "The Politics of English Studies in the British University, 1960–1984." In *Historical Studies and Literary Criticism*, ed. Jerome J. McGann. Madison: University of Wisconsin Press, 1985.

Symonds, John Addington. *Male Love: A Problem in Greek Ethics and Other Writings*. Edited by John Lauritsen. New York: Pagan Press, 1983.

———. *The Memoirs*. Edited by Phyllis Grosskurth. Chicago: University of Chicago Press, 1986.

Tanner, Tony. *City of Words: American Fiction, 1950–1970*. New York: Harper & Row, 1971.

Thwaite, Ann. *Edmund Gosse: A Literary Landscape, 1849–1928*. Chicago: University of Chicago Press, 1984.

Tisdale, Sallie. "Talk Dirty To Me." *Harper's*, February 1992, 37–46.

Tsuzuki, Chusichi. *Edward Carpenter: 1844–1929*. Cambridge: Cambridge University Press, 1980.

Tuveson, Ernest L. "The Millenarian Structure of *The Communist Manifesto*." In *The Apocalypse in English Renaissance Thought and Literature: Patterns, Antecedents, and Repercussions*. Manchester: Manchester University Press, 1984.

Urteaga-Ballón, Oscar. *Interpretacion de la sexualidad en la ceramica del antiguo Peru*. Lima: Museo de Paleo-patologia, 1968.

Vance, Carole S. "The War on Culture." *Art in America* 77 (September 1989): 39+.

Vermeule, Emily. "The World Turned Upside Down." *The New York Review of Books*, 26 March 1992, 40–43.

Wallen, Jeffrey. "On Pater's Use and Abuse of Quotation." *Arnoldian* 14 (Winter 1986–1987): 1–20.

Watney, Simon. *Policing Desire: Pornography, AIDS, and the Media.* Minneapolis: University of Minnesota Press, 1987.

Waugh, Tom. "Photography, Passion and Power." *The Body Politic*, March 1984, 29–33.

Weber, Samuel. "The Debts of Deconstruction and Other, Related Assumptions." In *Taking Chances: Derrida, Psychoanalysis, and Literature*, ed. Joseph H. Smith and William Kerrigan. Baltimore: Johns Hopkins University Press, 1988.

Weiskel, Thomas. *The Romantic Sublime: Studies in the Structure and Psychology of Transcendence.* Baltimore: Johns Hopkins University Press, 1986.

West, Cornel. "Ethics and Action in Fredric Jameson's Marxist Hermeneutics." In *Postmodernism and Politics*, ed. Jonathan Arac. Minneapolis: University of Minnesota Press, 1986.

White, Edmund. "An Essay," *Tribe: An American Gay Journal* 1 (Spring 1990): 10–14.

———. "The Political Vocabulary of Homosexuality." In *The State of the Language*, ed. Leonard Michaels and Christopher Ricks. Berkeley and Los Angeles: University of California Press, 1980.

———. *States of Desire: Travels in Gay America.* New York: Dutton, 1983.

White, Edmund, and Adam Mars-Jones. *The Darker Proof: Stories from a Crisis.* London: Faber & Faber, 1987.

Wilde, Oscar. *The Picture of Dorian Gray.* Edited by Donald L. Lawler. New York: Norton, 1988.

Wilde, Oscar, et al. *Teleny.* Edited by John McRae. London: GMP Publishers, 1986.

Willets, R. F. *Cretan Cults and Festivals.* London: Routledge & Kegan Paul, 1962.

Williams, Carolyn. *Transfigured World: Walter Pater's Aesthetic Historicism.* Ithaca: Cornell University Press, 1989.

Wittig, Monique. *The Straight Mind and Other Essays.* With a foreword by Louise Turcotte. Boston: Beacon Press, 1992.

Wittkower, Rudolf, and Margot Wittkower. *Born under Saturn: The Character and Conduct of Artists—A Documented History from Antiquity to the French Revolution.* New York: Norton, 1969.

Wollheim, Richard. *Sigmund Freud.* Cambridge: Cambridge University Press, 1971.

Woolf, Virginia. *Between the Acts.* London: Collins, 1987.

Wordsworth, Ann. "Derrida and Foucault: Writing the History of Historicity." In *Post-structuralism and the Question of History*, ed. Derek Attridge, Geoff Bennington, and Robert Young. Cambridge: Cambridge University Press, 1987.

Yingling, Thomas. "AIDS in America: Postmodern Governance, Identity, and Experience." In *Inside/Out: Lesbian Theories, Gay Theories*, ed. Diana Fuss. New York: Routledge, 1991.

INDEX

About the Author

Richard Dellamora completed this book during a year as Visiting Fellow in the department of English at Princeton University in Princeton, New Jersey. Dellamora lives in Toronto, Ontario, and teaches in the departments of English and Cultural Studies at Trent University. He is the author of *Masculine Desire: The Sexual Politics of Victorian Aestheticism* (1990).